Theologia

Theologia

The Fragmentation and Unity of Theological Education

EDWARD FARLEY

FORTRESS PRESS   **PHILADELPHIA**

COPYRIGHT © 1983 BY FORTRESS PRESS

Second printing 1989

Library of Congress Cataloging in Publication Data

Farley, Edward, 1929–
  Theologia: the fragmentation and unity of theological education.

  Includes index.
  1. Theology—Study and teaching—History. I. Title.
BV4023.F37 1983   230'.07   82–48621
ISBN 0–8006–1705–3

Printed in the United States of America   1–1705

Contents

Preface

The essay offered here is an occasional piece on theological education. It is part historical narrative and part constructive thesis. The thesis is a simple one. "Theology" has long since disappeared as the unity, subject matter, and end of clergy education and this disappearance is responsible more than anything else for the problematic character of that education as a course of study. The thesis, accordingly, embodies the historical narrative, which is an account of the origins and consequences of this decline and eventual eclipse of theology.

Even though the historical narrative does comprise part 1 of the essay, this narrative does not amount to a comprehensive "history of theological education." The purpose of the narrative is tendentious, since it attempts to expose problematic aspects of current clergy education by means of a historical genetics of its presuppositions. This is why the narrative concentrates on the literature and movement which once upon a time was called "theological encyclopedia." The origin, course, and final cessation of that 150-year-long movement is at the same time a story of the displacement and dispersion of *theologia*. Because this literature is not widely known, I have perhaps given it more attention than it deserves in a piece whose main purpose is not historical but evocative. On the other hand, the very fact that it is a moldy and forgotten literature signals the absence of the issue which it formulates, the issue of the structure of theological study. This is the issue which this occasional piece of reflection would resurrect as at least one (in my view the most important) strand of the critique and reform of church and clergy education.

I called this essay an occasional piece. Although a good bit of historical study was done for it as well as some monitoring of pertinent literature on contemporary theological education, it cannot pretend to be grounded in a thoroughgoing scholarly knowledge of the history of theological education or comprehensive empirical knowledge of the current situation. Nor can the essay pretend to speak on behalf of any constituency—denominational, theological, or educational. If it speaks on behalf of none of these, it is addressed at least to a wide audience. The narration of the career of *theologia*, at least after the Reformation, is almost exclusively Protestant. Yet the theological encyclopedic movement is as much a Catholic as a Protestant work.[1] As Roman Catholic theological education moved beyond the older patterns set by Aristotelian philosophy and Thomistic scholasticism to the post-Enlightenment European type of theological faculty as a group of specialists, it too experienced the dispersion of *theologia* into independent sciences and today shares with the Protestant faculties most of the problems articulated in this essay. The problem of theological education is, in other words, an ecumenical problem, embracing the major branches of Christendom.

In addition, the situation of theological schools described in these pages embraces schools of both conservative and liberal persuasions. Even though I myself am on the liberal or revisionist end of the theological spectrum and self-consciously approach theological education from that perspective, I am addressing the historical narrative, critique, and proposal just as much to "conservative" as to "liberal" schools, and just as much to denominational as to nondenominational, university-related schools. All of these schools are caught in the backwash of historical forces which have modified and maybe removed the original rationale for their patterns of theological study.

It seems pertinent to share with the reader two rather serious changes of mind which occurred in the course of the investigation. The first has to do with the theme of theological encyclopedia. When I began the study, I was quite convinced that the central conceptual problem of theological education was the need for a new theological encyclopedia, that is, a way of conceiving the major areas of study other than the traditional fourfold pattern of disciplines. Once the inquiry uncovered distinctions between *theologia* itself, theological disciplines as regions of knowledge and inquiry, and disciplines as areas of pedagogy in a course of study, this single "encyclopedic" task became several tasks. I concluded that the conceptual and theological problem facing clergy education was not a single problem of the pattern of sciences but a complex of problems in which several levels of analysis were required. These levels are the three criteria set forth in chapter 8, section 3. Because of this change, the essay does not pretend to be a solution to the problems it raises. That is, it does not offer a new encyclopedia or a pattern for the course of clergy studies. Instead, it proposes a way of conceiving theological education's subject matter and unity as *theologia* and certain consequent criteria for determining what happens in the course of study.

The second change occurred when I realized that theology in its original and most authentic sense referred to a sapiential and personal knowledge. Once I began to explore the effects of the loss of that meaning on theological education, I realized that over the course of time theology had come to be located in, and even defined by, clergy education. This set the stage for the distinction between *theologia* as such and its occurrence in various locations and modes; for instance, clergy education. Once this distinction was made, I saw that the argument had implications for much more than simply clergy education. The main thesis of the essay urged the restoration of *theologia* to clergy education. But the effects of the eclipse of *theologia* on that education had parallels in church education, higher education, and graduate theological education. The dispersion of theology into "sciences" which had produced such widespread confusion if not incoherence in clergy education had similarly affected these other undertakings. This second change then was a realization that the argument of the essay had broader application than simply in clergy education. Accordingly, while the essay is focused on clergy education, it is really about all education which purports to promote a Christian *paideia* or which would interpret the Christian religion.

A final comment on the question of the reform of clergy education is in order. I am persuaded that reform attempts will continue to be merely cosmetic until they address the fundamental structure and pattern of studies inherited from the past and submit to criticism the presuppositions which undergird that pattern. I am also persuaded that such a reform, guided by the recovery of *theologia*, is correlative with a reform of the institutionality of clergy education. This is because the three-year course of study occurring on the basis of a typical B.A. degree is drastically insufficient as an education in theological understanding for those who will later be responsible for facilitating it in others. The essay, however, is not preoccupied with this unavoidable issue. Its focus is on the conceptual, one might say theological, problem of theological education, which is the question of its nature, central task, and major desiderata.

Some written projects proceed from initial research to final editing with very little exchange with others in the process. The opposite is the case with the present work. It was born in interchanges with Robert W. Lynn of the Lilly Endowment and it continued to develop under his encouragement and closely formulated criticisms. Father William McConville, O.F.M., Paul Lakeland, and Anna Case Winters, graduate students at Vanderbilt Divinity School, contributed not only indispensable and extensive bibliographical work, but substantial investigations of Roman Catholic encyclopedia literature and the curricular patterns of contemporary theological schools. Glenn T. Miller of Southeastern Baptist Theological Seminary and a principal research member of the Auburn Project's history of the Protestant Seminary in the USA, gave invaluable help along the way in both conversation and written exchanges. Several people interrupted projects of their own to read and provide detailed responses to the penultimate version of this manuscript. They are John B. Cobb and Joseph M. Hough, Jr. of Claremont School of Theology, David H. Kelsey of Yale Divinity School, Joseph M. Kitagawa and Brian Gerrish of the University of Chicago, and Jack Forstmann of Vanderbilt Divinity School. The final rewriting of the manuscript was a major effort and almost all of the changes introduced were prompted by the criticisms of those mentioned above.

NOTE

1. The earliest encyclopedic works (1770s and 1780s) are both Protestant and Catholic. The periods of intense publishing of theological encyclopedias in Europe (1830s and 1880s) have both Catholic and Protestant authors. The Enlightenment-produced changes in European university education which evoked the movement in the first place penetrated the Catholic faculties and occasioned Schleiermacher-influenced works by members of the Catholic Tübingen school, J.S. von Drey and F.A. Staudenmaier.

Theologia

INTRODUCTION

1

Introduction: The Travail of
the Theological School

Complaints about theological education are as old as theological education itself.[1] Today they sound forth from many quarters: alumni who say they were not adequately prepared for church work, faculty who bemoan their professional isolation and loneliness, students who experience the ministry fields as trivial and academic fields as irrelevant, laity who are sure that the gospel has long been absent from the schools' agenda. Widespread and loud as these complaints are, they really do not add up to a call for a genuine reform of theological education. All of these constituencies seem to be content with both the basic institution itself (the seminary) and the inherited conceptual framework in which theological education occurs. In the past, reform has been no stranger to the institutions created for the education of priests and ministers. Reform movements in the church (like the Carolingian renaissance) created new institutions for that education. The history of theological schools is a history of constant reform. When theological study became attached to the first great European universities founded in the twelfth and thirteenth centuries, when it took on an entirely new structure in the first "modern" universities like Halle under the impact of both pietism and the Enlightenment, when it shifted from the informal and local education of clergy to the seminary in early nineteenth-century America, it was in these instances undergoing basic reform. Curiously, the present chorus of criticism does not call for reform in the sense of either a new institution or a new conceptual framework.

The reason the standard criticisms of theological education do not amount to a call for reform is that their focus is more on the symptoms than on the disease itself. These complaints constitute what might be

3

called a symptomology of the theological school's sickness. Insofar as symptoms are seen as themselves the problem, we are confronted with a complex hermeneutical challenge. We are pressed to penetrate the symptomology back to the underlying malady. This study will begin with but not dwell on the complaints, the manifest discontent, the symptomology.

The following statement succinctly expresses the travail of the theological school at the level of how it is experienced by its constituents. The typical product of three years of seminary study is not a *theologically* educated minister. The present ethos of the Protestant churches is such that a theologically oriented approach to the preparation of ministers is not only irrelevant but counterproductive. When we consider what appears to make ministers upwardly mobile, we suspect that the reward system for professional promotion and success is largely a matter of un- or anti-theological skills. Anticipating this, however vaguely, the theological student sees little point in "being a theologian." As students graduate into the reward system, they frequently discover the dispensability of their academic studies. At its very best, a theological education is only the beginning of a career-long discipline, and it is just this continuing "study of theology" which does not occur. Such is the problem at the level of the churchly and ministerial context of education.

In the school itself and at the experiential and symptomatic level, students, faculty, and alumni all agree about one thing. Education in the theological school is not so much a matter of "the study of theology" as a plurality of specific disciplines, each with its own method. These areas of study ("sciences," disciplines, courses, catalogue fields) are offered without any highly visible rationale which clarifies their importance and displays their interconnections. The faculty version of this is a kind of professional loneliness issuing in the perennial complaint about the absence of fruitful collegial relations. The students' and ministerial graduates' version is that the theological school did not adequately prepare them for the nitty-gritty problems and activities of churchly life, that the academic and practical were never really linked.

Theological schools have compared themselves for generations to schools of law and medicine, yet their graduates do not seem to have the divinity equivalent of the physician-scientist or the dialectician-lawyer. This is not to say that unity and synthesis are utterly lacking in theological education. It simply means that synthesis occurs in spite of and not because of the pedagogy and curriculum of the theological school. Theological education insofar as it is the "study of theology," a unitary, coherent study, is self-education, a synthetic accomplishment of the occasional individual student. Furthermore, the problem of a dispersed and incoherent educational experience is not simply the result of the free curriculum of the 1960s and 1970s. The cafeteria approach to curriculum offerings exacerbated the experience of a mere atomism of studies. But its alternative, the required and semi-required curriculum just now returning to the schools, is invariably the result of political negotiations between the area fiefdoms, not of any unitary vision of the whole. To require a pattern of courses among departments whose *raison d'être* and interrelations are neither clear nor self-evident does not reestablish a unified educational experience.[2]

But the indications of something not right in seminary land are not restricted to these experiences of dispersed and inadequate education. The symptoms are not hidden or subtle. The schools and their constituencies have been long aware of them. The many changes and experimentations in theological education in the recent past have been responses to these symptoms. Furthermore, the responses themselves represent a new layer of symptoms. Unfortunately, the responses have tended to take the symptoms at face value and have regarded them as the problem itself. The responses of theological schools to this symptom-as-problem have been along several major lines. The most fundamental and enduring response, one which has set the prevailing ethos of the schools, arises from reading the situation as requiring a pedagogy which translates the academic (theory) into the practical. Hence, the schools have manufactured various devices to bring the dead courses of the "academic" to life:field-based education, case study pedagogies, enlarged faculties in the areas of ministerial skills and activities, interdisciplinary courses, increased offerings in culture-oriented and culture-valued skills (therapeutic, literary, political). Various cycles of curriculum change, conferences on theological education, and special research projects (e.g., Readiness for Ministry) all bespeak this theory-practice ethos. These responses of the schools, a more recent stratum of the symptoms themselves, need not be discredited or dismissed as unimportant. Such efforts do share a common feature. They regard the symptom as the root problem. The problem itself thus remains hidden, with the result that a radical and fundamental critique does not occur. This is why these responses, both institutionally and conceptually, occur within traditional frameworks and do not amount to proposals for thoroughgoing reform.

1. Divinity, Scholarship, and Profession:
The Three Periods of American Theological Education

The problem of the theological school, perhaps like all major problems of complex institutions, has come about through centuries of historical accretion. It occurs as various past solutions obtain institutionalization and symbolization and persist alongside each other into the present. The description of this problem will therefore begin with a brief and simplified periodization of theological education in the United States. If the *location* of the training of ministers is our reference, theological education in the United States falls into two major historical periods, preseminary and seminary. The first period stretches from the beginning of the seventeenth century to about 1800, and the second covers the founding of the first seminaries to the present. However, if the *nature of the education* is our reference, there seem to be three periods: the period of pious learning (divinity), the period of specialized learning, and the period of professional education.

The period of pious learning roughly coincides with the preseminary period.[3] From the founding of the first colonies to the rise of the first seminaries, the congregations expected the minister to be educated. The initial generation of Anglican, Dutch, and Congregationalist ministers was in fact educated abroad. Furthermore, the minister's education was not just in divinity but coincided simply with the education occurring in the (Protestant) university. With the founding of Harvard and Yale, New England at least had schools for the training of ministers on this side of the Atlantic. Even if only a certain percentage of ministers completed the college degree, it was assumed that the education of the minister occurred at a school. The models for American schools were the universities of England, Scotland, and Northern Europe

(Holland). This meant that the basis of education was thorough grounding in biblical and classical languages, and the education in divinity was primarily the study of Scripture and the guides, handbooks, or compendia of dogmatics and ethics being written by continental and English theologians. In this period the first step was taken to distinguish ministerial education from college education, the practice of doing "graduate study" in the subject of divinity. Thus many returned to the college for a special two-year course in divinity. In the mid-eighteenth century there arose the practice of seeking education in divinity with a pastor who was willing to accept one or more students. Modeled on an English practice, these schools of the prophets answered to a new population of believers and clergy created by the Great Awakening. In many cases this too was "graduate education," in that ministers with college degrees sought further work in divinity with a well-known pastor-teacher. And there appears to be close continuity between some of the most famous of these schools of the prophets (such as the Log College of the Tennents in Pennsylvania) and those centers founded by official acts of denominations prior to the rise of the first true seminaries in the early nineteenth century.

In this first period, the education of Protestant clergy is education in divinity. Insofar as it takes its cue from institutions, the universities of seventeenth-century Europe are the imitated models.[4] The American schools looked more to England than to the continent, although the confessions, compendiums, and controversial writings of continental Protestant universities were directly influential on the Presbyterians, Lutherans, and the Dutch. The Dutch clergy looked back directly to Leyden and Utrecht; the Presbyterians looked to the Scottish universities which in turn were under the sway of Holland. Oxford and Cambridge were the models for Harvard and Yale. The result is that both orthodox and scholastic modes of thought and puritan and pietistic modes of thought set the primary ethos for the American education of clergy.

Divinity named not just an objective science but a personal knowledge of God and the things of God in the context of salvation. Hence, the study of divinity (theology) was an exercise of piety, a dimension of the life of faith. The literary expressions of the study of divinity fall into two types, one coming forth from continental Reformed and Lutheran theologians, the other from pastors and teachers of England. The continental writers of the late sixteenth and seventeenth centuries wrote about "the study of theology."[5] The English writers submitted a more informal and piety-centered type of work, a manual of pastoral advice to ministers or students concerning the ministry and its required preparation.[6] American pastors and teachers, looking as they did more to England than to the continent, imitated the pastoral advice type of work. One of the most famous and influential of these works in America was Cotton Mather's *Manuductio ad ministerium* (1726).[7] These guides are especially concerned with the piety, the spirituality of the minister, and they view the study of divinity as an exercise in humility, remorse, and glorification of God. They do not hesitate to recommend books to study, but are not as concerned about the nature or structure of *theologia* or divinity as are the "study of theology" works of the continent.

Specialized scholarship is the approach to the education of ministers characteristic of the second period. It does not strictly coincide with the rise of the theological seminary, partly because it begins a generation or so after the founding of the first seminaries, and partly because it is highly qualified in the seminaries of the third period. Sociologically speaking, the age of specialized scholarship is still with us in that the institutions created by this approach still persist. What in fact is this second approach? It does not describe the concept of the minister as specialist, the specialization of ministries, but rather an approach to the education of the minister in which the student is exposed to a considerable number of scholarly methods and disciplines, known now as the departments or areas of the theological school. So much is this an engrained way of thinking about theological education, it is difficult to imagine that it was not always with us. The transition from the approach of divinity to specialized fields did not occur instantly. The major steps marking this transition are the following.

In the approach of pious learning, theological education coincides simply with university or higher education. While divinity is a distinguishable part of that education, it nevertheless pervades that education and is its apex and crown. The study of classical languages, of rhetoric and grammar, and even of mathematics and astronomy (natural philosophy)—all is ordered toward divinity, toward reading and understanding sacred Scriptures and reading the signs of God's work in the world. At Harvard a tutor would take a class through all these studies year by year. The first sign of a specialized, separated divinity occurred when it became customary for the president of the institution to teach divinity, especially in the more specific sense of positive and controversial theology, in a concentrated way in the final year of the student's college work. This trend finds institutional expression when finally a chair of divinity is instituted, first at Harvard (1721) and then at Yale (1755).[8] With this act, divinity becomes a designated professor's sole responsibility. He attends to it and not to mathematics, astronomy, or rhetoric. This delimited responsibility anticipates the later fields of expertise. The trend is exacerbated when the schools do what Edinburgh did in 1694, add a second chair of divinity, thereby creating areas of emphasis and expertise within divinity itself.

A second step toward the specialized approach, also occurring in the first period, is the development of a graduate component of ministerial education. This occurred both in the form of further study at the existing colleges—a two-year course in divinity—and in the form of study with a well-known pastor, which continued even into the period of the seminaries. This includes the late eighteenth-century centers of study (New Brunswick in New York City and Service Seminary [Xenia] in Western Pennsylvania) which were created by official acts of denominations but which lacked the essential features of what later became seminaries in the full sense of the word.

The third step was the founding of the seminaries themselves, with Andover (1808) providing the New England alternative to the then unitarian Harvard, and Princeton becoming the seminary sponsored by the Presbyterian General Assembly. Thus was inaugurated the age of seminaries in which twenty-two such institutions were founded in the first thirty years of the nineteenth century.[9]

The three steps mentioned so far—the separation of divinity into a distinct area of pedagogy, the postcollege graduate education of the minister, and the rise of seminaries—all create the conditions for a specialized learning approach to ministerial education. They themselves are not the decisive cause. In the transition from the divinity approach to the specialized approach, Europe replaces England and

Scotland as the primary model of theological education. "Replace" may not be an accurate expression. England and Scotland continued to play important roles for Episcopalians and Presbyterians. However, in the second generation of the founding of the seminaries, something happened which introduced an entirely new model and approach for the education of ministers. Faculty members from the first seminaries (Andover, Princeton) went to Germany to study, and when they returned, they programmatically set out to introduce that model to the American schools.[10] Not only did the seminaries begin to take into account German theological scholarship, the German system itself began to influence the very conception of a program of theological study. Hence, after the middle of the nineteenth century, the standard German fourfold division of theological sciences (Bible, dogmatics, church history, practical theology) was widespread.

These developments eventuated in a new paradigm for ministerial study. The divinity approach is largely replaced with a plurality of "theological sciences" requiring specialist teachers. The shift was not from piety to learning. A learned ministry was never seriously questioned in many of the church traditions. The shift was from one meaning of learning to another, from study which deepens heartfelt knowledge of divine things to scholarly knowledge of relatively discrete theological sciences. After the 1860s this approach received further institutional support from the rise of Ph.D. education which, building on the distinction between studies for the ministry and graduate study, created programs of education for scholars and professors. Thus emerged a system of scholarly guilds which reinforced the emerged theological sciences.[11]

Some may want to argue that the period of specialized areas of theological scholarship is still with us. The institutions of this period have in fact persisted into the present. Ph.D. programs still supply teachers for specialized areas. Theological schools are still organized for the most part around the traditional theological sciences. However, it appears that we are now either in a new period or we are living in the transition to a new period. Another paradigm shift seems to have occurred within the past forty or so years. The A.T.S./Carnegie Foundation study of the 1950s noticed it occurring in the pastoral director image of the ministry. The Auburn Project finds a harbinger of the

shift in William Rainy Harper's speech, "Shall the Theological Curriculum be Modified and How?" (1899).[12] That essay was of critical
importance, for it made a plea for what in fact eventually came about
in theological education: an approach based not on the structure of
theological sciences (cf. the German system) but on the highly varied
religious situation of modernity which requires different kinds of minister specialists and which focuses more on current problems than on
scholarly disciplines.

Emerging here is what recent decades have called the minister as
professional.[13] The educational paradigm which this requires is new,
distinguishable from both the divinity and specialized sciences approaches. This new paradigm is not simply an affirmation that the
ministry bears the sociological marks of a profession. On the basis of
that affirmation, it recommends an education whose rationale lies in
its power to prepare the student for designated tasks or activities which
occur (or should occur) in the parish or in some specialized ministry.
To the degree that this is the case, the theological student neither
studies divinity nor obtains scholarly expertise in theological sciences,
but trains for professional activities.

In sum, these three periods reflect the directions of change affecting
religion, the church, the ministry, and the school. Religion and its
environment have undergone a transition from a highly parochial, virtually "Christian" culture to a highly pluralistic, largely secularized
culture whose fate is bound up with worldwide issues and crises. The
church's direction of change in these periods has been from a parochial, denominational if not even confessional absolutism to a more
relative if not ecumenical spirit. The way this change appears in theological schools is not so much in positive ecumenical convictions and
institutions but in the participation by faculties in a transdenomina-
tional world of scholarship established by each faculty member's graduate training, scholarly guild, and specialty. Therefore, what was once
feared as one of the main problems besetting theological education,
narrow denominationalism, seems to be considerably alleviated.[14]

As to the ministry itself, the direction is, as Donald M. Scott says,
from office to profession. The direction of change was from the minister
as comprehensive interpreter and shepherd of faith to manager of a
local society or some related institution. The theological school was in

the first period a place of comprehensive education where divinity education was based primarily on classical languages and classical studies and was taught without specialties in such a way that it was largely self-education. The direction of change was toward a cluster of special subjects, taught in a postcollege institution by specialists of scholarship and church practice. Although the three periods represent a changing direction, it would be a mistake to say that succeeding periods simply replace everything occurring in former periods. The first two approaches have, to a certain extent, survived into the present but in most cases as subordinate to the third approach. While divinity has disappeared as the unifying concept, it persists in the form of a discrete area of studies. However, it is thought of as a discipline or science separated from piety, and this separation promotes the general yearning for churchly and personal relevance and the present nostalgia for "formation." The specialized sciences are all here, supplied by enduring Ph.D. programs and maintained by the guild identities of the faculties, but their rationale and unity are far from self-evident either to students or to faculty. The professional paradigm is the present-day theological school's response to these problems, but it is more an assumed ethos than a self-consciously and theologically established solution.

2. Faith and Institution: Two Dimensions of the Problem of Theological Education

The present study does not attempt a comprehensive treatment of the problems of the theological school, but focuses on one stratum of the problem: the unity and structure of theological study. That stratum may come into view more clearly if we take a brief look at other dimensions of the problem of contemporary theological education. The problem of this study appears to be only one of three major problem areas. They are the problem of theology and faith, the problem of the institution itself, and the problem of the *ratio studiorum*, the rationale for the unity, content, and divisions of theological study.

It seems evident that the deepest, most severe and debilitating problem besetting theological schools is the one they share with Christendom itself, the question of the very possibility and viability of

Christian faith. We cannot so formulate this problem that it appears to rise and decline with the noble efforts of schools and churches. Nor would we so formulate the problem as to make it appear that some ages are ages of faith and some are not. "Ages of faith" tend to turn out to be ages of religion. My concern is with more immediate and symptomatic realities. It simply seems to be the case that faith is not now the binding reality, the primary agenda-setting power at work in contemporary churches and theological schools. To express it differently, the churches have undergone acculturation (which is, in itself, inevitable) in such a way as to lose their ecclesial character.[15] It is this loss or diminution which is at work when the theological school finds itself perplexed as to what its education is really about.

The school has of course a legacy from the past which provides it with a tradition about Christian faith, the ministry, and the church. But these things are present in very formal ways and not as convictional visions of the work of the ministry. One need only glance at almost any of the works of the past on the ministry or on the study of theology (in Luther, Baxter, Mather, Mason) to discover a convictional vision. Even the eloquent pleas of such modernists as Charles A. Briggs and William Adams Brown are informed by such a vision. For them the problem was not a vacuum, an absence of consensus about the task and content of faith and ministry, but a narrow, oppressive denominational restriction of that task. Today the need for such a vision arises not so much from sectarian narrowness as from the problems and crises in Christianity itself resulting from the influence of modern culture. Feuerbach, Marx, Freud, and Heilbroner are names which signal these issues. To the degree that the theological school lacks a vision which can incorporate and deal with these matters, its ethos, activities, and pedagogies will be characterized by a certain unreality.

The second dimension of the problem is institutional and pedagogical. It is a set of problems which attends the way we have been going about theological education in the United States since the early nineteenth century and the origin of the seminary movement. I am referring to the education of Protestant ministers in a postcollege seminary course of three years which offers Bible, church history, theology and a plethora of practical courses. When we ponder four intertwined features of this (seminary) institutionality as it exists today, the conclusion is all but inescapable that present-day theological schools simply cannot provide a *theological* education.

First, almost no theological school can presuppose anything about an admitted student's educational background except the bare fact of the B.A. degree. Most schools list desiderata for the student's college preparation, but these are not specific conditions for admission. A college education, even a liberal arts education, now means an enormous variety of things. The range in quality goes from virtual high-school level education to graduate education. And except for the ability to read English and write sentences, the school cannot presuppose with confidence any specific body of knowledge or skill. It cannot assume and build on a classical education, any specific language, European history, philosophy, psychology or sociology, hermeneutical skills, or dialectic or "thinking." Most students will have a smattering (introductory-course level) of most of these things, but not enough to serve as a base for further education. The occasional student will have majored in one of these areas, but the theological school cannot assume such a coverage for all students. In short, there is some question as to whether seminary-level work can presuppose the liberal arts education which theological studies have always required.

Second, the curriculum of the theological school is an aggregate of more or less independent disciplines, each of which has its method, bibliography, history, scope, current issues, and so forth. Although these disciplines tend still to be classified in the traditional fourfold pattern, they are further dispersed into ten to fifteen areas of teaching: education, preaching, counseling, religion and society, ethics, historical theology, Christianity—and courses, New Testament, Old Testament, various courses covering church history, black studies, feminist theology, church administration, worship, etc. Most of these courses do not occur in some larger theological discipline, but are themselves introductions to a larger world of possible inquiry.

If a student's educational experience is comprehensive, three to four of the six semesters are spent in this sort of course, in being introduced to some new discipline or skill. Further, if students' continuing work attempts any comprehensiveness, they will take one more course in these areas. If the student concentrates—on Old Testament, for instance—this simply means being content with the one-course exposure to many of these areas. Occasionally a student comes to the school with extensive work in religious studies or one of its areas, but this does not alter the more typical pattern. The result is that theological education has the character of a mélange of introductions. The German ideal of the minister as master of several basic theological sciences is certainly not realized. Such education neither produces scholarly control (with the exception of the student who singlemindedly takes an enormous number of courses in some one area) nor does it eventuate in theological thinking or understanding.

Third, in early New England Congregationalism and Presbyterianism, there was a primary harmony between the popular churchly demand for a learned ministry and the goals of Harvard and Yale. Such harmony has been replaced by a fundamental conflict between theological schools, insofar as they retain elements of either a divinity or a specialized sciences approach, and the churches and congregations, insofar as they require institutional-maintenance oriented professionals. In fact, the "theologically" oriented graduate may actually be punished by the ecclesiastical system which rewards un- and anti-theological approaches to ministry. To the degree that the efforts of the theologian-minister do not find confirmation, approval, or encouragement in the churchly setting, a malaise with respect to theological study begins in student years themselves. The student discerns, either vaguely or clearly, that academic studies have little or no relevance to the successful prosecution of the ministry. Undercut at the beginning of study is the motivation needed to persist at serious and difficult theological study.

Finally, for whatever sociological, economic, and other reasons, the ministry is not now attracting (in comparison with science, law, medicine, industry) the most talented and gifted of the population. Furthermore, most of those who are attracted do eventually find acceptance from theological schools which, under financial pressure and facing an oversupply of clergy and dwindling population, are tending to take close to 100 percent of their applicants. The occasional schools which accept one of every three or four applicants are rare.

Recall now the four items: a large proportion of academically marginal students, absence of an academically concerned career-reward

system and motivation, absence of preseminary educational requirements and standards, and the mélange of introductions comprising
much of the three-year course. One can only conclude that a theological education under such conditions is virtually impossible. We are
not making the banal point that the education of ministers today could
be better than it is. We are arguing that its typical result is simply not
a theologically educated minister. There are those, no doubt, who
because of their notions of both church and ministry do not see this
as a problem, who have in effect abandoned the older ideal of a theologically educated ministry. For those of us who retain it, this is a
critical problem, and it is a problem of the *institution* in which theological education occurs. If this reading is correct, it is a situation
parallel to other times in the history of Christendom—the early Middle Ages, Europe prior to the rise of universities, the United States
prior to the coming of the seminaries—when a whole new institutionality was called for.[16]

3. *Ratio Studiorum:* The Third Dimension of
the Problem of Theological Education

This essay is primarily concerned with a third dimension of the problem of the theological school. A symptomology of the travail of theological education takes note of the complaints, the malaise, and the
recent wave of proposed solutions occurring in theological schools.
Altogether these complaints add up to an experience of theological
education as an atomism of subjects without a clear rationale, end, or
unity. This dimension of the problem concerns the content of education for ministry, the unity and divisions of that content, and their
rationale. This in itself is not the problem as it besets the theological
school but the sphere in which the problem occurs. It is neither a
single problem, something to be formulated in a single assertive sentence, nor a highly visible and self-evident state of affairs. It has to do
with a whole cluster of anomalies which have arisen due to the way
in which antiquated solutions of the past have been retained in the
present. It also has to do with the vacuum created by the loss of the
traditional subject matter of the theological school, that which made
a theological school theological. This loss (of *theologia*), attended by

and in part produced by the rise of independent theological sciences, has brought about the situation of which malaise and complaints are symptomatic. That situation is the irreconcilability between an existing unity (subject matter, content) of theological education and the presence of free, independent realms of scholarship, each one pursuing and obeying its own rules. It is just this impasse between divinity and specialized sciences which brought about, in part at least, the abandonment of both for the professional, strategy-oriented programs of recent decades.

This situation has both traditional and modern dimensions. In a traditional sense, the general problem of the content, unity, and structure of whatever is being studied attends any and all education of clergy, whether it occurs in a ninth-century monastery or a twentieth-century denominational seminary. At the same time, this inherited and intrinsic problem has a peculiarly modern form. Theological education today occurs in the wake of the Enlightenment, the rise of the modern university, and the ideal of autonomous scholarship. It thus takes for granted the use of historical methods in theology and the emancipation of various enterprises of interpretation and inquiry which properly pertain to the education of the minister. This modern version of the problem is what called forth on the continent the literature of "theological encyclopedia" with which we shall concern ourselves in subsequent chapters. This is the third dimension of the problem of the theological school, and it is this perennial problem now occurring in a distinctively modern form which is the focus of this essay.

To use an older expression, the third dimension of the problem of the theological school has to do with the study of divinity or "the study of theology." However, the term *divinity* has dropped out of contemporary discourse, and the term *theology* has undergone an unfortunate narrowing and specialization. "Theological education" is now the new language, but since that connotes the whole phenomenon of contemporary seminaries and their curricula, the term is not really equivalent to divinity or the study of theology. Our subject in other words has lost its language, and this fact itself is indicative of the problem. The very nature of the developments in theological education in the third professionalist approach removes "the study of theology" from the agenda of reform, centered as this approach is on the technical problems of bridging theory to ministerial practice. Accordingly, the content, unity, and rationale for the study of theology are not grasped as a problem or task because the professionalist approach unifies the inherited studies under the category of the "academic," presupposes these studies as self-evident, and moves on to the strategic problem of relating such studies to tasks of ministry.

This professionalist approach combines both conservative and liberal elements. It is liberal in its concern for the present and for situations of ministry in the present. Its overall impact is conservative since it leaves unquestioned the structure of theological science inherited from the past. Accordingly, the whole third dimension of the problem is obscured, and this poses for us the special hermeneutical task of recovering that dimension; that is, the peculiarly modern form of the problem of the study of theology. Because the third dimension of the problem is itself multiple, its recovery is not an instantaneous insight but a gradual process. It is closely bound up with the way in which a complex and multistratified heritage functions (or exists nonfunctionally) in the present. What needs to be recovered is what continental theologians call the issue of theological encyclopedia. However, this does not imply a commitment to the antiquarian program of restoring the epoch or literature of theological encyclopedia.[17] We distinguish, therefore, between the encyclopedic *issue* and theological encyclopedia as a particular historical movement in the history of the study of theology.

4. The Reform of Theological Education: Resistances and Resources

The theological school, like all institutions, offers resistance to reform. Four elements of the general ethos of the theological school constitute reactionary forces and they are equally present in "liberal" and "conservative" schools. More associated with the conservative school is the traditionalist commitment to pre-Enlightenment approaches to religious faith. In these schools there is either resistance to or ambivalence about submitting traditional canons of authority (dogmas, passages of Scripture) to historical methods. To the degree that conservative schools adopt and retain the fourfold pattern, they are paradoxically taking into themselves a pattern of studies and mode of thought which originated in the postorthodox dispersion of divinity or theology. Present throughout American theological schools (although more in evidence in denominational than university-related schools) is a second element which would resist reform: the pragmatic, strategy-oriented ethos of theory-practice. This element has virtually become the American theological encyclopedia. As a mind-set, this approach is almost entirely blind to the encyclopedic issue (i.e., the issue of the unity, end, and divisions of theological studies), since it sees the problem of theological education as the technological task of discovering a pedagogy which will train students for the activities of ministry viewed as tasks of an institutionally defined profession.

A third element of resistance to reform, also present in all theological schools, is the scholarly-guild mind-set. According to this mind-set, the *scholarship* involved in one's teaching and research has proven itself, and this confirms the validity of the historic past and the graduate education which set the parameters of the disciplines of ethics, systematic theology, Old Testament, American church history, and so forth. Thus is generated negative resistance to any line of thought which would undermine the traditional pattern of studies which the particular realm of scholarship presupposes. Furthermore, it is almost impossible for the scholarly-guild mind-set to think about theological education in any other way except through the self-evident categories of the guild discipline. Such things as divinity or theology tend to be invisible to scholarly specialists, who find it very difficult to transcend the specialized discipline to the question of the larger pattern of study. In other words, the guild mind-set finds it difficult to entertain the more comprehensive questions of the overall *ratio studiorum*. What is hell for the student (the pedagogical experience of an atomism of courses) is heaven for the scholarly specialist (the freedom and autonomy of specialized research and teaching). One must acknowledge that from the *religionsgeschichtlich* point of view, the ideal of sciences born in the Enlightenment and the European universities, there is a self-evident validity about a designated scholarly activity. What is not self-evident is the validity of that activity as part of the total pattern of theological study.

Finally, resistance to the question of the rationale for studies is offered by those who focus exclusively on what we called the second dimension of the reform of the theological school, the reform of the whole institutional pattern. In this view, the primary problems are political and institutional structures, not theoretically problematic patterns inherited from the past. When the dynamics and course of actual change are considered, this surely is the case. However, it also seems clear that any reform of the theological school which omits the question of the very content, pattern, and goal of theological study must inevitably turn out to be trivial, technological, and cosmetic.

On the other hand, there are powerful forces of discontent in current theological education which provide impetus for criticism and change. Three educational and literary movements have potentially far-reaching effects on the reform of theological education. None of the three, however, has applied its own programmatic to the reform of theological study. The first movement, paradoxically, is at the same time one of the previously-mentioned resistances to reform. It is roughly coincident with the third period of theological education and the model of theory and practice. While it is the case that this professionalist formulation has tended to freeze the present structure of study into the academic and the practical and has promoted technological (professional skills) models of the ministry, it also amounts to a radical criticism of traditional theological education, and that criticism may itself suggest items for reform. We are referring here to the enormous expansion of areas of practical theology and the appropriations of various culture sciences (linguistics, social science, phenomenology, new rhetoric, literary criticism, political science, etc.). Because of the larger problem—the loss of *theologia* and the resulting dispersion, autonomy, and isolation of disciplines—these appropriations have resulted in practical theology's loss of its theological component. In current theological schools, practical theology frequently becomes simply a pragmatics of ministry. Yet these developments are not simply absurd or invalid, and they contain potentialities for criticism and reform.

A second movement and potential source of criticism and change is frequently thought of more as a competitor and enemy than as a friend of the theological school.[18] This is the religious studies movement in the colleges and universities. This movement may have an even more severe problem of subject matter and rationale for studies than the theological school. For its purported unity, religion, is far from established as a real or functional subject matter, and thus there seems to be no single "science" of such, much less an agreed-upon division of specific disciplines constituting those studies. On the other hand, these programs for the scholarly study and teaching of religion confront the theological school with its parochialism in two ways. First, the parochialism of the theological school appears not only in the loss of *theologia* but in the loss of the question of religion. Some theologians (e.g., Karl Barth) may dismiss the question of religion as anthropocentric and untheological. But surely it is an impoverished approach which insists that faith and Christian faith utterly repudiate everything analogous to or related to the ancient and widespread experience of the sacred. Second, there is a parochialism about a faith, ministry, or education built on the traditional true religion and false religion approach. The alternative to this need not be a senseless eclecticism which repudiates determinate faith and ecclesiality. The Christian churches, however, still have the overall effect of relating themselves to other faiths and world cultures in modes of utter exclusion and alienation, contributing to and confirming exploitive, competitive, and rapacious postures which have so long characterized the nations of Christendom. We are saying, therefore, that the understanding of world religious faiths has a legitimate presence in the study of theology.[19]

A third potentially reforming movement and literature is liberation theology. This term includes both general programmatic appeals to reconceive the nature of theology itself and specific agendas of theological feminism, black theology, and Third World theology. The literature of these movements is severely critical of traditional Western "academic" theology and yet has mounted almost no serious criticism of or proposals about theological study. The enemy targeted is, in other words, the narrowed-down academic specialty, theology. Preoccupied with the critique of the specialty, this literature has yet to address itself to the real culprit, the whole institutionality, legacy, and pattern of study of "theology" in the broader sense of that word; in short, the theological school. But the criticisms proffered by this literature, especially as they raise the question of praxis and the issue of the living context of theological study, have potentially explosive ramifications for the reform of the study of theology.

None of these three locations of criticism have yet made comprehensive proposals for the reform of the theological school. The practical theologies and the professionalization of the ministry have in fact effected changes in the school. Religious studies and the consideration of world faiths is largely a literary movement, as is liberation theology. The exception to the latter is that minor changes of course offerings, faculty, and languages have been effected in some schools by theological feminism and black theology.

The chapters which follow will offer no blueprint of theological study, no detailed plan for curricular reform. They will attempt two things: an account of the aforedescribed third dimension of the problem of reform, the encyclopedic problem of the pattern of studies and its rationale; and some suggestions concerning the restoration of *theologia* as the unity and end of theological study, requisites for working with the problem, and implications about a pattern of study. The problem itself will only gradually emerge as the strata of the past still at work in the present are uncovered. One stratum concerns the loss of *theologia* in both its classical meanings of "knowledge" and discipline. For this reason, a chapter on the career of *theologia* begins the description. Behind this loss of *theologia* in theological education is the demise of the classical Christian way of authority and the emergence of the critical principle and its attending disciplines in the treatment of the authorities themselves.[20] The painful paradox this produces for the theological school is that *theologia* which was replaced by the emancipated areas of scholarship is at the same time needed as the subject-matter unity of theological study.

The choice between *theologia* and the critical principle is a bitter one. The story of the rise of the modern theological school is a story of the dispersion of theology into independent sciences. The literature reflecting that dispersion and even attempting a rationale for it is the literature of eighteenth- and nineteenth-century theological encyclopedia. This displacement of *theologia* by theological sciences plays a central role in the present-day problem of theological education. This is why several chapters of this essay will record this displacement through an account of the encyclopedia movement. This movement was itself a proffered solution of the problem created by the loss of *theologia*. That solution can be summarized as: (1) the conception of theology as an aggregate term for sciences related to the ministry, a step decisively taken by Schleiermacher, and (2) the fourfold pattern of Bible, church history, dogmatics, and practical theology. This solution is retained in current theological schools and the incoherencies and intrinsic difficulties of the solution therefore pervade the schools. In addition, theological schools have attempted to transcend the old encyclopedic solution in a theory-practice encyclopedia which threatens to turn all theological education into pragmatics and technology. But to grasp the difficulties and engage in these criticisms requires first the archaeological recovery of the historical strata operative in current theological study.

NOTES

1. "Theological education" is what is under review throughout this essay. I should clarify now that I am addressing primarily North American Protestant institutions for the education of clergy. However, it seems to be the case that most of what is argued also pertains to European theological schools and to Roman Catholic schools, and has implications for the study of theology in other contexts than simply clergy education, such as lay education and theology as it might occur in departments of religious studies.

2. The conclusion of the H. Richard Niebuhr study of theological education in the 1950s under the sponsorship of AATS and the Carnegie Foundation was along these lines. "The greatest defect in theological education today is that it is too much an affair of piecemeal transmission of knowledge and skills, and that, in consequence, it offers too little challenge to the student to develop his own resources and to become an independent, lifelong inquirer, growing constantly while he is engaged in the work of the ministry" (Niebuhr, D. D. Williams, and J. M. Gustafson, *The Advancement of Theological Education* [New York: Harper & Brothers, 1957], p. 209).

3. For a fairly detailed account of this preseminary period see William O. Shewmaker, "The Training of the Protestant Ministry in the United States of America before the Establishment of Theological Seminaries," Papers of the American Society of Church History, 2d series, vol. 6 (1921). Also pertinent to this period is M.L. Gambrell, *Ministerial Training in 18th Century New England* (New York: Columbia University Press, 1937); Donald M. Scott, *From Office to Profession: The New England Ministry, 1750–1850* (Philadel-

phia: University of Pennsylvania Press, 1978); Frederick G. Gotwald, "Early American Lutheran Theological Education, 1745–1845," *Lutheran Quarterly*, vol. 45 (1916); David Hall, *The Faithful Shepherd: History of the New England Ministry in the 17th Century* (Chapel Hill, N. C.: University of North Carolina Press, 1977); J. Johnson, "Early Theological Education West of the Alleghenies," *Papers of the American Society of Church History*, 2d series, vol. 5; and B. Sadtler, "The Education of Ministers by Private Tutors, Before the Establishment of Theological Seminaries," *Lutheran Church Review* 12 (April 1894).

4. For a detailed account of the Protestant universities of Europe in the seventeenth century, their history, faculties, and academic programs, see F. A. Tholuck, *Das akademische Leben des siebzehnten Jahrhunderts* (Halle, 1853). See also P.D. Bourchenin, *Études sur les académies protestantes en France au XVIe et au XVIIe siècle* (Paris, 1882) for the French reformed schools. For Holland, C. Sepp, *Het godgeleerd onderwijs in Nederland gedurende de 16e en 17e eeuw* (Leyden, 1874). See also F. Paulsen, *The German Universities and University Study* (New York: Charles Scribner's Sons, 1902).

5. Hyperius (Andreas Gerhard), claimed by both Reformed and Lutheran churches, wrote one of the first great works of this sort, which became a model for the later literature: *De theologo, seu de ratione studii theologici* (Basel, 1556). A fairly extensive summary of it can be found in Robert Preus, *The Theology of Post-Reformation Lutheranism* (St. Louis: Concordia Publishing House, 1970), vol. 1. The work is especially significant for being the first to propose the classical fourfold division of Bible, dogmatics, church history, and practical theology. Beza published his *De theologe sive de ratione studii theologi* in the same year. Other reformed theologians who wrote works of this sort are J.S. Alsted, Bullinger, Crocius, Gaussen, Heidegger, Keckerman, Perizonius, and Voetius. Lutheran theologians who wrote such works are J. Andreae, Berckelmann, Calov, Chryteaus, Johann Gerhard, Selnekker, Thamer, and Weller. Luther, Erasmus, and Melanchton had all addressed the subject in shorter writings.

6. The best-known work of this sort is probably Richard Baxter's *The Reformed Pastor* (1655). In addition, two other works stand out as being especially important for the colonies: Henry Dodwell, *Two Letters of Advice* (1672) and Thomas Bray, *Bibliotheca parochialis* (1697).

7. This work was translated from its original Latin into English under the title, *Dr. Cotton Mather's Student and Teacher* (London, 1781). Almost as important as Mather's work is Samuel Willard's *Brief Directions to a Young Scholar Designing the Ministry for the Study of Divinity* (Boston, 1735).

8. This too is an imitation of English practices. The first chair of divinity at Edinburgh was instituted in 1620 and in 1694 a second chair was created there.

9. For what I am calling the second period, especially as it has to do with the founding and development of Protestant seminaries, I am especially in-

debted to unpublished materials collected and written by the authors of the Auburn Project under the direction of Robert Lynn. The Project, soon to be published, will be the fullest history of North American Protestant theological education to date. The account of three periods offered here owes much to the Project's work, but in no way does justice to that study.

10. Two examples of programmatic articles urging an imitation of the German approach to the education of ministers are the following: A Society of Clergymen, "Thoughts on the State of Theological Science and Education in our Country," *Bibliotheca sacra,* vol. 1 (1844); Edward Robinson, "Theological Education in Germany," *Biblical Repository,* vol. 1, nos. 1, 2, 3, and 4 (1833).

11. I owe this notion of the importance of the Ph.D. movement beginning at Yale and Johns Hopkins to an unpublished lecture by one of the Auburn Project researchers, Prof. Glenn Miller of Southeastern Baptist Seminary.

12. *American Journal of Theology* (1899).

13. See especially Charles F. Feilding, *Education for Ministry* (Dayton: AATS, 1966).

14. Charles Briggs's eloquent statement, "A Plea for the Higher Study of Theology," *American Journal of Theology* (July 1904), sees ecclesiastical domination of theological science as the main foe of the scientific or scholarly ideal of theological study. W.A. Brown saw narrow denominationalism as one of the two primary evils of the system of ministerial training in his day ("The Seminary Tomorrow," *Harvard Theological Review,* vol. 12, no. 2 [April 1919]).

15. The term *ecclesial* occasionally finds its way into this study. It is used in place of the now more diffuse term *Christian* to refer to features constitutive of a certian type of universal and redemptive mode of corporate existence. As such it is both an ideal-normative and historical-descriptive term. It points to ideal (eschatological) features of an actual historical community. For elaboration, see the author's *Ecclesial Man: A Social Phenomenology of Faith and Reality* (Philadelphia: Fortress Press, 1974).

16. By institutionality I mean the solving of a community problem by the creation of a new enduring social structure, a new way of institutionalizing. For instance, the rise of the seminaries in early nineteenth-century North America was a new institutionality designed to solve the problem of the training of ministers.

17. The term *theological encyclopedia,* current in Europe from the late eighteenth century on and in English-speaking countries in the last part of the nineteenth century, is still in use by continental theologians who write about the study of theology. Gerhard Ebeling, *Studium der Theologie: eine enzyklopädische Orientierung* (Tübingen, 1975), English translation by D. A. Priebe, *The Study of Theology* (Philadelphia: Fortress Press, 1978); Wolfhart Pannenberg, *Theology and the Philosophy of Science,* trans. F. McDonagh (Philadelphia: Westminster Press, 1976), pp. 14ff; Friedrich Mildenberger, *Theorie der Theologie: Enzyklopädie als Methodenlehre* (Stuttgart: Calwer Verlag, 1972).

18. For an excellent discussion of the relation between theology and religious studies, see Schubert Ogden's "Theology and Religious Studies: Their Difference and the Difference it Makes," *Journal of the American Academy of Religion*, vol. 46 (March, 1978).

19. At one time, the study of world religions was considered an important element in theological study. Thus, for instance, see the following: Alfred Cave, *An Introduction to Theology* (Edinburgh: T. & T. Clark, 1886); E. O. Davies, *Theological Encyclopedia: An Introduction to the Study of Theology* (London: Hodder & Stoughton, 1905); Paul Wernle, *Einführung in das theologische Studium* (Tübingen: J.C.B. Mohr, 1921); James Drummond, *Introduction to the Study of Theology* (Macmillan, 1884). One of the few current proposals on the structure of theological study to give the study of other faiths a prominent role is George Rupp's convocation address at the Harvard Divinity School, Fall, 1979.

20. The expression "way of authority" is used several times in this study, especially in chapter 6. It is little more than a code word for certain features of classical Catholic and Protestant ways of grounding claims, namely in some specifiable entity (Scripture, text, church father) whose truth character was an a priori quality. As an authority, the text could be a norm for truth but could not itself be subject to something outside itself to determine its truth.

PART 1

THE DISPLACEMENT OF *THEOLOGIA:* A STUDY IN THE HISTORY OF PRESUPPOSITIONS

2

Theologia: The History of
a Concept

It should be clear that a thoroughgoing analysis, criticism, and reconstruction of theological education requires a descriptive uncovering of concepts and imageries formed in past epochs and still operative in the theological schools. A theological school is not simply a multiplicity of pedagogical and institutional undertakings but a particular way the theological past is sedimented. Patterns of meaning, convictions, and images, confessional and otherwise, pervade the literature, curricula, and enterprises of a theological school. They provide the rationale, stated or hidden, for what the theological school is and does. Some of these concepts and images are self-consciously held and defended (e.g., the importance of Scripture) and some have rarely if ever been thematized (e.g., the nature of the distinction between the academic and the practical). The concepts are present in all sorts of modes and meanings: hidden, defended, outmoded, unformulated, disguised in modern terminology. This means that straightforward, fact-oriented description of the theological school fails to do justice to its complex character.

The descriptive sorting out of this multiplicity is in part a historical task, a consulting of theological education's historical past to help uncover strata operative in the present. And yet it is more than a straightforward historical depiction of major periods, literary landmarks, and important developments. The theological school as a school for the education of the church's leadership (the priesthood, the ministry) is itself a way of conceiving things: the church, the ministry, Christian faith, theology. Basic conceptions determine the school's interpretation of the end, the unity, the subject matter(s), the course of what used to be called "the study of theology." These conceptions include metaphors, paradigms, convictions resting on classical orthodoxies, models pedagogical and political. Their present meaning, function, and even absence are the outcome of a long history. Hence, what is necessary is a historical sifting which traces the career of the fundamental concepts and imageries now at work in theological schools. For example, the very notion of the *unity* of theological study and, as part of that, the nature of theology itself, has a historical career. The transformations which "theology" has undergone are an important part of the story of theological education and an important clue to its present-day problems. Current meanings of and approaches to "theology" are the outcome of this historical career in which very different notions vie with each other, some winning and others losing out.

None of these events and developments simply remain in the past. For example, if present-day theological schools do not understand theology to be a personal, cognitive disposition toward divine things, that negation is not just a past event but a present presupposition. Furthermore, the very fact that the personal disposition toward divine things is not seen in connection with "theology" but is located in other ways (as "spirituality") in the theological school refers us to the career of the notion "theology." Instead of a straightforward historical narrative, our task is one of tracing the accumulating, changing career of the important concepts and presuppositions of present-day theological education. That is the historiography needed for a program of theological critique and reform of theological education. It is, to use Michel Foucault's term, an archaeology of the theological school.[1]

A glance at present-day theological schools shows us that various lines of history are pertinent to our task. To put it differently, the story of the theological school can be told in a number of ways, each one with its own focus: the founding and development of the schools themselves as institutions, the *literature* of the study of theology, the career of theology itself, even the total enterprise of interpretation in the Christian churches. The first option, an institutional history of theological education, will in no way be attempted here.[2] Because the way "theology" is conceived determines any approach to "the study of theology" and theological education, the career of "theology" as it pertains to theological study will be traced in a general way. Chapters 3 through 5 contain an account of post-Reformation writings on the

study of theology and its succeeding literature, theological encyclopedia. This little-known literature is an aspect of an almost buried past
of theological education, yet it forged concepts which still structure
theological schools, especially theory-practice and the fourfold curricular pattern. The archaeology of theological study will proceed
then on two lines. The first will trace the career of *theologia*, the
shifting meanings of its major strands.[3] The second will set forth
the way in which the study of theology was thematized, articulated in
a literature in which originated basic proposals still operative in
theological education.

The literature which pursues, interprets, and is entitled "theology"
seems endless. Such a massive and complex articulation clearly indicates that the term *theology* is fundamentally ambiguous. This ambiguity does not simply mean that systematic theologians dispute the
nature and method of theology, but rather that the term refers to
things of entirely different *genres*. There are two fundamentally different premodern senses of the term.[4] We must first review these
senses and monitor the career of each sense before we are ready to
consider the peculiarly modern usages. The two senses are these.
First, theology is a term for an actual, individual cognition of God and
things related to God, a cognition which in most treatments attends
faith and has eternal happiness as its final goal. Second, theology is a
term for a discipline, a self-conscious scholarly enterprise of understanding. In the former sense theology is a habit *(habitus)* of the human soul. In the latter it is a discipline, usually occurring in some sort
of pedagogical setting. The ambiguity, the double reference and genre
of the term *theology* does not originate with theology itself, the church
and its teachers. It is the outcome of a similar ambiguity and double
reference occurring in the language of human "science" in premodern
Western philosophy.

In the West the vision of human being as a cognitive animal, the
vision of the possibility of science distinguished from opinion and rhetorical manipulation, is primarily the work of Plato and Aristotle. In
Aristotle the term for knowledge, *episteme*, obtains the double meaning of true knowledge (contrasted with *doxa*, opinion) and an organized
body of knowledge or deliberate inquiry producing such. *Episteme* can
be quite properly translated both as knowledge and as science or dis-

cipline. The two senses were of course related. *Episteme* as knowledge meant a grasp of something's causes, hence the possibility of an inquiry (discipline) into causes. This same double meaning persisted in the Latin term which translated *episteme*, namely, *scientia. Scientia* thus means knowledge, a habit of the soul, by which the true is distinguished from the false. Citing pseudo-Grosseteste, Richard McKeon says that "knowledge *(scientia)* is a passion or a perfection resulting from the union of something intelligible and an intellectual power."[5] But *scientia* can refer to the enterprise of investigation or reflection which produces the knowledge. And as these enterprises can be directed to different sorts of things, types of *sciences* arise.

It was this tradition and this language which was applied to the term *theologia* in medieval Christianity, and with the application came the double reference. Without clarifying the double usage, the question of whether or not theology is a science is not at all a clear question. And because of the double meaning, the ambiguity, there can be no straightforward history of "theology." Rather, there can be, on the one hand, a history of the church's claim that faith facilitates an individual cognitive act and, on the other, a history of interpretation (inquiry, argument, scholarship) in the church.[6] And though related the two histories are not identical.

In the following brief exposition the two premodern senses of theology will be distinguished and the career of each one will be traced in three major periods—periods in which very different treatments of the particular sense in question emerge, and with them new meanings. The one sense will here be called "theology/knowledge" and the other sense "theology/discipline." Furthermore, it will be argued that the three periods are marked by changes in the institutional setting of theology (e.g., the rise of universities), and that there are correlations between the two senses in each period. The three periods do not coincide exactly with the conventional epochs of church history, but are distinguished by the prevailing institutional environments of theology. The first period covers early patristic and early medieval Christendom prior to the rise of the medieval universities. The second period ranges from the origin of the universities in the twelfth century (Bologna, Paris, Oxford) up to the so-called modern university, of which Halle is a prototype.[7] In the third period the seminary arises, after Trent in Catholicism, and in the nineteenth century in Protestantism. Modeling itself on the Enlightenment-type university of Europe, the seminary developed faculties, disciplines, realms of scholarship parallel to the universities. Although the seminary is different from the university as an institution for the education of clergy, it too embodies and exemplifies what happened to theology in the third period.

1. The Early Christian Centuries

Theology/Knowledge

It may seem misleading to speak of theology in the period of the first eleven centuries of Christianity. The term itself rarely occurs, and when it does it refers to pagan authors, like Orpheus, who dealt with religion. The exceptions to this are occasional Greek fathers (Eusebius, pseudo-Dionysius) who mean by it the true, mystical knowledge of the one God. But however rare the term, the phenomenon itself, the knowledge of God, was very much a part of the Christian movement and Christian (patristic) literature. In other words a salvifically oriented knowledge of divine being was part of the Christian community and tradition long before it was named theology.

Theology/Discipline

The second sense of the term *theology* picks up that meaning of *episteme* and *scientia* which refers to a cognitive enterprise using appropriate methods and issuing in a body of teachings. Although this sort of thing had some existence in the church prior to the Middle Ages, it did not go by the name "theology." Some appropriation of classical learning had occurred in the church since the second century. And learning of a sort was promulgated in the monasteries.[8] The door through which classical learning and classical literature entered monastic education was reading, memorizing, expounding, and meditating on Scripture. Furthermore, the great teachers of the church from patristic times on had engaged in what now could be called inquiry, a discipline of thought and interpretation occurring in their commentaries on Scripture and in their polemical and pedagogical writings. In Boethius's time this was more apt to be thought of as (Christian) philosophy. Whatever the term, there was in this early period, in addition to knowledge of God (the cognitive act, the illumined mind), the effort of discerning and setting forth the truth given to the world by God through Jesus. This effort had primarily the character of exposition, the interpretation of the received text from Scripture or council.[9] The truth of the revealed texts could be assumed, hence the task was to discern and properly formulate its meaning.

2. From the Middle Ages to the Enlightenment

From one point of view the period from the twelfth century to the Enlightenment and the modern university is an identifiable epoch in the history of Christianity. Even though another branch of Christianity, Protestantism, arose in that period, it still falls very much in this epoch and shares its characteristics. What gives the period its unity is the coming together of the classical patristic doctrinal scheme and the school. The result is the appropriation of learning, especially from philosophy, into a framework to explore and express the classical scheme. The result, in other words, is *theologia* as *scientia* in the distinctive scholastic sense of a method of demonstrating conclusions. The distinction between theology as knowledge and theology as discipline becomes sharpened. And as theology as discipline grows in the school, it is also opposed by those who see theology as a salvific knowledge. Prior to the universities were schools of another kind: palace schools, cathedral schools, monastic schools, traditional centers of learning, like Paris, which would become universities in the Middle Ages. And later in the university period are movements, especially the Renaissance, in which momentum is gathering toward the Enlightenment. Once the university came on the scene and with it the circle of Aristotelian sciences reformulated by Roger Bacon and others, a new literature arose—anticipated, however, by.encyclopedic works of Cassiodorus and Isadore of Seville. Some writings described the circle of sciences and the place of *theologia* therein.[10] In addition came works reflecting the new methods of inquiry in the schools, works of sentences, summas, introductions. And as the Thomist line developed theology more and more as a *scientia* in the sense of a discipline, a theoretical science, so came reaction against this from the Augustinian-monastic line (Bonaventure) which insisted that *theologia* had to do with the mind's road to God.

Theology/Knowledge

From its beginnings, the Christian community has laid claim to a knowledge of God, to a divine illumination of the human intellect operative in the salvation of the human being. Pseudo-Dionysius called this knowledge the "mystical theology." But in the second period, and with the coming of the universities and the renaissance of Aristotle, an appropriated philosophical scheme establishes the precedent of calling this knowledge of God *theologia.* The philosophical apparatus includes not only the concept of *episteme* but the Aristotelian anthropology of three powers of the soul. In that anthropology *episteme,* knowledge, is a *hexis,* one of the three states or enduring characteristics of the soul.[11] Thus, for example, virtue in contrast to a particular act of virtue is an enduring, defining, structural feature of the human soul. The school theologians appropriated this anthropology, and translated *hexis* by the Latin term, *habitus.* Hence, they portrayed knowledge *(scientia)* as a habit, an enduring orientation and dexterity of the soul. It was natural then to see theology as a *habitus,* a cognitive disposition and orientation of the soul, a knowledge of God and what God reveals.

This meaning of *theologia* was not just a reflection of differences between one strand of medieval thinkers and another. Those like Thomas who thought of *theologia* as a discipline, a theoretical science, did not abandon the notion that it was also a cognitive state. The following definition attempts to capture the standard meaning of theology throughout this second period, from the twelfth through the seventeenth centuries: *theologia* is a state and disposition of the soul which has the character of knowledge. There were, of course, many debates about this throughout the period: between Thomists and Augustinians, Thomists and nominalists, Catholics and Protestants, Lutherans and Reformed, but the issue turned on what *kind* of knowledge (habit) theology was. And if there is a dominant position, it is that theology is a *practical,* not theoretical, habit having the primary character of wisdom.[12] It is not our task here to sort out these controversies. The most important point is that in the second period theology characteristically refers to a practical, salvation-oriented (existential-personal) knowledge of God. It is not an easy point to grasp, since this usage of the term has been long absent from the Christian community, its churches and schools.

So far I have stressed that the one sense of theology, theology/knowledge, pervades the second period. There were, however, real differences of emphasis, especially between the Thomist school and what Congar calls the Churchmen of the Augustinian line.[13] This line continues the first period's notion of a divine illumination of the intellect and sees the theology/discipline emphasis of the schools as a serious distortion. Both lines agree that theology is a *habitus,* an aptitude of the soul, but the Churchmen see it more as a directly infused gift of God, tied directly with faith, prayer, virtues, and yearning for God. It is just this understanding of theology which is at work later in the seventeenth-century Reformed thinkers like Alsted and Polanus who see God as the exemplar theologian. They mean by this that God's own self-knowledge is the pure archetype of theology.[14] Furthermore, this emphasis on theology as concrete knowledge of God leading to salvation is taken up again as the primary emphasis of European pietism. Spener, Francke, and those influenced by them in the first half of the eighteenth century (Budde, Gundling, Rambach) explicitly say that the purpose of theology is salvation. The study of theology is thus a *cultura animi* (Francke). The pietists' focus on the theologian, the life of the student, the training in the Christian life, assumes this Augustinian-monastic view of theology.

We can say, however, that in the second period the sense of theology as knowledge of God continues but also departs from the understanding of the first period. God's illumining operation on the intellect is affirmed from the time of the church fathers. But with the universities and Aristotelian philosophy, this illumination is understood as a *habitus* of the soul.[15] And while Thomists and Churchmen may debate whether it is simply a divine gift or a cognition advanced by human effort, it still is something which occurs in connection with schools. It is connected with insight into Scripture and that in turn is served by commentaries on Scripture. In other words, in this second period theology may be (in the one sense) wisdom, but it is a wisdom which can be promoted, deepened, and extended by human study and argument. This is why a literature on "the study of theology" connotes study which pertains to this salvific knowledge (wisdom) of God and of things pertaining to God.

Theology/Discipline

Regardless of how "theology" was conceived and carried out, there were in the church prior to the twelfth century enterprises of learning and teaching. There were "theologians" who engaged in controversy (Gottshalk, Erigena), refuted heresy, and even offered more or less systematic expositions of Christian doctrine (Origen). But prior to the twelfth century these enterprises were not thought of as a part of a "science" in the Aristotelian sense of a demonstrative undertaking. With the second period and the coming of the universities, this earlier learning, teaching, and exposition continued, but a great change took place in how they were conceived. Along with law, medicine, arts (including philosophy), "theology" names a faculty in a university and some ordered procedures which yield knowledge. It was not simply the direct cognitive vision of something given to it, a cognitive *habitus* of the soul, but a deliberate and methodical undertaking whose end was knowledge. Promoted especially by Thomas Aquinas and the schoolmen, theology in this sense became a discipline.

The transition of Christian learning and teaching based on Scripture (*sacra pagina*) into an Aristotelian science (*sacra doctrina*), while primarily the work of Thomas and the thirteenth-century schoolmen, was made possible by a number of preceding historical accomplishments.[16] The rise of *centers* of learning after the reform of Alcuin in connection with both cathedrals and monasteries was an important anticipation of the universities, most of which originate in the thirteenth through fifteenth centuries all over Europe.[17] These abbey and cathedral schools were not only the settings for Peter Lombard, Abelard, Hugh of St. Victor, and Gilbert of la Porrée, whose work laid the foundations for theology as a discipline, but they were the recipients of the renaissance of Aristotle.[18] The coming of Aristotle to Christian learning may have been the decisive catalyst for the precipitation of the new theological science, but it was not the only stimulus. The use of classical learning had long been accepted, even in the monastic schools. Such learning may have entered the schools as a servant, but it held the seeds of the independence later asserted in the Renaissance and Enlightenment.

One part of this classical learning was dialectic, serving initially as an instrument of exposition but then thematized by Abelard as an independent method. And with this comes the epoch-making distinction between commentary-exposition *(lectio)* and rational inquiry which uncovered what had been previously hidden *(quaestio)*, between expounding the text and displaying the intelligibility of the content. In the beginning the questions had only an arbitrary order, but soon works appeared providing some rational sequence to the questions, a sequence which displayed the very structure of the articles of faith in relation to each other.

In this way theology as science/discipline was born. Theology could occupy a legitimate place, in fact the reigning place, along with law and liberal arts in the new institution of learning, the university. As a discipline it could have a method of its own, hence method itself could be thematized and become the occasion of controversy. *Sacra doctrina* is a discipline sufficiently parallel to physics and metaphysics to be a science.[19] As such it had founding principles and it could proceed to connect the principles with conclusions. It may be argued that this is not "science" in a very full sense. Thomas suggests this when he assigns sacred doctrine the status of a subalternate science. The very thing that qualifies its scientific character, the supernatural origin of its principles, is, however, also what makes it the reigning queen and provides it with a superior knowledge.

Needless to say, there was enormous fallout from the rise of theology as an Aristotelian, university science. The very fact that it occurred in universities and not institutions presided over by bishops or abbots created a new distance between theology and the church. The fact that it occurred in a faculty as an inquiry with its own methods meant that theology (discipline) was a matter of study and part of one's overall studies. Pertinent to theology now is the question of a *ratio studiorum*, a rationale for the studies which are theological. And with this question comes a new literature, the literature of "the study of theology."[20] Theology as Aristotelian science continued throughout what I am calling the second period, from the thirteenth to the eighteenth century, and in both Catholic and Protestant universities and schools.[21] We must not forget, however, that this meaning of theology did not displace what was the more primary sense of the term in this same period, theology as a practical *habitus* of knowledge whose end is salvation. The two senses exist side by side and are present in the literature of both Catholic and Protestant scholasticism.

3. From the Enlightenment to the Present

The third period covers roughly the seventeenth century to the present. In this period the two genres of theology continue but undergo such radical transformation that the original senses of theology as knowledge (wisdom) and as discipline virtually disappear from theological schools. Theology as a personal quality continues (though not usually under the term *theology*), not as a salvation-disposed wisdom, but as the practical know-how necessary to ministerial work. Theology as discipline continues, not as the unitary enterprise of theological study, but as one technical and specialized scholarly undertaking among others; in other words, as systematic theology. These developments are the outcome of theology's long career. They are peculiarly modern and, to some degree, even distinctively North American. But they are the result of events and movements occurring throughout the eighteenth and nineteenth centuries, and are not unrelated to the theology-as-Aristotelian-science development of the second period.

Two movements of human cultural and religious life inaugurated the third period: continental pietism and the Enlightenment. Each one had ancestral movements in the past. Pietism gathered up traditions from Catholic mysticism, the Reformation, English puritanism, and even the modern turn to the subject. The Enlightenment drew on the revivals of classical learning which had been occurring since the twelfth century. Both movements constituted a basic critique of the scholastic theologies of the second period, and this had a cataclysmic effect on the study of theology. The institutional setting for the Enlightenment's modification of the study of theology was the modern university. The university of Halle in Germany, founded in 1694, is sometimes called the first modern university, and the University of Berlin later became the prototype of faculties of specialized scholarship. In such universities originated critical ideals of scholarship, specialized faculties, and scholarly inquiries relatively free from confessional restrictions. This was the setting which so drastically altered both theology/knowledge and theology/discipline. The institutional setting of pietism was originally also the university, but the final stage of the transformation of theology/knowledge occurred not in the modern university but in the denominational seminary. The third period, therefore, is united not by one single type of institution but rather by two types, related to each other by somewhat contradictory agendas and goals: the ideal of theological scholarship (the post-Enlightenment continental university) and the ideal of the practically-trained minister (the twentieth-century Protestant seminary).

Theology/Discipline: From Unitary Discipline
to Aggregate of Specialties

In the narrower and more precise sense of the word, "Enlightenment" names a widespread eighteenth-century cultural movement in Western society which challenged traditional authority-oriented modes of thought and in their stead proffered critical, rational, and historical ways of understanding. In this narrow sense, there were Enlightenment theologians and philosophers who occupied a specific period of time and were the object of criticism by later thinkers. But in a broader sense Enlightenment is not simply a discrete period but a continuing part of modernity. Enlightenment introduced modes of thought into culture, education, and religion which are still very much with us in the form of ideals of scholarship, evidence, and criticism. With these ideals came the idea of the university in the modern sense, a community of free scholarship based on universal canons of evidence and inquiry.

It had been customary since the founding of the universities in the Middle Ages to differentiate the faculties: canon law, medicine, theology. Furthermore, within theology itself, the seventeenth century, drawing in part on the Middle Ages, applied all sorts of qualifying adjectives to the term *theology*.[22] However it sounds, this nomenclature does not partition theology into scholarly disciplines or sciences in the modern sense. It rather designates different ways in which the cognitive *habitus* of the knowledge of divine things can be oriented to its object or on different aspects of that object which can be the

subject of knowledge. In other words, theology itself was not divided
into disciplines. In the eighteenth century two things occur which
result in a totally new conception of theology/discipline. It is somewhat
ironical that continental pietism played its own role in the rise of
theology in the modern sense of specialized disciplines. Pietism attempted to correct a scholastic-scientific approach to the study of theology in which rational demonstrations were more central than faith
and personal formation. Central to pietism was the individual's progress in spiritual matters, hence the emphasis on prayer and discipline
as the setting of theological study. However, the pietists also wanted
to correct any notion of the minister as primarily a knower, a resident
scholastic theologian, hence they very much stressed preparation and
training for specific tasks of ministry. This introduces, in addition to
personal formation, a second telos of the study of theology: training
for ministerial activities. This in turn sets the stage for conceiving the
study of theology as a plurality of studies preparatory for such activities. It is not surprising, therefore, that theologians in the first half of
the eighteenth century influenced by Spener and Francke are the very
first to speak of theological *sciences.*[23]

The primary movement, however, which effected the pluralization
and specialization of theology was the Enlightenment. The Enlightenment was in part a revolt, an emancipation of thought and inquiry
from institutional and even cognitive authorities. In pre-Enlightenment theologies, the *norms* for theology/discipline were the *articuli
fidei* themselves. These doctrines of church tradition were not products, accomplishments of theology, but the *principia*, the givens. They
were, accordingly, the norms for interpreting Scripture and determining Christian responsibility and Christian truth. With the Enlightenment and the modern university came the ideal of autonomous science, of scholarship, proceeding under no other canons than proper
evidence. With this came historical sense and historical-critical methods of interpretation. And these things in turn revolutionized the human and historical sciences into disciplines (sciences) in a new sense.
A science was a cognitive enterprise working on some discrete region
of objects under universal and critical principles. One result of this
revolution was that new sciences, new bodies of data, and new methods were available to theology: philology, history, hermeneutics. In

the mid-eighteenth century, Ernesti and Semler appropriated these for biblical interpretation. And once this happened it became apparent that the Bible itself could be the object of a "science," a collection to which critical, autonomous methods of interpretation could be applied. It was only a short step to realize the same thing was true about church history, about preaching, about dogmatic theology.

We have then as the consequence of pietism and the Enlightenment a new model of the end of theological study (providing training and skills for ministerial tasks) and a new model for what it means to be a discipline. The result was that theological study in the university came to mean the study of a number of discrete disciplines pertinent to the ministry. The literary expression of this pluralization and specialization of theology was the theological encyclopedia literature which arose in the wake of the Enlightenment. Once the theological school and the course of theological study is thought of as a plurality of sciences, theology as a single science (discipline) is lost. It becomes an aggregate term for a family of scholarly pursuits. Furthermore, a secondary usage arises. Theology becomes *one* of the specialties along with biblical studies, ethics, pastoral care, etc. And in any given course of study, theology in this specialty sense may be required as one of several important areas of study or regarded as a merely technical and therefore dispensable pursuit.

Theology/Knowledge: From Sapiential Habitus to Practical Know-how

In the second period and especially in the Augustinian and monastic view, the end of the study of theology is salvific union with God. The rise of theology as an Aristotelian science in the medieval universities is a step toward the third period's pluralization of theology. What happens to theology as knowledge during the Enlightenment and after when theology names an aggregate of more or less independent sciences? The specialization of theology in the continental university creates a problem similar to high scholasticism. Monastics and pietists, Catholic and Protestant, suspect scholasticism of losing religion itself in a labyrinth of dialectic and ratiocination. Likewise, the university is suspected of training scholars at the expense of faith and the ministry. The pluralization and specialization of theology comes to resemble a new scholasticism. And it was a scholasticism with a much more severe problem than those inherent in medieval and seventeenth-century scholasticisms. In those times there was at least one unitary science to pursue and it was correlative with an individual *habitus*, wisdom. But with its pluralization into sciences, theology as a disposition of the soul toward God simply drops out of "the study of theology." Furthermore, there is no unitary science but an aggregate of disciplines whose unity is their pertinence to the tasks of ministry. But concern for the individual's experience and faith and discontent with a merely academic approach to the study of theology has been present in schools of theology throughout the third period.

This concern has found three major expressions. The first is the attempt to make *each of the theological sciences* in some way personally relevant, pertaining to the faith, development, and life situations of the individual. A second is the attempt to create a special part of the educational experience called formation, a theme long present in Roman Catholic schools and recently flirted with in Protestant schools. The third and most pervasive expression is present in the unifying model of most theological schools where the tasks of the ministry are the *ratio studiorum,* the rationale for the disciplines. In that model there is a place for theology as a personal, cognitive disposition, the theology/knowledge genre. According to that model, it is necessary for the minister or prospective minister to know certain things. This knowledge is simply knowledge ordered toward and required by the tasks of ministry. What the tasks of ministry are changes from one church body to the next and from generation to generation.

The most recent generation in America appears to have a primarily institutional/administrative view of the tasks of ministry. To the degree that this is true, the personal knowledge required for such tasks has a strategic, technical character. And this is the fate, the end-point to date of theology/wisdom. Theology/wisdom has become a *Kunstlehre,* a technology. It is not called theology. Terminologically, the Enlightenment's pluralization of theological study is determinative, so that theology has come to mean "systematic theology." Its older usage as a disposition of the soul toward God has been transformed, without retaining the word, into the know-hows required for tasks of ministry. If the transformation of theology as a discipline into a plurality of disciplines was primarily the work of the post-Enlightenment, continental university, the transformation of theology/knowledge into strategic know-how is primarily the work of the twentieth-century seminary. Each of these transformations, however, pervades the programs of study of both seminaries and universities.

We have traced the two fundamental meanings of theology through three major periods.[24] We should not be surprised to find that there is some correlation between these two meanings in each period. In the first period theology as exposition of the faith as found in Scripture presupposes a divine illumination of the mind. In the second period theology as cognitive *habitus* and theology as an Aristotelian science correspond with each other. For the *habitus* originates partly from a supernatural gift and partly as an effort of inquiry. The disposition thus is both a motivating impetus to theology as science and something which is extended and deepened by the results of the science. In the third period the pluralization of theology into independent disciplines whose end and unity is training for ministerial tasks is closely connected with strategic, technical knowledge.

The most serious and sobering aspect of this account of the career of theology is simply the disappearance of theology as wisdom and theology as discipline (science) from the theological school—their disappearance, that is, as the overall unity and rationale of theological study. In a very restricted way theology, even in these two ancient senses, persists, but in the form of idiosyncratic aspects of the curriculum, something available for certain kinds of students and certain kinds of ministers. It is not too strong to say that the theological school will make little progress in understanding its present nature and situation if it overlooks the disappearance of the very thing which is supposed to be its essence, agenda, and telos.

NOTES

1. Needless to say, this archaeological undertaking will be pursued in a modest way. Our goal is not a comprehensive archaeology or history of theological education but one sufficient to uncover what, in our view, are the central problems to be addressed, problems which call for reform. Foucault applies his archaeological approach to medicine in his *The Birth of the Clinic:*

An *Archaeology of Medical Perception,* trans. A.M.S. Smith (New York: Pantheon Books, 1973).

2. There is nothing that even approaches a comprehensive history of theological education. R.C. Briggs's two-volume work, *History of the Study of Theology* (London: Gerald Duckworth & Co., 1916), is more a history of literature than of education, although education is included. The Auburn Project when published will offer a comprehensive account of Protestant theological education in the United States since the founding of the first seminaries. There are some fine period studies, for instance, M.L. Gambrell's *Ministerial Training in 18th Century New England* (New York: Columbia University Press, 1937).

3. Unless specifically qualified, the terms *study of theology, theological study, divinity,* and *theological education* are being used more or less interchangeably.

4. That the term *theology* stands for different *kinds* of things does not seem to be noticed in the reference work literature, the articles on the subject in the multivolume dictionaries and encyclopedias. One of the few passages where this ambiguity is formulated is found in René Latourelle's *Theology: Science of Salvation* (Staten Island, N.Y.: Alba House, 1969), pp. 3ff. He distinguishes a subjective sense—theology as God's own knowledge of God and our dependent and analogical knowledge—and theology proper, theology as a science of God. See also Eberhard Jüngel, *Unterwegs zur Sprache* (Munich: Chr. Kaiser, 1972), "Das Verhältnis der theologischen Disziplinen intereinander," pp. 36ff. Jüngel speaks of the ambiguity of theology as a science, the problem being that theology springs from faith, yet as science requires an unrestricted employment of reason.

5. Richard McKeon, *Selections from Medieval Philosophers* (New York: Charles Scribner's Sons, 1930), vol. 2, p. 402.

6. On the history of the concept and term *theology,* the fullest account available in English is the expanded version and translation of Yves M.J. Congar's long essay in the *Dictionnaire de Théologie Catholique* entitled in English, *A History of Theology* (Garden City, N.Y.: Doubleday & Co., 1968). It is superb on the Roman Catholic usages and on the Middle Ages, less helpful on Protestantism. Supplementing Congar's study is the more recent work by G.R. Evans, *Old Arts and New Theology: The Beginnings of Theology as an Academic Discipline* (Oxford: Clarendon Press, 1980). Almost as important is the long essay by F. Kattenbusch, "Die Entstehung einer christliche Theologie," *Zeitschrift für Theologie and Kirche* (NF) 11 (1930): 161–205. In addition see J. Stiglmayer, "Mannigfache Bedeutung von Theologie und Theologen," *Theologie und Glaube* XI (1919): 296ff. The following more specialized studies are likewise recommended: J. Turmel, *Histoire de la théologie positive,* 2 vols. (Paris: Gabriel Beauchesne, 1906); Johannes Wallmann, *Der Theologiebegriff bei Johann Gerhard und Georg Calixt* (Tübingen: J.C.B. Mohr,

1961), especially chap. 1; Robert Preus, *The Theology of Post-Reformation Lutheranism* (St. Louis: Concordia Publishing House, 1970), vol. 1; Otto Ritschl, "Literarhistorische Beobachtungen über die Nomenklatur den theologischen Disziplinen im 17. Jahrhundert," *Zeitschrift für systematische Theologie*, 1918.

7. These three periods do not represent a real history of education in Christendom. The principle of distinguishing them is not just education itself but the transformation of theology in both of its senses.

8. For an account of monastic learning see Jean Leclercq, *The Love of Learning and the Desire for God* (New York: Fordham University Press, 1960), especially chaps. 5 and 6.

9. The term for this expository learning is *sacra pagina*. Thus says Congar, "Up to the end of the twelfth century theology is essentially and, we may truthfully say, exclusively biblical. It is properly called *sacra pagina* or *sacra scriptura*" (*History of Theology*, p. 51).

10. Thus, Hugh of St. Victor, *Didascalion*; Rabanus Maurus, *De universo*; Vincent of Beauvais, *Speculum mundi*; Roger Bacon, *Opus Maius*; William of Conches, *De philosophia mundi* (twelfth century); and Thomas Aquinas, *In librum Boethii de trinitate*, quest. 5 and 6.

11. For a good discussion of how this anthropology with its notion of *habitus* entered into Protestant theology and especially Melanchthon, see Wallman, *Theologiebegriff*, pp. 66ff.

12. In the Middle Ages it was Thomas and his successors who argued for theology as a primarily theoretical habit. But the Augustinian nominalist line, Scotus and Alexander of Hales, saw theology as a practical habit of the soul and, as such, a wisdom. See Preus, *Post-Reformation Lutheranism*, p. 249, n. 191. This is also the characteristic Lutheran scholastic view, for instance, that of John Gerhard and Calov. For Gerhard, theology is a God-given habit, a wisdom, which excels all knowledge. (Preus, pp. 118–9). While Preus plays down this motif of theology as wisdom in the Reformed scholastics, I find the most widespread view among them is that theology is mixed aptitude. That is, *theologia* is both theoretical and practical, and its genus is wisdom, although some identify it as prudence.

13. See Congar, *History of Theology*, pp. 114ff. The Churchmen include Bonaventure, the prime representative, and also Alexander of Hales, Grosseteste, and Roger Bacon. It continues in the nominalists, Ockham, Gerson, and even Nicholas of Cusa.

14. This view that God is the archetypal theologian is widespread among the seventeenth-century Reformed school theologians. Not only is it affirmed by Turretin, Alsted, Polanus, and Wolleb, but the Leyden Synopsis incorporates it in the disputation over sacred theology. According to it, theology is a knowledge *(notitia)* and its archetypal instance is God's perfect self-knowledge.

15. One of the most detailed schemes setting forth an analysis of *habitus*

is found in Goclenius's *Lexicon Philosophicum* (Frankfurt, 1613). After acknowledging other usages of the term, Goclenius expounds its anthropological meaning as a disposition or state of the human being, the most general category for affirming any human state, be it of the body (like a sickness) or of the soul. Habits of the soul fall into either habits of will or of reason. It is in connection with the *habitus intellectus* that theology occurs. The intellective habit is a state of knowledge which can be either certain or uncertain, and if certain can further be of a simple or a complex kind. Theology is a knowledge which occurs in the mode of certainty, and which is of a *composite* nature because it combines both a knowledge of conclusions (thus, *scientia)* and knowledge of principles *(noetikos).* The name for this composite cognitive state or disposition is *sapientia* or wisdom. Hence, when seventeenth-century Reformed theologians argue, as they do, that *theologia,* is in genre, wisdom, they are arguing for its composite character as a cognitive habit or state of the soul.

16. For three excellent descriptions of the twelfth-century renaissance and its place in the transition from theology as *sacra pagina* to Aristotelian science, see Congar, *History of Theology,* pp. 61–88; M.D. Chenu, *La Théologie au douzième siècle* (Paris: J. Vrin, 1957), especially chap. 15; and Evans, *Old Arts and New Theology.*

17. See Hastings Rashdall, *The Universities of Europe in the Middle Ages,* 3 vols. (Oxford: Clarendon Press, 1936). Rashdall's monumental study gives an account of the sources, origin, and faculties of each university in Europe country by country. See also Gabriel Compayré's *Abelard and the Early History of Universities* (New York: Charles Scribner's Sons, 1899), which argues that Abelard is the most important predecessor in the origin of the universities, especially the University of Paris.

18. See F. van Steenberghen, *Aristotle in the West: The Origins of Latin Aristotelianism* (Louvain: Louvain University Press, 1955).

19. *Sacra doctrina* is Thomas's term for this science in both the *Summa Theologica,* part 1, question 1, and in his commentary on Boethius's *De Trinitate.* The term does not refer simply to a body of doctrine. The *articuli fidei* describe that. *Sacra doctrina* is in these passages clearly the name for a cognitive discipline.

20. This literature is primarily a Protestant literature, at least in the sixteenth and seventeenth centuries. Its occasion is the need for a rationale for the studies taking place in the new universities and *Hochschule* being founded in Europe in this period.

21. With the exception of particular streams of continued Protestant scholasticism, theology as a single (Aristotelian) science more or less ended in Protestantism with the Enlightenment and the pietist movement. It underwent challenges in Catholic theology but nevertheless continued into the twentieth century as school theology and textbook theology.

22. Thus, *theologia . . . acroamatica, christiana, didactica, speculativa,*

thetica, etc. Otto Ritschl offers a more or less complete list of these qualifiers, some 68 in all, "Nomenklatur," p. 77.

23. The Lutheran theologians Nicholai Gundling, Johann Lorenz von Mosheim, and Johann Georg Walch are all influenced by pietism. Although the seventeenth century dominates their theological world, they do depart from it to speak of the *sciences* of divinity *(Gottesgelahrtheit)*. Gundling entitles the theological part of his *Historica Litteraria, Die Geschichte der übrigen Wissenschaften, fürnehmlich der Gottesgelahrtheit* (Bremen, 1742). He sees *theologia* as a collection of sciences. Although divinity is the main science, it has subdisciplines within it. Mosheim also speaks of theological sciences (dogmatics, morals, hermeneutics, homiletics, polemics, etc.). But the real break occurs when he defines divinity as setting forth the skills needed for pastoral work *(Kurze Anweisung die Gottesgelahrtheit* [Helmstadt: Weigand, 1763], chap. 1). Walch's work is entitled, *Einleitung in die theologischen Wissenschaften* (Jena: Güth, 1753). He retains the older notion of divinity as a single science of true religion, yet speaks of subdisciplines: dogmatics, exegesis, catechetics. As far as I can determine, Walch is the first to apply the term *science* to the specific branches or subdisciplines of divinity. These works all precede the literature of theological encyclopedia proper, but their language of "theological sciences" anticipates it.

24. These two fundamental meanings of theology mark the career of theology. The developments in the third period have introduced other senses which have the character of trivializations and corruptions. First, the use of theology to designate a university faculty or type of professional school is the aggregate use. Theology in this sense is like medicine or law. Second, theology sometimes means a specific field or discipline within such a faculty which struggles normatively and synoptically with the contents of faith. In this sense theology's predecessor is dogmatics and *Glaubenslehre.* Third, theology refers to doctrines themselves which are the contents of faith, the object of assent, the subject matter of confession. This is a degenerative usage in that originally *doctrina* and *habitus* were not separated, since *doctrina* was divine truth as occurring in the cognitive reception of the faithful human being. (See Wallman on Gerhardt, *Theologiebegriff.*) In the modern usage the *habitus* drops out, leaving theology as simply the fixed content to be taught. In this objectivist sense the study of theology means the study of church teachings.

3

From "The Study of Theology" to Theological Encyclopedia

The travail of the current theological school is further compounded by the retention of antiquated patterns of conceiving and organizing theological study, and by responses to those patterns which have created new incoherencies and given them new institutional expression. The central thesis is that all of this is itself the result of the displacement of *theologia* both as knowledge and as single discipline as the unity and end of theological study. The organization of studies still taken for granted in most theological schools falls into the four basic disciplines of Bible, systematic theology, church history, and practical theology, with an overlaid pattern of theoretical and practical disciplines. This fourfold pattern, anticipated as early as Hyperius (1556), actually originated with the theological encyclopedic movement in Gemany in the second half of the eighteenth century. Anticipating a critical assessment of the pattern, this and the next two chapters attempt a historical account of the origin and career, the conditions and presuppositions, of this pattern.[1]

The general historical thesis can be succinctly expressed. The theological encyclopedia movement of Europe constitutes a virtual cataclysm in the history of theological schools. It is not an exaggeration to say that it (or the mode of thinking behind it) is the most important event and the most radical departure from tradition in the history of the education of clergy. The *problem* which called forth the encyclopedia movement and literature is the discovery of a coherent pattern and rationale for various theological *sciences* (disciplines, faculties, areas of scholarship). The departure we are referring to is simply theology's dispersion into a multiplicity of sciences. The one thing (*theologia*, divinity, *Gottesgelahrtheit*) thus became many things. Theological encyclopedia addressed the question: How do we justify and interrelate these many things? This question expresses a major shift from one way of conceiving education of clergy to another, from "the study of theology" to theological encyclopedia.[2] Since this shift is the clue to everything that followed, I shall begin the account with a brief look at the situation prior to the rise of theological encyclopedia.

1. The Post-Reformation Study-of-Theology Literature

The post-Reformation study-of-theology literature occurs in the second period of the career of *theologia*, the period of universities. Protestant universities and *Hochschulen* spread rapidly from the time of the Reformation—some newly founded, some formerly Catholic schools. With these schools came occasional writings, mostly of a polemical character, on what it means to study theology. Some of the major figures of the first generations of the Reformation, including Luther himself, made declarations, usually brief, on the subject of the study of theology.[3] The Reformation did not originate this type of work. The question of the study of theology in the Middle Ages was primarily the question of locating theology among the circle of sciences, the comprehensive term for which was *philosophy*.[4] The Middle Ages produced a number of major works of a general encyclopedic character whose specific concern was not the study of theology. However, the close of the Middle Ages saw widespread discontent with scholasticism as an approach to the study of theology. Reflecting the antischolasticism of the new humanism, revived Platonism, and mystical theologies, a few works on the study of theology were produced which had the character of protest and reform.[5]

The brief and occasional writings of Erasmus, Luther, Melanchthon and others on the study of theology were harbingers of major Protestant works on the subject to be written in the sixteenth and seventeenth centuries. Ten years after Luther's death came a seminal Protestant work, Hyperius's *De theologo seu de ratione studii theologici*.[6] This work by a theologian claimed by both Lutheran and Reformed churches paved the way for major publications from both communions. The theme of the study of theology was taken up by a number of Reformed theologians but, with the exception of Hyperius, not in major and independent publications.[7] The real progeny of Hyperius are the two great Lutheran dogmaticians of the seventeenth century, John Gerhard of Jena (d.1637) and Abraham Calov of Königsberg and Wittenberg (d.1686).[8] These study-of-theology works represent more than simply a retention of the medieval past or the pursuit of interconfessional polemics. In the seventeenth century the teaching of theology typically included lectures on "isagogic science," that is, introductions to theology. This is what is behind those many seventeenth-century publications entitled *medulla, compendium, isagoge, methodus, apparatus, syntagma*, etc. And one kind of introduction is "introduction to the study of theology." Hence to introduce *theologia* Hoffmann, Gerhard, and Calixt all lectured on the method of the study of theology.[9]

What is this "theology" which is under review in these introductions? To draw on distinctions made in the previous chapter, it is theology/knowledge, the "wisdom" that disposes the life of the individual as the result of revelation and redemption.[10] And while a supernatural act of grace is its indispensable condition, this knowledge sufficiently resembles ordinary knowledge as to have a "principle," a given, and something which mediates that given and its interpretation. The knowledge originates in God both historically (as revelation in Christ) and individually (as the illumining work of the Spirit). But it has an available and continuing deposit, Holy Scripture, and whatever will help uncover and rightly interpret this deposit will at the same time extend and deepen the knowledge. This is why theology as knowledge is not a sheer illumination of the intellect but a matter of "study." There are, accordingly, appropriate things for human beings to do to extend, seal, even demonstrate this knowledge which is theology. And this is the subject of these works "on the study of theology." Because theology is a sapiential knowledge on the part of an individual which has its very archetype (cf. *theologia archetypa*) in God's own knowledge and its telos in the final vision of God, it is not primarily a science in any modern sense nor could it contain within itself "sciences."

Keeping in mind that what is under consideration is a single thing, theology/knowledge, I note features which attend most of these study-of-theology works. Even though the setting of these works is the school, and even though the schools in question are the much maligned environments of "Protestant scholasticism," all of these works begin with and very much emphasize the personal religious conditions of the study of theology. To this degree Luther's three rules, *oratio*, *meditatio*, and *tentatio*, preside over the whole literature. Even when the study is a reading of Scripture, this must be done in prayer, for the study of theology is a process of spiritual formation.

Second, the primary activity of the study of theology *qua study* is the study of Scripture. There are in this literature some faint indications of what later were distinct areas of studies, but finally there is only one major activity of study from which the knowledge-wisdom is formed, and ·his is the reading and interpretation of Scripture.[11] Hence, exhortations to read philosophy, or the church fathers, or to study the loci of doctrine, are not recommendations of different subjects but of different ways to extend, interpret and apply one's knowledge of God in Scripture. The reason for this centrality of Scripture to the study of theology is clear. Theology is sapiential knowledge of God and the things of God, and Scripture is the place where the primordial deposit of the content of this knowledge is to be found.

Third, the study of theology is not simply interpreting Scripture as an aggregate of texts. Grasping the written Word occurs under the doctrinal principle. The reason is that theology itself is a knowledge of divinely communicated truths pertinent to salvation. The units of this knowledge are articles of faith, and it is the grasp of these to which the study of Scripture is ordered. For this reason, there is a dogmatic moment in the study of theology, a step in which Scripture is brought to systematic arrangement. This dogmatic moment is clearly not a discrete discipline or science within theology. Rather, theology has a dogmatic element because the knowledge of God from Scripture appropriately occurs along the lines of the articles of faith, and literatures which set these forth are pertinent to that knowledge.

Fourth, because of the importance of *rightly* interpreting Scripture and understanding its true doctrines, *theologia* is always attended by the responsibility to refute error inside and outside the church. Such "controversial theology" (*theologia polemica, theologia elenctica*) occurs in a historical situation marked by the Catholic and Protestant doctrinal struggles and also including interconfessional controversies within Protestantism. The result is that preparation for controversy, for the defense and demonstration of the truth of the Christian religion and of one's own confessional version thereof, is an important aspect of the study of theology. Responsibility to establish and defend the church's confessions provides the main reason in this literature for proposing the reading of church fathers, church history, and the works of Catholic scholastics. Actually, it does not itself add to and constitute the knowledge which is theology. Rather, it helps prepare the theologian, the person with such knowledge, to employ that knowledge for a certain purpose, namely to refute pagans, heretics, and papists. *Theologia polemica* is an applied theology, even a *telos* of theology, rather than theology itself.

Finally, these writings all give some attention to what was later called propaedeutics, the *educational* (and not just personal and religious) requisites for the study of theology. Because the study of theology itself is primarily the study of Scripture, a collection of ancient texts, certain bits of knowledge and skills are called forth. This is the way Protestant writers introduce the question of theology's relation to the circle of sciences. However, because the study of theology means the study of Scripture, the propaedeutic question becomes: What is necessary for the study of Scripture? Hyperius proposed as preparatory sciences philosophy, organized along Aristotelian lines (mathematics, logic, physics, and ethics), then history, including sacred history, and finally languages. Proposals such as these were standard in the study-of-theology literature and continued in this fashion (preparatory sciences) into the later literature of theological encylopedia.

We recall that the literature of the study of theology constitutes a *ratio studiorum.* It offers a ground, definition, and rationale for the studies. But when we consider what this *theologia* is for which a ground of studies is proffered, we discover that the *ratio* has more the character of personal exhortation than an analysis of pedagogy. It says in effect: "These are the things you must do to deepen and sustain the disposition already set in you by the Spirit, to lay hold of and understand the things made available to you in revelation." The "studies" therefore include prayer, learning biblical languages, reading books which set forth doctrines, and, above all, reading the Scriptures. The transition from the study of theology to theological encylopedia engendered an entirely new meaning of *ratio studiorum*. The rationale for studies becomes a justification for an organization of specific "sciences" within an overall university faculty and science.[12]

2. Pre-Modern Anticipations of Change

It has been stressed so far that the study of theology is the study of one thing, *theologia*. When it is successful, there occurs a divinely enabled sapiential knowledge, a practically oriented habit or disposition. Yet one cannot read this material without noticing an enormous number of distinctions between what look like disciplines of theology. In fact different *disciplines* or sciences are not being proposed. Some of the distinctions refer to *levels* of the one knowledge. Such is the case with archetypal and ectypal theology (Alsted, Polanus) and with the distinction between scholastic or academic theology and ecclesiastic or didactic theology. Some of the qualifications refer to different *purposes* which theology (knowledge/wisdom) can serve. Accordingly, there can be a straightforward setting forth of truth (thetic theology) or a refuting of errors (polemical theology). Some of the distinctions are themselves polemical, offered for the sake of repudiating another view of or approach to theology. For the Reformers, "scholastic theology" connoted unduly philosophical, speculative, systematizing theology and they contrasted this with "positive theology." In some cases different approaches to theology are acknowledged as valid but distinguished as supplementary; thus, scholastic theology is supplemented by mystical or ascetic theology. None of these cases constitute proposals for distinct theological sciences.

Recall again the thesis. The problem of the study of theology, the one thing, eventually gives way to the problem of theological encyclopedia, the interrelating of the many things. However, there are powers at work from the Middle Ages through the seventeenth century which anticipate the transition of *theologia* into theological sciences. Three occurrences deserve special mention. First, an important development is the medieval notion that theology is a "science" not just in the sense of being a personal cognitive *habitus*, but in the sense of one of the Aristotelian disciplines, thus occurring in the larger circle of disciplines.[13] In the Thomist scheme, theology was one of the theoretical sciences. Although this was opposed by Augustinian-monastic theologians like Bonaventure and later by both Catholic and Reformation antischolastic theologians, it still persisted to the degree that theology came to reside in schools of learning, with many parallel features to other areas of learning.[14]

A second occurrence anticipating the later rise of a plurality of disciplines was the distinction in medieval philosophy between various *levels* of habit. The nominalists especially tended to divide knowledge into levels, each with its own object. Thus God is the object of several levels of human act: assent, doctrinal assertion and defense, the grasp of principles, the logical derivation of conclusions. And it is this sort of thinking which makes possible the above-mentioned distinctions between scholastic and ascetic theology, moral theology, and dogmatic theology. For instance, Hugh of St. Victor distinguishes theology (along with mathematics and physics) as a higher wisdom, in contrast to the practical wisdom of ethics.

Third, the humanist movement of the Renaissance, and the Reformation with its focus on Scripture, restored texts to the very center of learning. Once this happened, the historical task of obtaining as true a text as possible and the task of properly carrying out that task took on enormous importance in the process of learning. This occurred long before the historical-critical movements of the German Enlightenment, and it created "scholarly" tasks in relation to texts themselves which were not simply synonymous with theology. This development reinforced the one distinction at work in this period which resembled a distinction of disciplines, that between *sacra pagina* (Scripture studies or theology as Scripture interpretation) and theology of the sentences, the dialectical demonstration of conclusions.[15]

Finally, these distinctions, especially that between the interpretation of Scripture and dogmatics, obtained some institutional expression in both Catholic and Protestant schools of the sixteenth and seventeenth centuries. There were chairs which professors occupied which covered special teaching responsibilities. This happened in the Jesuit schools of the late sixteenth century, especially in the *cursus maior* or "academic" course.[16] In the course of the seventeenth century the territorial princes issued statutes establishing distinct professorships in the Protestant schools, sometimes requiring that a given professor, for instance the second or third professor appointed, had responsibility for moral theology or for homiletics.[17] These appointments anticipate but do not constitute the distinct theological sciences of the late eighteenth century and after. The concern here is not so much to have an expert in a specific discipline as to assure that a certain field of study is taught in the schools. Although the local statutes containing these specifications were in no sense advocating separate theological sciences, they do represent the beginning of the practice of distributing different areas of teaching among the faculty, a practice not to come into American theological education until the mid-nineteenth century.

In spite of these anticipations, *theologia* in this period was still one thing, a sapiental knowledge, produced by revelation and the Spirit and extended by study. Something decisive and new must yet occur for theology to be inclusive of "disciplines." When this happens, theology/knowledge will give way to its replacements.

3. The Eighteenth-Century Background of the Theological Encyclopedia Movement

When we move from John Gerhard's *Methodus studii theologici* (1620) to Johann Nösselt's *Anweisung zur Bildung angehender Theologen* (1771), we find ourselves in a different theological world. Gerhard sets forth a method of study and life pertinent to forming a disposition (*habitus*) in which God and the things of God are known for the practical purposes of edification, salvation, and glorifying God. Nösselt offers an analysis of the requirements of the "scholarly knowledge of religion" as these fall into various "sciences." What happened between the one work and the other to effect the change and what was the change which was effected? Our question concerns that mostly German literature which called itself theological encyclopedia. It is difficult to identify an absolute beginning of this literature.[18] Beginnings can be discerned in the middle decades of the eighteenth century, hence by the 1780s works entitled "theological encyclopedia" have become fairly common in both Catholicism and Protestantism. There is, however, a transition literature, published in the first half of the century, which departs in certain respects from the study-of-theology approach and which is not yet theological encyclopedia. Accordingly, the immediate background of the encyclopedia movement is constituted by the movements of early eighteenth-century Germany. Four are decisive in bringing about the transition from *theologia* to theological sciences. They are the ethos and learning of the new, modern universities, new genres of scholarly publications, continental pietism as a reform movement in the education of Protestant clergy, and the German philosophical and theological Enlightenment.

The New Learning

This new problem reflected in the theological encyclopedia movement of the late eighteenth and nineteenth centuries came about as a result of dispersion of *theologia* into the theological sciences. This dispersion cannot be understood apart from the new ethos of the eighteenth-century universities. This ethos is broader than simply the German *Aufklärung* as a philosophical, cultural movement. It includes a widespread antischolastic and antimedieval temper and a new learning breaking out of the dominantly Aristotelian sciences of the former period. With this new learning comes the modernization of the universities. According to Paulsen, the eighteenth century is the second great period of the universities. In the previous period from the Reformation to the seventeenth century, the universities were dominated by the established churches of the various German states, and the most important faculty was the faculty of theology. In the eighteenth century, modern culture, new sciences, a new spirit promoting reason and inquiry as independent principles permeate the universities, and faculties of philosophy and law gain in importance and prestige.[19] It is generally agreed that the first modern university in Germany is the university of Halle, followed a generation later by Göttingen and Erlangen.[20] In these three universities there comes about a spirit of free inquiry, German replacing Latin as the language of instruction. Also came new sciences such as philology and modern church history, new teaching methods such as seminars replacing the old disputations, and new, modernized approaches to both philosophy and theology.

Two New Genres of Scholarly
Literature

Expressing the spirit of the new, modernized university as well as offering a vehicle for making the new learning available are the many encyclopedias founded in the century. Symbolic of the anticlerical spirit of the eighteenth century is the *Encyclopédie* of Diderot and d'Alembert. Beyond this, the eighteenth century was a century of great dictionaries and encyclopedias, both general and special.[21] Encyclopedias of one sort or another had been appearing all along from the Middle Ages through the seventeenth century, but the eighteenth-century works were the first cooperative multivolume attempts to publish the results of scholarship with articles assigned to the specialists themselves. Furthermore, encyclopedias gathering up the knowledge of particular sciences also began to appear in the eighteenth century (special encyclopedias) in philosophy, law, medicine, and, as we shall see, theology.[22]

In addition to the cooperative deposits of knowledge, the encyclopedias, a second literature also signaled the intellectual ferment of the eighteenth century, the *historia literaria theologica*. These are works, frequently multivolume, comprised of historical accounts of various areas of study (moral theology, exegetical theology, etc.) plus extensive bibliographies.[23] This genre of publication is important for the later movement of theological encyclopedia, partly because many of the encyclopedias incorporated these works—that is, histories of disciplines and bibliographies—into themselves, and because this literature displays ways of organizing major divisions of study. It may be the case that this is the earliest literature to speak about theological *sciences* in the plural.[24] We also find it, alongside the pastoral type of work on the requirements and education of the minister (e.g., Baxter's *The Reformed Pastor*), in English-speaking countries in the early eighteenth century. In the United States a well-known work of this type was Thomas Bray's *Bibliotheca parochialis*. A great number of "theological historical bibliographies" appear in Europe from DuPin (1693) to the encyclopedic movement.[25] This literature anticipates the later theological encyclopedia because it represents a break with the older way of listing books, namely, by centuries. These works functioned as manuals, handbooks, introductions to the literature of theology, and they list books according to branches of study.

The Effect of Pietism on the Teaching of Theology

A third powerful impetus in the transition from theology to theological sciences was provided by continental pietism. Pietism's role in the breakup of *theologia* is not without its irony. While pietism placed the reform of theological study high on its agenda, it did not set out to dissolve theology into various scholarly sciences. The central concern of its founding fathers, Jacob Spener and August Hermann Francke, was to restore salvation as the one, basic end of the study of theology. This does not represent a substantial departure from the study-of-theology literature. Like Lutherans before him, Spener saw theology as a practical *habitus*.[26] The departure was more an emphasis, a concentration on the *conditions* of theology, what must be done to implement this habit in the life of the student. From this emphasis came two criticisms of theological schools which recur in the works of Spener and Francke. First, they strongly criticize those approaches which would make theology primarily a matter of human power, effort, talent. Rather, the heart's knowledge of God is a divinely created thing.[27] Second, and somewhat at tension with the first, they repudiate any approach to theology which prevents theology from becoming a matter of the heart and a matter of practicing life.

When these criticisms and themes began to be implemented in an actual university, the central figure was not Spener but Francke. The faculty of theology of the university of Halle was the main vehicle of the Spener school. And at the center of the reform of theological study at Halle was A.H. Francke.[28] Francke's writings on theological study do not in substance look very different from those of Gerhard and Calov. All would agree that theology is a salvation-oriented disposition. But the pietists intersperse between theology, the "practical habit," and ultimate salvation what appears to be a penultimate goal, namely, practice. Theology is in essence the conversion of the heart, but its end is a life which can by example inculcate pure doctrine and wisdom in others.[29] Furthermore, this practice is not only a matter of individual example, but of ministerial conduct, thus the conclusion of the whole course of theology is practical theology, homiletics, and catechetics. And it is just this focus on practice, especially the practice of the minister, that was picked up by pietist theologians of the middle decades of the eighteenth century and which promoted the dispersion of *theologia*. To this line of Lutheran pietist theologians we now turn.

In the first half of the eighteenth century, works on the study of theology continue to appear in Germany.[30] Most of them are by Lutheran theologians who are strongly influenced by the Spener school. These works, differing both from the study of theology writings of the seventeenth-century school theologians and from the later theological encyclopedias, represent a transition literature. That is, they mark the transition from the seventeenth-century way of unifying theological study as a practical habit to the dispersed sciences of theological encyclopedia. In many respects, this literature looks unchanged from the seventeenth century. Doctrinally speaking it has a pre-Enlightenment character, hence marks little substantial departure from the tradition of Protestant orthodoxy.[31] As in the seventeenth century, the branches of theological study tend to be simply lists of pedagogical enterprises. The writings themselves continue to be written expressions of a synoptic introduction to the "theology" going on in the schools.

These similarities, however, should not cover up what is virtually a new world in this post-Spener, Lutheran pietistic literature. In this new world, the pedagogy of the schools departs from the seventeenth century's approach to the making of the theologian. The clue to the difference is the treatment of the end and the means of theology. Like the seventeenth-century authors, these theologians acknowledge that the end of theology is salvation, being united with God, honoring God. But this means not so much the final, ultimate vision, a knowledge which is analogous to God's own self-knowledge, but the present practice of the Christian life. The end of theology is *Gottseligkeit*, personal piety, and this includes certain qualities of life like knowledge, prudence, and wisdom. Thus what constitutes *theologia* in the seventeenth century now becomes its end, implying that *theologia* itself is something other than wisdom.[32] The end of theology is knowledge of God (of the seventeenth century) *so as to do God's will;* to honor God . . . *in all our acts.* Thus the course and conduct of the Christian life is that to which theology is ordered. This shift then sets up the expected question: What are the *means* of obtaining this end? The usual answer is taken from Luther's three rules: prayer, reflection, and disciplined testing. Academic studies of exegesis, dogmatics, and so on are placed under reflection and thus are "means" for the realization of the end of theology, the holy life. What then is theology itself, falling as it does between the end (wisdom, prudence, qualities of holy life) and the means (studies)? That a change is under way is signaled by the new term for theology, taken from Spener by Gundling, Walch, and Mosheim, and used interchangeably with theology, the term *Gottesgelahrtheit*.

Ironically, the pietist theologians have in this term objectified theology. It defines theology, that which falls between the end and means, as a *Lehre*, a teaching, a doctrine, a collection of theological truths. Gundling's definition is: "everything known, believed, acted on in order to obtain piety."[33] Walch says that divinity (*Gottesgelahrtheit*) is a teaching, grounded in religion, which communicates and contains the divine truths.[34] In these early and mid-eighteenth-century Lutheran pietist works, a step is taken beyond even the objectivism of the Protestant school theologians. It is true that the pietists downplay the doctrinal and polemical aspects of theological study and put more emphasis on Scripture and practical theology. At the same time, they alter the genre of *theologia* from a practical *habitus* or disposition to a content, and once that is done, the problem is immediately created of discerning practical *ends* beyond theology, and the means of obtaining those ends. With this shift, theory-practice in the modern sense is born. For once theology is thought of as itself simply a deposit, a collection of truths, the modern problem of building a bridge from those truths to practical ends is created.

The modification of *theologia* is the major step taken in this literature, but it created the conditions for two other important changes in the approach to the study of theology, both of which anticipate theological encyclopedia. The first is the development of the concept of *disciplines* of theology. Once theology (*Gottesgelahrtheit*) names simply the divinely given content, the divine truths, the way is paved for disciplines. Disciplines can arise from distinction of the end, content, and means of having these truths. Qualities of the holy life (the end), divine truths occurring in different levels of relevance (the content), and various studies (the means) enable one to propose sciences within *Gottesgelahrtheit*. Gundling, Walch, and Mosheim all take this step. They are the first to speak of "theological sciences."[35] The most general classification in these midcentury works distinguishes theoretical and practical sciences. All three authors, Gundling, Walch, and Mosheim, classify the theological sciences into those pertaining to practice and those pertaining to theory. And it is clear that these authors are in fact thinking of discrete disciplines. Walch not only uses the term *discipline,* but proposes the object of each discipline and discusses its specific literature. The disciplines are distinguished by means of the seventeenth-century nomenclature: *theologia theoretica, catechetica, practica,* and so on.

The second important change in the approach to the study of theology is an alteration of the meaning of practice as the end of the study of theology. More specifically, this change is effected when the tasks of ministry become the unifying end of theological study. Because this way of conceiving the unity of theological study has now become standard, it may not be easy to imagine that its origination required a cataclysmic change of thought. And while it is not until Schleiermacher that this way of conceiving the unity of theological study received comprehensive formulation, the notion first occurs in this midcentury transitional literature, specifically in Mosheim. Theological study had always been study offered for those preparing for church vocations, for priests, monks, ministers of the Word. But in the Middle Ages and the early centuries of the Reformation there was little effort directly to correlate specific items in the preparation with specific clerical tasks.[36] Such a correlation was certainly not the way the "study of theology" was defined, unified, grasped as an idea. The study of theology was a matter of prayer, personal discipline, and study, all for the purpose of forming that sapiential knowledge called *theologia*. In these former periods it is *that, theologia*, which the priest or minister must have to exercise the vocation of ministry. But with Mosheim something new is proposed.

The pietist movement as a whole had placed great emphasis on the practical needs of the church. Both Mosheim and Semler formulate explicitly the education of ministers as the end of theological study. Mosheim begins his work with a discussion of theological method, which he calls a "science" and which he identifies with divinity. He describes this method as a science of teaching, of setting forth certain skills to beginners. The skills and capabilities he is talking about are those needed by the "shepherds of the community," those who teach in the churches and exercise spiritual leadership.[37] Theological study is not the formation of a habit or disposition (the knowledge of God which attends piety and salvation) but a mélange of sciences pertaining to the education of leaders. With this as his clue, Mosheim proceeds to derive the theological sciences, working from dogmatics and ethics to hermeneutics, homiletics, polemics, catechetics, and finally church history.[38] Writing also in the mid-eighteenth century Semler too sees the "dexterity proper to teachers of the Christian religion" as the end of the study of theology, and to that end proposes theological sciences as independent studies.[39]

The German Aufklärung

A third power contributing to the breakup of *theologia* and creating the conditions for the theological encyclopedic movement is the German *Aufklärung*, especially in its philosophical and religious expressions. We should distinguish a narrow sense of the German Enlightenment which more or less identifies it with the "rationalistic" philosophies of Leibniz and Christian Wolff and the midcentury Neologist theologians and a broader sense which stands for the spread of critical principles throughout German academic life. Lessing, Herder, and Schleiermacher were all critical of the "Enlightenment theologians." In the broader sense, their work is very much in the stream of the *Aufklärung*. Theologically speaking, we are talking about a movement and literature arising in the mid-eighteenth century which opposed both orthodoxy and pietism and went beyond even the "transitional theologies" of the first half of the century. The universities of Halle and Göttingen are the important centers of this movement. Leibniz and Wolff are its philosophical roots. And the actors themselves are the so-called Neologist theologians.[40] When we consider the impact of this movement on the study of theology and the education of ministers, the two most important works from this movement are Ernesti's *Institutio interpretis Novi Testamenti* (1761) and J.S. Semler's *Versuch einer näher Anleitung.* . . .[41]

Two features of the German Enlightenment especially stimulated a new approach to the study of theology: its commitment to the general principle of "reason" in matters of religion and its strong focus on historical consciousness and method. The German theological *Aufklärung* is frequently and pejoratively called "rationalism" and is compared to deism in England and the French encyclopedists. In the German movement as in the others, this "rationalism" amounted to an extensive criticism of supernaturalist, scholastic theologies, a criticism which specifically questioned the traditional doctrines of Catholic and Protestant orthodoxy.[42] Accordingly, in the Enlightenment theologies the older term *positive theology* took on a new and pejorative meaning. Positive religion, the institutional religion based on supernatural and historical revelation, is contrasted to natural religion which rises above the incoherencies of supernaturalism and dogmatism. One of the outcomes of this reappraisal of positive religion was the location of the grounds of religion in some natural human power and region of experience. In Kant's version, the moral consciousness is that ground. The "rationalist" aspect of the German theological Enlightenment was extreme, and it later evoked powerful opponents in theologians like Schleiermacher.

The second feature of the Enlightenment was not so provisional or vulnerable: the application of historical methods to matters of religion. The movement of historical criticism began more or less modestly. There was the search for a critical text of the New Testament (Wettstein), manuscript classification (Griesbach), and criticism of the synoptic Gospels. Textual criticism of the Old Testament occurs in Michaelis and all of this leads to a comprehensive proposal concerning a historical-critical method of interpreting Scripture by Ernesti. But it was Semler who recognized the import of this whole line of inquiry.[43] He articulated the effect of these modes of inquiry on the very categories of inspiration, canon, Scripture, and offered historical ways of understanding the origin and nature of what hitherto were simply authorities: the New Testament books, the great dogmas of the church, and so forth. It was only a short step from this to suggest that *theology itself* was historical, something correlative with the culture, situation, and institutions of a historical period. Theology, then, is distinguished from religion. Religion may contain insights, disclosures, realities which have to do with faith, salvation, the sacred, but theology is a matter of useful concepts pertaining to the historically ever-changing doctrines of Christendom. In other words, "theology is a specialist or vocational affair which is neither useful nor necessary for the Christian as Christian."[44]

The impact of these two features, rationalism and historical method, was a hermeneutics of destruction, a de-supernaturalizing of canon, authority, and Scripture. *Theologia* as both *habitus* (knowledge) and unified science was challenged and displaced. What displaced it were discrete efforts of inquiry and scholarship, each applying rational and historical principles; in other words, exegesis, textual criticism, church history, and the like. Nor should this be a surprise. Once *theologia's* unifying principle, its authoritative texts of Scripture construed as a priori authorities, is lost, what remains are discrete scholarly enterprises.

In summary, we find occurring in the early and mid-eighteenth century in Europe, especially Germany, a complex of events, movements, and literatures which brought to an end *theologia* in the older senses and which introduced theological sciences as relatively independent undertakings. Once this happened, the setting was created for "faculties" in the modern sense of collections of specialists. Furthermore, two new and very serious problems were created for those who study and teach theological subjects. First, the pedagogical problem of introducing students to "theology" by a synoptic survey became a different sort of problem, namely, how to provide a rationale for the study of what had become separate theological sciences. Needless to say, this was a very different undertaking from the old "study of theology" books which described the conditions of piety and study necessary for sapiential knowledge. Second, a new theological problem developed. How could the unity and interrelationship of the new theological sciences be conceived? The subsequent epoch, beginning in the 1760s and continuing through the nineteenth century, self-consciously took up both the pedagogical and the theological problem and even gave a name to the inquiry into that problem: "theological encyclopedia."

NOTES

1. There is no adequate history of "the study of theology" either as a literature or as a movement, nor of the literature of theological encyclopedia. The most comprehensive history available is found in Abraham Kuyper's *Encyclopedie der heilige godgeleerdheit,* 3 vols. (Amsterdam: J.A. Wormser, 1894). While volume 2 of this work is available in English translation, the history of encyclopedia (vol. 1) has never been translated. R.C. Briggs's *History of the Study of Theology,* 2 vols. (London: Gerald Duckworth & Co., 1916) is a helpful bibliographical source for all periods. Fairly useful bibliographically oriented surveys can be found in K.R. Hagenbach, *Theological Encyclopedia and Methodology,* ed. G.R. Crooks and J.F. Hurst (New York: Hunt & Eaton, 1884), appendix to part 1; D.C.F. Heinrici, *Theologische Encyclopädie* (Frieburg: J.C.B. Mohr, 1893), pp. 337–61; J.F.Räbiger, *Encyclopedia of Theology* (Edinburgh: T.&T. Clark, 1884–5); and Phillip Schaff, *Theological Propaedeutic* (New York: Charles Scribner's Sons, 1983), introduction. Räbiger is probably the most extensive history of the study of theology and theological encyclopedia literature in English. A brief history of theological encyclopedia is Henrici's article, "Encyclopedia, Theological" in the *New Schaff-Herzog Encyclopedia* (New York: Funk & Wagnalls, 1908-1914), vol. 4. Most of these accounts have the character of annotated bibliographies. They disclose little about the origin of the fourfold encyclopedia, the similarities and differences between Roman Catholic and Protestant approaches, the major types of proposed patterns, the relation between the literature of encyclopedia and the actual course of studies in schools.

2. The expression *the study of theology* can be an equivalent term to *theological education.* So is it used in Briggs, *History of the Study of Theology.* I am using the expression in a more specific manner to refer to a certain genre of post-Reformation publications on the subject. Thus, for instance, Bullinger's *Ratio studii theologici,* 1594. Since "theology" usually means in these works of the sixteenth and seventeenth centuries theology/knowledge, the *habitus* of sapiential knowledge of God, this literature is very different from the theological encyclopedias which later replaced it. And the expression means something different in the later genre of literature, for instance, in Schleiermacher's *Brief Outline of the Study of Theology.*

3. Luther himself wrote a short piece on the study of theology in which he advanced the three famous rules for study: prayer, reflection, and disciplined testing *(tentatio, Anfechtung).* A translation is available in G. Ebeling, *The Study of Theology* (Philadelphia: Fortress Press, 1978), postscript. Me-

lanchthon wrote what may be the first Protestant expression on the subject, *Brevis discendae theologiae ratio* (1530). On the Reformed side, both Theodore Beza and Heinrich Bullinger wrote works on the subject.

4. The typical scheme of Aristotelian medieval theologians was the division of philosophy (science) into logic, ethics and theoretics. Theology was one of the three theoretical sciences along with mathematics and physics. See for instance Vincent of Beauvais, *Speculum doctrinale*.

5. Two of the best-known antischolastic works of this sort came from the early fifteenth century: Jean Gerson's letters on the study of theology written about 1400 against Franciscans at the University of Paris (See *Oeuvres complètes* (Paris, 1960–1962), vol. 2; and the Italian humanist theologian Nicolaus de Clemangiis's *De studio theologico*. It is in this line of antischolastic humanism that Erasmus's brief work on the subject belongs. It occurs as a preface to his edition of the Greek New Testament (1522) and is entitled, "Ratio seu methodus compendio pervendiendi ad veram theologiam."

6. This is a lengthy work, divided into four books. Book 1 treats of preparatory studies such as philosophy, mathematics, physics, history, and languages. The remaining three books divide the study of theology into what later became the fourfold pattern. This work is distinguished by an extensive description of hermeneutics and what is involved in reading and interpreting Scripture, by the inclusion of church history (in book 4), and by the inclusion of studies pertaining to church governance. Because of this part of the work and also because of his *De formandis concionibus sacris* (1555), Hyperius is called the father of practical theology.

7. J.H. Alsted's views are found in book 2 of his *Theologia praecognita* (1614). Franz Burman, the dogmatician of the Cocceian school of Holland, offers his "collection on the study of theology" as an appendix to his *Synopsis theologiae* (1681). Several Reformed theologians wrote works on the subject in the last part of the seventeenth century; from Holland, Voetius (1644), Crocius (1651), and Perizonius (1669).

8. Gerhard's work is *Methodus studii theologici* (1620); Calov's is *Paedia theologica, de methodo studii theologici* (1652). This is the second volume of his *Isagoges theologicae*. For an excellent summary of the views of these two theologians, see Robert D. Preus, *The Theology of Post-Reformation Lutheranism* (St. Louis: Concordia Publishing House, 1970), vol. 1.

9. F.A. Tholuck, *Das akademische Leben des siebzehnten Jahrhunderts* (Halle, 1853), p. 100.

10. In their technical disputes over *theologia*, the seventeenth-century theologians did not all accept the view of theology as wisdom. Calov, for instance, explicitly denied it was wisdom since that sounded like a natural human power. But in the sense set forth in chapter 2, theology is still in genre a "wisdom," that is, a personal and insightful way of being disposed toward all things, made possible of course by a divine operation. Thus Calov can say, "Theology proceeds from God, teaches us about God, and leads us to God."

(Preus, *Post-Reformation Lutheranism*, p. 271). Hyperius says explicitly that theology is wisdom, the wisdom of God prepared before all ages and revealed through the Spirit. In addition, see Friedrich Paulsen, *Geschichte des gelehrten Unterrichts*, 3d ed. (Leipzig: von Veit, 1919), vol. 1, book 2.

11. This is clearly the case in the brief essays of Luther, Melanchthon, and Erasmus. The longest truly central part of Hyperius's work is book 2 on the study of Scripture. Book 1 pertains to tools which prepare one to read Scripture, and Book 3 on theological loci of doctrine concerns books which arrange Scripture in a certain way. Of John Gerhard's five parts on the course of study, three set forth steps of studying Scripture, and the final two on controversy, homiletics, and church fathers subject these matters to the first three. Chrytaeus's ten rules for beginners in theology likewise center on Scripture study. Calov says plainly that theological study is mainly biblical study.

12. As we would expect, there is in the sixteenth and seventeenth centuries a Roman Catholic literature of the study of theology. It tends to continue the late medieval criticism of scholasticism. One of the earliest is the anti-Erasmus work of Latomus, *De trium linguarum et studii theologici ratione dialogus* (1519). Also in the sixteenth century is Larentius a Villavicentio's *De recte formando theologiae studio libri quatuor* (1565) and also works which describe the Jesuit course of studies: P. Canisius, *De ratione studiorum theologicorum quaedam notationes* (ca. 1589). Canisius and other works of this type are collected in J. Pachtler, *Ratio studiorum et institutiones scholasticae, societatis Jesu*, 3 vols. (1887). In the seventeenth century the most important Catholic work is probably Jean Mabillon's *Traité des monastiques* (1692) written for the monks at St. Maur, and going through several Latin editions in the eighteenth century. Another frequently cited work is Possevinus, *Apparatus sacer ad scripturas V. et N.T.*, 2 vols. (1608). This too is a Jesuit work and represents a return to scholastic modes of thought.

13. The term *facultas*, originally meaning a capability or power, may have been the first term in the Middle Ages to express theology as a discipline. Gilbert de la Poreé uses the term to speak of particular disciplines like mathematics or theology. By the thirteenth century the University of Paris is employing it as a technical term, and Honorius's Bull of 1219 speaks to the faculties of Paris, meaning here a corporation. The expression *theological discipline* (*facultas theologica* and even *theologica disciplina*), is fairly common by the second half of the twelfth century. For these materials on the term *facultas theologica*, see Bernhard Geyer, "Facultas Theologica; Eine bedeutungsgeschichtliche Untersuchung," *Zeitschrift für Kirchengeschichte*, 75 (1964).

14. A similar distinction between faith/theology and academic theology occurred in early eighteenth-century Lutheranism. Earlier, theology (as practical *habitus*) and faith were more or less identified. But in the early eighteenth century John George Neumann, an antipietist theologian, proposed what he called a theology of the unregenerate (*theologia impiorum*). That is, the un-

regenerate or the lapsed Christian could still retain the *habitus* such that there could be a theology of the intellect if not of the will. This opens the way to thinking of theology as something distinguishable from faith—an acquired, intellectual enterprise. For an exposition of Neumann, see Preus, *Post-Reformation Lutheranism.*

15. Evans proposes three approaches to or traditions of theology in the twelfth century. In addition to the distinction made here between biblical or expository theology and dialectic, she adds polemical and missionary theology whose audience is primarily the unbeliever and heretic (*Old Arts and New Theology* [Oxford: Clarendon Press, 1980], chap. 4).

16. This was the period, however, when moral theology, primarily viewed as casuistics, began to be thought of as a special area of pedagogy, obtaining in some cases one of the chairs. For a full account of Catholic education in the sixteenth century, especially as it pertains to moral theology, see Johann Theiner, *Die Entwicklung der Moraltheologie zur eigenständigen Disziplin* (Regensburg: F. Puster, 1970).

17. Tholuck, *Akademische Leben,* pp. 118ff.

18. The work usually nominated as the beginning of theological encyclopedia is Mursinna's *Primae lineae encyclopediae theologiae* (Halle, 1764). This is the first work with theological encyclopedia in the title. However, the Roman Catholic theologian, Martin Gerbert, a crucial figure in the reform of Catholic education in southern Germany (St. Blasien) entitled a chapter of his *Apparatus ad eruditionem theologicam* (1754) "theological encyclopedia." Further, works without this title but reflecting the new scholarly, critical approaches to different areas of theology appear in the 1750s. It might be argued that Gerbert, who wrote a series of works in the 1750s on different areas of theology, and Mosheim (*Kurze Anweisung die Gottesgelahrtheit* [1756]) are as much founders of the encyclopedia movement as Mursinna.

19. On the history of the German universities and the rise of the first modern universities see Paulsen, *Geschichte des gelehrten Unterrichts,* especially vol. 2, b. 4; Paulsen, *The German Universities: Their Character and Historical Development* (New York: Macmillan Co., 1895). See this work for Paulsen's analysis of the three periods of the historical development. See also Philip Schaff, *Germany: Its Universities, Theology, and Religion* (Philadelphia: Lindsay and Blakiston, 1857), p. 1. The articles on the Universities of Halle and Göttingen in *Religion in Geschichte und Gegenwart*[2], are also pertinent.

20. Halle was formed as a university by reform-minded professors from Leipzig. The three most important names of this early period are Thomasius (law), Francke (theology), and Wolff (philosophy). Thomasius, involved in violent disputes at Leipzig, was in full rebellion against both scholastic philosophy and the stress on eloquence by humanists, and was the first professor in Germany to use German in his lectures. Christian Wolff was an antischolastic philosopher whose commitment to reason as an independent principle advanced philosophy as a self-sufficient discipline (rather than simply a pro-

paedeutic to theology) and influenced Protestant universities throughout Germany. Francke and pietism in its own way had a modernizing effect on university life. Göttingen, founded in the beginning time of the German *Aufklärung* (1734), offered a spirit of free inquiry, new sciences like philology and oriental studies, and some of the great scholars of the day in Mosheim, the "father of modern church history," and Michaelis, the orientalist.

21. The Chambers *Cyclopedia* of 1728 was the stimulation for the Diderot work which appeared from 1751 to 1766. The first cooperative encyclopedia was Zedler and Ludovici, *Grosses vollständiges universal Lexicon*, 64 vols. (1732–50). In 1768–71 the *Encyclopaedia Britannica* appeared in three volumes, and between 1865 and 1876 the Larousse encyclopedia was published: *Grand dictionaire universel du XIXe siècle*, 15 vols. For a summary account of the history of this literature, see the article, "Philosophical Dictionaries and Encyclopedias," in *The Encyclopedia of Philosophy*, ed. P. Edwards (New York: Macmillan Co., 1967), vol. 6.

22. Thus, J.G. Sulzer, *Kurzer Begriff aller Wissenschaften*, 2d. ed. (Leipzig, 1759); J.G. Feder, *Grundriss der philos. Wissenschaften* (Coburg, 1767); H. Boerhaave, *Methodus studii medici* (Amsterdam, 1751).

23. For a brief account of the history of this literature which lists the main works, see Alfred Cave, *Introduction to Theology* (Edinburgh: T.&T. Clark, 1886), p. 13.

24. Nicholai Gundling's *Die Geschichte der übrigen Wissenschaften, fürnehmlich der Gottes gelahrtheit* (Bremen, 1742) is a work of this sort. At the same time it presents a whole structure of theological study which we shall take up when we look at the eighteenth-century pietist theologians. Buddeus's *Isagoge historico-theologica* (Leipzig, 1727) includes similar material, and while it does not speak of "theological sciences," its title does indicate the parts of theology.

25. The highlights of the publications appearing from the last decade of the seventeenth century to Mursinna are the following. The first great publication is the nineteen-volume work by Ellie DuPin, *Nouvelle bibliothèque des auteurs ecclésiastiques*, 2d ed. (Paris, 1693–1715). William Cave, *Scriptorum ecclesiasticorum historia literaria* (London, 1688) is significant for being the best guide to manuscripts prior to printed books. J.A. Fabricius's *Bibliotheca ecclesiastica* (1718) builds on and adds to a famous seventeenth-century work by Miraeus, published at Amsterdam in 1639, which itself had collated even earlier works. Important also was J.G. Walch, *Bibliotheka theologica selecta literariis* (Jena, 1757–65).

26. Jacob Spener, *Pia desideria*, trans. T.G. Tappert (Philadelphia: Fortress Press, 1964), p. 105.

27. This is the main theme of Spener's *Die allgemeine Gottesgelehrtheit aller gläubigen Christen und rechtschaffenen Theologen* (Frankfurt am Main, 1705). This work is a reply to Dilfeld who had written a polemical work against Spener, and the main issue is whether theology is a natural science.

28. Francke from the very beginning of his career was concerned with the reform of theological study. Thus he began almost every semester with lectures on the subject, introducing the study of theology, and he wrote a number of works on this theme. See especially his *Idea studiosi theologici* (1718) and his *Methodus studii theologici* (1723). For a good account of Francke on the study of theology, see Erhard Peschke, *Studien zur Theologie August Hermann Franckes* (Berlin, 1966), chap. 4.

29. Francke, *Methodus studii theologici*, chap. 1.

30. The main works are as follows: C.M. Pfaff, *Introductio in historiam theologiae literarum*, 3 vols. (Tübingen, 1724); Buddeus, *Isagoge historico-theologica*; J.J. Rambach, *Studiosus theologiae* (Frankfurt, 1737); Gundling, *Übrigen Wissenschaften*; J.G. Walch, *Einleitung in die theologische Wissenschaften* (Jena, 1753); Johann Lorenz of Mosheim, *Kurze Anweisung die Gottesgelahrtheit* (Helmstadt, 1763).

31. Martin Kähler acknowledges this point, the essential orthodoxy of pietism, but stresses that there was a kind of indifference to dogmatics, the effect being that the traditional Lutheran and Reformed dogmatic controversies were deemphasized (*Geschichte der protestantischen Dogmatik im 19. Jahrhundert* [Munich: C. Kaiser, 1962], introduction, p. 11).

32. Thus Buddeus appealing to Francke introduces the distinction between the final end of theology (salvation) and the proximate end which is to provide the setting for obtaining certain qualities of life: knowledge, wisdom, divine prudence. The proximate end, in other words, is the holy life (*Isagoge historico-theologica*, bk. 1, chap. 1, secs. 9 and 10).

33. Gundling, *Übrigen Wissenschaften*, p. 325.

34. Walch, *Theologische Wissenschaften*, p. 5.

35. The term *theological sciences* is in the title of both Gundling's and Walch's works on the study of theology. See also Mosheim, *Kurze Anweisung*, pp. 111–19, on the theological sciences.

36. An exception would be the *cursus minor* or "seminary" course of Jesuit education in which there was close relation between the priest as a father confessor and the textbooks in casuistry which were written to help prepare for that role. Similarly, there is some attention to preaching in the Protestant school of the sixteenth and seventeenth centuries. However, these correspondences between a specific task and an item of education remain discrete and do not rise into a way of conceiving the total course of theological study.

37. Mosheim, *Kurze Anweisung*, chap. 1.

38. *Ibid.*, pp. 111–14. This derivation of theological sciences is only an anticipation of the later theological encyclopedias and the kind of analysis one finds in Schleiermacher's *Brief Outline of Theological Study*. However, it is more than the usual list of studies so common until the mid-eighteenth century.

39. J.S. Semler, *Versuch einer nähern Anleitung zu nützlichem Fleisse in der ganzen Gottesgelahrtheit* (Halle, 1757).

40. Hirsch lists as the major *Neologen*, Ernesti, J.J. Spalding, J.D. Michaelis, J.G. Töllner, and J.S. Semler. For an account of each representative, see Immanuel Hirsch, *Geschichte der neueren evangelischen Theologie* (Gütersloh: Wohn, 1968), vol. 4, pp. 9ff. According to Hirsch, neology is a fairly vague term for a mid-eighteenth century movement, roughly 1740–86, which carries into theology the general revolution of thought going on in German culture and education.

41. Ernesti's work was translated into English, *Principles of Biblical Interpretation* (Edinburgh: T. & T. Clark, 1771).

42. There were controversies over the Lord's Supper, the devil, the Trinity, Christology, the knowledge of God, canon, and the inspiration of Scripture.

43. According to Hirsch, Semler posed the three following implications concerning the nature of theology: (1) Theology contains much that is not revealed by God or deduced from Scripture; (2) It is relative to historical situations and conditions; (3) It is neither fixed nor immutable (Hirsch, *Geschichte der neueren evangelischen Theologie*).

44. Hirsch, *Geschichte der neueren evangelischen Theologie*, p. 53.

4

Schleiermacher and the Beginning of the Encyclopedia Movement

In the last third of the eighteenth century, theological study was promoted in a new agenda and a new literature. Appropriating a nomenclature already applied to works in law and medicine, it called itself "theological encyclopedia." This type of work—like its predecessor, the bibliographical-historical introduction—was a published expression of the introductory survey-of-the field course offered in German universities. The publication of theological encyclopedias falls in a fairly clearcut period, lasting from the 1760s to World War I. Germany was the primary location of these works, partly because of the great vigor and creativity of German theology in the nineteenth century, and partly because of the practice of introducing students to their course of study by means of an encyclopedic survey. Outside Germany, theological encyclopedias were produced in France, Holland, and Sweden after 1830, and in England and the United States after 1870.[1] Both Protestant and Catholic theologians were part of the movement from its beginning.

Two periods of rather intense publication organize this 135-year-long period. The first covers roughly the last third of the eighteenth century and goes from the midcentury to Schleiermacher's *Brief Outline of Theological Study* of 1811. The second period appears to be occasioned by the *Brief Outline*, even if not materially influenced by it in any great degree, and it includes two intense periods of publication: the 1830s and 1840s, and the 1870s and 1880s. In the second period the movement expands to other European countries and to the United States.

To speak of a definite historical period of the theological encyclopedia movement, with a beginning and an end, requires some clarity about the very concept of theological encyclopedia. That concept will remain muddled as long as "encyclopedia" refers to a mere collection of knowledge like, for instance, the *Encyclopaedia Britannica* or the *Realencyklopädien* of Germany. Nor is theological encyclopedia simply an amassed collection of knowledge about theology. The *problem* addressed by the special encyclopedia is the intellectual problem of discerning the sciences proper to a field of knowledge, and two things must happen for that problem to occur. First, the overall field itself must come into the foreground as a distinctive area in its own right; thus law, medicine, theology. Second, particular sciences or disciplines must be established within the overall field. Once this happens, questions arise as to what these sciences are, why the field requires just those sciences and not others, and how they are related to each other. In a nutshell, that is the encyclopedic problem. When the mid-eighteenth-century German pietist theologians began to offer study-of-theology works presenting theology as made up of "sciences" whose interrelation posed a problem, we can say that the age of theological encyclopedia had begun. When the literature that struggled with that problem was replaced in the twentieth century by collections of essays (usually by faculties of schools) on each discipline, we can say that the age of encyclopedia ended.

Even though there is an identifiable historical period in which works of this sort occur, we cannot say that theological encyclopedia is an utterly unambiguous *literary* genre. The reason is that some works like Schleiermacher's *Brief Outline* restrict themselves to the intellectual, theological problem of deriving and interrelating the disciplines of theology (cf. "formal encyclopedia"). Most of the works, however, combine proposals about the structure of the disciplines with bibliographical and historical summaries of their content ("material encyclopedias").[2] In this initial, pre-Schleiermacher period, a scheme of four basic disciplines became more or less standard. There have been occasional departures from that scheme, but, for the most part, it has been the standard classification of theological sciences throughout the whole period and after. So much is this the case that the *theological* problem of determining the disciplines of theology has been presumed to be settled. Actually, the fourfold scheme was not itself the outcome of rigorous theological scrutiny, but of an appropriation of the past having the nature of a compromise. This is the overall thesis that will be argued in this brief historical treatment of this period and literature of theological encyclopedia.

1. The Earliest Theological Encyclopedias

We turn now to the first and originating period of theological encyclopedia, from the middle of the eighteenth century to Schleiermacher. Even though no enduring classics of theological encyclopedia were written in this period, it nevertheless has enormous importance, and for three reasons. First, it was the time in which the problem of the study of theology was construed as an "encyclopedic" problem, a problem of justifying and relating relatively independent "sciences" or disciplines. Second, there originated in this period the basic pattern of theological disciplines which became standard in both Europe and the United States: the fourfold pattern of Bible, church history, dogmatics, and practical theology. Third, the period's theologians and philosophers formulated most of the issues and problems which became the occasion for a truly monumental work, Schleiermacher's *Brief Outline of Theological Study* (1811).[3]

No single work can be nominated as the one which begins the period of theological encyclopedia. The Reformed theologian Mursinna, imitating the special encyclopedias of law and medicine, was the first to use the term *encyclopedia* in a title of a theological introduction.[4] In the strict sense, however, Mursinna's work is not an encyclopedia, for while he speaks of particular theological "sciences," he makes no attempt to justify their presence or show their interrelation. Actually, the midcentury works of Lutheran theologians influenced by pietism have a more encyclopedic character than Mursinna's 1764 monograph. These writings all speak the new language of a plurality of theological sciences. Gundling proposes an important step when he distinguishes between classifications according to literature and according to method.[5] The literary way is what we find in previous authors whose divisions are inherited from seventeenth-century nomenclatures around which bibliography can be organized. Thus, *theologia patristica, theologica exegetica,* and so forth organized not "sciences" but authors and their works.[6] Gundling's category of distinguishing fields by distinct *methods* went beyond the organizing of bibliography to identifying the fields as sciences (*Wissenschaften*). Further, Gundling also contributes to a theological basis for classifying these sciences. They fall naturally, he says, into sciences of theory and sciences of practice.[7] The one thing, divinity (*Gottesgelahrtheit*), embraces two kinds of content: doctrines of faith (*Glaubenslehren*) and rules for living (*Lebens-regeln*).[8] This language and this twofold division became standard for the rest of the eighteenth century.[9]

The theory/practice scheme is, then, the first real step away from simply listing areas of theological literature, the sort of thing going on in the "introductions to the literary history of theology." It is also one step removed from the pietist movement in which all the theological areas were "practical," furthering the purpose of religious life.

Another midcentury author, Mosheim, is equally important in the origin of theological encyclopedia.[10] Although he does not speak of theological encyclopedia, he does self-consciously propose a discipline, theological method, which is the science of the education of church leaders, and which therefore sets forth the needed skills, qualities, and studies needed by a pastor. Further, he makes a beginning at a theological derivation of the disciplines. He thus finds Gundling's doctrines of faith and rules of life to be a way of organizing what God has disclosed in Scripture. This in turn sets requirements for disciplines which facilitate the understanding of Scripture (hermeneutics), and which produce skills of defending its truths (polemics), teaching them (catechetics), and preaching them (homiletics). In addition, because this revelation continues in the Christian religion and its history, activities of attesting to what is believed are not really possible without knowledge of that (church) history.

Because these two midcentury Lutheran theologians go beyond the previous listing of fields by proposing a way of organizing theological sciences based on method and attempting to derive that organization theologically, we can say that the origin of theological encyclopedic thinking occurs here. Although Mursinna used the title "theological encyclopedia," his work is less a true encyclopedia than these earlier examples.

The Origin of the Fourfold
Pattern

Distinctions within the one science (or *habitus*) of theology are common from the Middle Ages to the eighteenth century. These distinctions refer to different literatures to be studied and different "habits" of knowing. But all the distinctions refer back to the one habit, theology, the knowledge of God and the things of God. They do not refer to different "sciences," each with its own method. Once the mid-eighteenth-century theologians did begin to speak about "theological sciences," a new problem was immediately engendered. What are the sciences of theology and how are they organized? By the time Schleiermacher began to lecture on this problem in the first decade of the nineteenth century, the fourfold way of organizing theological disciplines was more or less standard. How did such a pattern originate?

The practice of organizing theology by *literatures* (patristic theology, prophetic theology) was commonplace. At the beginning of the eighteenth century we find simplified patterns for arranging the many bibliographical categories. C.M. Pfaff's *Introduction to the Literary History of Theology* (1724) arranges theology into five divisions: exegetical, dogmatic, polemical, church historical, and pastoral theology. This is the fourfold division plus a separate category for polemics. This division is not original with Pfaff. Hyperius's work, *On the Theologian* (1556), had proposed the fourfold way of organizing theological literature. It must be repeated, however, that these schemes are an organizing of literature, not of disciplines.

The first steps taken by Gundling and Mosheim beyond a mere listing of areas of literature have already been noted: the concept of theological sciences, the arrangement into theoretical and practical types, the rationales for just these sciences and not others. If there is any one distinctive encyclopedic pattern in this first period, it is just this—the distinction between disciplines of theory and disciplines of practice. And this classification plays an important role in the evolution of the fourfold pattern. For it to do so, the Gundling and Mosheim version of that distinction had to be altered. According to them, divine revelation issued in two kinds of teaching (*Lehre*): that presented for belief, and that presented for action and life. This is an organizing of theology viewed not as itself a habit, a knowing, a wisdom, but as an object, a set of truths.[11]

The critical development occurred in the second half of the century with the altered meaning of the practical side of theology. It changed the moral category concerned with life, rule, and duties to a clergy category. In the older *historia literaria theologica* works, "pastoral theology" included such things as church jurisprudence, catechetics, and homiletics.[12] However, Gundling places these undertakings under the practical side of theology conceived as applied theology.[13] In early versions such as Walch, the practical side covered both moral theology and disciplines of church and ministry.[14] But by the time of Nösselt (1771), the older sense of practical (moral) is placed under systematic theology, and only the sciences of ministry including the care of souls are the applied sciences.[15] Practical theology has thus become a term for ministry or clergy disciplines. Hence theory (theoretical sciences) describes Scripture studies, church history, and dogmatics. The fourfold pattern originated from this twofold division between *theoretical* and *applied* disciplines.

So far the focus has been on the role of the theory-practice distinction in organizing the three "theoretical" sciences on the one hand and the applied sciences on the other. Since the term *practical* had come to describe disciplines which *applied* the truths of revelation by exercising clergy responsibility, it became the inclusive term for homiletics, catechetics, and the care of souls. What determined the three theoretical disciplines—Scripture, dogmatics, and church history? Nothing new needed to happen to establish Scripture and dogmatics as necessary and important areas of investigation and knowledge. The study of Scripture had been self-evidently important throughout the history of Christian schools and took on a new primacy after the Reformation. Dogmatics had originated in the Middle Ages when speculative (rational, dialectical) theology was distinguished from *sacra pagina,* the exposition of Scripture. The Protestant theologians distinguished dogmatics from exegesis as the undertaking which arranged the topics (*loci*) of Scripture.[16] This does not mean, however, that the study of Scripture and the study of dogmatics were thought of as distinct sciences. For that to happen, the critical principle and historical methods of the Enlightenment had to be applied to the study of

Scripture.[17] Once that occurred, exegetical theology could become a separate scholarly discipline with its own sources and methods, and dogmatics could be distinguished from it by a larger complex of materials (e.g., confessions) and a different method (analytic and synthetic).

But how did church history become part of this trinity of theoretical sciences? To be so established, church history had to obtain the status of an independent scholarly enterprise and also had to obtain parallel importance alongside Bible and dogmatics. Many historical movements conspire in the making of church history into an independent scholarly discipline: the legacy from patristic historians, the Renaissance turn "to the sources," the use of church history in the polemical warfare between Catholics and Protestants, and the rise of historical-critical methods and consciousness in the Enlightenment. Most sixteenth- and seventeenth-century theologians agreed that the study of secular and sacred history was important, though there was little consensus as to why. Accordingly, we find church history usually present as one of the categories organizing authors and works in the historical-bibliographical type of works. In the eighteenth-century theological encyclopedic movement, it survived to become one of the three theoretical sciences of theology. But it obtained this status without clear agreement about the nature of its subject matter or the basis of its importance.

There is clearly a shift in the assessment of church history from the beginning of the eighteenth century to the end. By the time of Francke and the pietist movement, church history is no longer a mere servant of polemics. Church history was primarily the history of God's salvation, a historical account of the events recorded in the Old and New Testaments.[18] But after Semler and the German Enlightenment, a more secularized view arose. Church history leaves the Old and New Testaments to the biblical area and turns to the practices, sects, institutions, and doctrines of the Christian religion. Two primary justifications for the importance of church history arise in the eighteenth century and both go beyond the earlier demand for a weapon to wage sectarian polemical warfare. With Francke and pietism comes the claim that the knowledge of church history helps one assess the difficulties of the present and shapes the person in piety.[19] The encyclopedic movement of the second half of the century adds to this a justification which reflects the new understanding of theology as a totality of scholarly disciplines. The study of church history is important because it contributes to other theological disciplines. That is, the knowledge of schisms, hierarchies, events, doctrines, and the like supplements the historical knowledge of the Christian religion obtained *Bible* in the study of the Bible and also contributes to the ability to formulate *dogmatics.* the truths of Christianity in dogmatics.[20] We note that these two justifications argue the *value* of knowledge of church history but do not frame a real argument for its necessity in the pattern of sciences. Some authors in the period play down its importance and view it as propaedeutic to theology proper.[21] However this may be, by the end of the century, church history was well established as one of the three theoretical disciplines of theology and part of the fourfold pattern.

The New World of Issues and Problems

This initial period of theological encyclopedia is also important because it formulated the problems and issues which evoked the work of Schleiermacher and his successors and which still deserve careful scrutiny. We have already delineated some of these problems—those which attend the new enterprise of an encyclopedic organization of theological disciplines. Four additional problems need to be kept in *Heretical issues* mind before we consider Schleiermacher: (1) the collapse of orthodox theology; (2) the altered meaning of "theology"; (3) the clerical paradigm as the unity of the study of theology; and (4) the new problem of theology's status in the university.

The theological encyclopedia literature of the eighteenth century was not written, for the most part, by orthodox Lutheran or Reformed theologians. Although few were as extreme as Karl Friedrich Bahrdt, most of these authors participate to some degree in the criticisms, implied or explicit, of Protestant orthodox theology growing out of the historical temper of the Enlightenment.[22] While they write works on the study of theology which reflect a postorthodox temper, not many spell out precisely how the collapse of the orthodox theology affects the conception of theological study and the education of the clergy. Semler's writings on the subject, although not encyclopedias, are the most explicit in this regard. Yet none of these authors see "theology"

KB!

as a divinely imparted knowledge, the archetype of which is God's knowledge. None of them see Scripture uncritically, as if the knowledge which is theology coincides with knowledge of the subject matter of Scripture. Therefore, none of them see systematic theology as simply the ordering of that scripturally determined knowledge. Even though they retain the literary divisions of the older study-of-theology works (exegetical theology, etc.), the new meaning of these divisions as "sciences" (scholarly disciplines) implies a postorthodox orientation.

This is not to say that encyclopedias of this initial period did in fact accomplish a clear and cogent conceptuality which embodied all the implications of the collapse of orthodoxy. Rather, the proposals have a mixed and compromised character. *Sola Scriptura* is in some sense retained, and yet the study of Scripture is described as a collection of philological, historical-critical disciplines. The fourfold pattern, in other words, mixes the older way of authority with the newer historical-critical consciousness. But the problem and issue were there even if not explicitly formulated. In the light of these altered (postorthodox) ways of conceiving the ground and method of theological thinking, how does one formulate what theology is as a whole and the specific disciplines which comprise it?

Buried in the sea change of the eighteenth century is the issue of the meaning of *theology* itself. Most of the works on theological encyclopedia do expound the nature of theology. What is astonishing is that they do not seem to be aware of the radical departure from the Middle Ages and the Reformation occurring in their redefinition. In brief, this shift is from theology viewed as a *habitus*, an act of practical knowledge having the primary character of wisdom, to theology used as a generic term for a cluster of disciplines. Crucial to this shift is the definition of theology by its reference and not by the subject's act. This objectification of theology appears to be the outcome of the sectarian (Catholic and Protestant, Lutheran and Reformed, orthodox and heterodox) controversies of the sixteenth and seventeenth centuries. That is, dogmas, articles of faith (pure and mixed), the teachings of the church obtain a certain primacy. "God and the things of God" had always defined the reference and content of theology, but theology itself had been a sapiential knowledge which attended salvation. When the step is taken to define theology by its reference, it becomes the doctrinal truths themselves. As was argued earlier, this is presupposed in the nomination of three theoretical sciences of theology. But as the Enlightenment and historical consciousness gain ascendance, these sciences become more and more independent disciplines with their own methods, concepts and subject matters. And when that happens, theology no longer names simply the doctrinal truths but a faculty of studies. It has, in short, become a cluster term.

This departure was not explicitly articulated by the works of the eighteenth century, although it was implied by the pluralization of theology into "sciences." Nor does this new meaning of theology settle the question of the subject matter of this generic faculty enterprise. Two types of solutions were already beginning to develop in the eighteenth century, both of them to be used later by Schleiermacher. The first proposed that theology's subject matter is religion or the Christian religion.[23] The second proposed that theology as a faculty is unified by the requirements of the training of clergy. And this is our next major issue and problem.

The eighteenth century in German theological education began with a pietist reform at Halle under Francke. The agenda of that reform included both the element of personal piety and strong emphasis on the tasks of ministry. Once theology itself became a term for a faculty of studies embracing particular scholarly disciplines, an obvious candidate for what unified these disciplines was their goal or end. This way of thinking is itself a major departure. Insofar as theology is a *habitus* of practical wisdom which attends salvation, it has no additional end since the existential, saving knowledge of God is itself the end for which the human being is created. In that way of thinking, theology itself is the end (*telos*) of the study of theology.

On the other hand, when theology names an objective referent, doctrinal truths, and when it is a generic term for a faculty of disciplines, then it does need an end beyond itself, and the training of clergy is an obvious solution to that problem. Interestingly enough, it was not Schleiermacher who first proposed this solution but Mosheim and the Enlightenment theologian Bahrdt.[24] According to Mosheim theological method as a science explains how leaders of the church obtain the skills they need. Theology has to do with the church's leaders preparing for their responsibilities. Bahrdt's work is aimed at reforming ministerial education, which he thinks is in a bad way. He explicitly says that the criterion for determining the disciplines of theology is their contribution to clergy as good teachers and ministers. Neither Mosheim nor Bahrdt represents what we shall call the clerical paradigm for theological studies in a fully articulated sense, yet they are important early anticipations of it.

A final set of issues has to do with theology's (the faculty of theology's) place in the university. Clearly, this is a new problem. In the medieval university, theology is the very apex of the sciences because this *habitus*, the knowledge of God, founds and determines the principles and content of all other knowledge and sciences. After the Reformation many universities and *Hochschulen* of Europe were either appropriated or specially founded for confessional purposes and the training of Protestant clergy. But with the Enlightenment and the rise of "modern" universities like Halle and Göttingen, not only the reigning place but the very existence of theology began to become problematic. In Germany the traditional four faculties (philosophy, medicine, law, and theology) made up the university. But theology's right to be there was to some by no means self-evident. "Science" (*Wissenschaft*) was the new self-understanding of these universities. It required an open, critical, historical, and universal method and temper. The theological encyclopedic works of the second half of the century had all claimed that theology was made up of "sciences," but this did not exactly harmonize with the orthodox and pietistic heritage which insisted that theology had to do with piety and Christian life, and was correlated with a supernaturally given revelation and the authorities created by that revelation.

At the turn of the century, anticipating the founding of what was to be a model of scientific work, four authors published important monographs on this issue.[25] Kant poses the question of the relation of philosophy (pure scholarship operating under the principle of reason) to the other three faculties, including theology.[26] He advances the view, taken up by the other authors including Schleiermacher, that the three higher faculties—medicine, law, and theology—are united by their contribution to the state. That is, they address some indispensable need or aspect of human being.[27] Schelling retains this view and attempts to ground the three faculties sponsored by the state by arguing that the transition to objectivity produces a threefold organization of the areas of philosophy, each with an "objective" cultural expression.[28] These three areas are simply immanent aspects of the absolute and can be discerned by reason. When the state actually sponsors teaching and research in these aspects, they become "faculties."[29] What has been only brewing in Kant and Schelling comes to the surface in Fichte in a sharp attack on any conception of theology which works from mere authority. If theology's ground is simply an arbitrary divine will communicated in ancient writings, the understanding of which is the condition of human salvation, then it cannot possibly be a science and has no justification as a faculty of a university whose most essential feature is its commitment to science.[30] The issue posed by these turn-of-the-century works can be formulated both generally and specifically. Generally, it is the question of the justification of the theological faculty in the university. Specifically, it asks how theology, oriented as it is to a specific ("positive") religion and to special claims of revelation, can be a "science," a scholarly discipline.

2. Friedrich Schleiermacher's *Brief Outline of Theological Study*

Most interpreters agree that Schleiermacher's *Brief Outline of Theological Study* is a seminal work.[31] Why it is a seminal work is not easily and quickly stated. Its immediate influence was negligible and, because its threefold scheme of theological disciplines was never widely adopted, it might be argued that it had little long-term effect. Any estimation of the importance of the work depends on its interpretation and, like so many of Schleiermacher's writings, this little work does not make itself easily available for interpretation. It is written in such a formal, abstract, and compact way that each sentence is virtually a new thesis and a new insight. Hence, the details of the work tend to overwhelm and obscure its radical and novel character. Interpreting this brief and compact monograph requires getting behind the details to certain overall paradigms and insights. In addition, Schleiermacher's retention of traditional language for the theological disciplines and his threefold scheme makes his proposal look much more conventional than it actually is, especially insofar as it is viewed as simply a formal scheme.

The seminal character of Schleiermacher's contribution to theological encyclopedia is contained in two major insights which amount to two quite different ways of conceiving the unity of theology and of theological study. The first, which we shall call the "clerical paradigm," proposes a teleological solution to the unity of theology. The second, the "essence of Christianity motif," proposes a substantial or content solution to the unity of theology. The two insights constitute Schleiermacher's answers to two major questions or areas of questioning which he had inherited. The first is simply theology's status as a science, which, at the same time, is also the question of theology's place in the university. The second is the destructive effect of the collapse of the traditional bases of theology on the nature and unity of theology. To put it differently, if theology has become dispersed into various independent disciplines, how can there be any single subject matter of those disciplines or criteria to which they are bound? The following exposition is organized by these two questions.

The Teleological Unity of Theology: The Clerical Paradigm

Schleiermacher began lecturing on theological encyclopedia in 1804, when he first joined the Halle faculty, and continued to do so through the remainder of his career—twelve times in all. It is these lectures which obtained written form in the *Brief Outline* of 1811. If there is any one event to which these lectures are a response, it is probably the thirty-two-page course of theological study published by the Halle faculty in 1805.[32] But Schleiermacher's first publication on these issues was a lengthy article which appeared in 1808 after he had gone to Berlin, and the occasion of that article was the "conflict of the faculties" issue posed by Kant, Fichte, and Schelling and the situation of the newly founded university of Berlin.[33] This essay, "Occasional Thoughts on the German Universities," is important because it contains a clear and extended account of the first of Schleiermacher's two great insights and departures on theological study, and this is expressed in much more succinct form in the *Brief Outline*.

The "conflict of the faculties" issue poses the question of the general relation of the four faculties (philosophy, medicine, law, theology) and asks for the grounds for including theology in the university. Schleiermacher approaches this issue in a way which both retains and departs from the philosophers of German idealism. He retains the motif present in all three monographs that the university and its faculties exist under the sponsorship of the state and in some way receive their justification from that sponsorship.[34] He rejects, however, Schelling's speculative way of deriving the three higher faculties from "the transition to objectivity." Schleiermacher's departure yields a new definition of positivity and "positive science," and this is the main significance of the "Occasional Thoughts" essay. In contrast to philosophy, the faculty of pure science, the three higher faculties are described as faculties of "positive science." Here Schleiermacher sides with that long-running tradition (since medieval scholasticism) that acknowledges that theology is not a "pure science." In the eighteenth century, especially in the Enlightenment movement, "positive" meant something specifically historical or cultural, in contrast to the universal.[35] Schleiermacher gives this meaning a new dimension when he says that the positive faculties originate in the need to give cognitive and theoretical foundations to an *indispensable practice*. Human culture contains certain identifiable areas of practice which pertain to fundamental human needs, for instance, needs having to do with the conditions of health of the body or the conditions of social order. These areas of practice call for a specially trained leadership, and that leadership in turn requires "knowledge" pertinent to that area of practice. Since all areas of human culture occur under the protection and sponsorship of the state, the education of leaders for these indispensable regions of practice likewise occurs under the state. Faculties of law and medicine educate a clientele in the *theoria* of each one's practice.[36]

In what way then does a theology faculty find legitimation in the university? At this time Schleiermacher has already written his famous *Speeches,* in which he proposes a fundamental ontology of religion as an irreducible distinct dimension of human spirit. Curiously, he does not make use of this in the "Occasional Thoughts" essay. He simply asserts that the matters with which the church is concerned call for an educated leadership, as do medicine and law, and a university faculty which provides the cognitive foundations of that education. The distinctive thing about this proposal for a rationale of the three positive faculties is that the knowledge with which they are concerned has its unity in a social enterprise and practice external to the faculty. These three faculties are "sciences" (scholarly disciplines), not in the sense of pure theory, but rather in the sense of a theory for an area of social practice.

This solution to the problem of what the three "positive" faculties have in common and how they are justified becomes, in the *Brief Outline,* the basis for a whole new paradigm for understanding what theology is and what kind of unity its disciplines have. The major elements of that paradigm are the following:

1. Theology is a science in two formal respects: it is an enterprise whose methods yield cognitions, knowledge, and it gathers the details or particulars of its area into a systematic whole. But it lacks the feature necessary for a *pure* science, namely, a basis of its knowledge in what is universally accessible or given.

2. It is a *positive* science. Schleiermacher's definition of religious positivity embraces at least two features. First, because "positivity" names a culturally determinate form of experience, it has to do with a specific religious community with its distinctive mode of faith, tradition, piety, not "religion in general." This is the positivity which the Enlightenment identified with supernaturalism and tried to overcome. Second, the knowledge which theology accumulates is the knowledge (theory) needed by the leadership operative in the social ordering and survival ("governance") of that specific religious community. In other words, what unifies the various disciplines of theology is the pertinence of their discovered knowledge for clerical tasks and responsibilities. Theology is unified by the social situation of clerical praxis external to the university and the faculty of theology.

This teleological way of conceiving the unity of theological studies is what we shall call the *clerical paradigm.*[37] It had been developing since the pietist movement in the early eighteenth century. Now, it is clearly articulated in the first of the purely formal theological encyclopedias.

We recall now the complex problem Schleiermacher inherited and is self-consciously addressing. The one problem is theology's place in the university and its status as a science. This problem divides into two major problems:

1. How can theology be a science, a scholarly discipline with a genuine subject matter and proper method which yields genuine cognitions, if it is governed by a prescientific religious interest? This problem reflects the continued tension between the religious priorities of pietism and the critical principle of the Enlightenment.

2. Given the rise of independent sciences within theology, the dispersion of theology into a multiplicity of disciplines, how can theology have any unity?

As we have seen, Schleiermacher's general answer to the overall problem of theology's status as a science is his argument that theology is a legitimate positive science in the same sense as medicine and law. The clerical paradigm is Schleiermacher's solution to both of these specific problems. He mediates the tension between the interests of piety and the interests of scholarship by taking the issue beyond the level of *individual* motivations and commitments to a sociological level of training for church leadership. The requirements of a community for guidance by a leadership do not function as criteria of hidden agenda in the scholarly work of theological disciplines. Scholarly work with ancient texts or the theory of preaching is just as open to objective evidence as similar work in other positive facilities. As to the second problem, the unity of the various theological disciplines, the clerical paradigm proposes their unity to consist in their end or aim, the educational requirements of church leadership.

The Material Unity of Theology:
The Essence of Christianity

According to this analysis, Schleiermacher's *Brief Outline* is marked by two comprehensive insights. Another way to express this is to say that Schleiermacher has not one but two solutions to the problem of the unity of theological disciplines. The clerical paradigm offers a teleological way of understanding that unity. We consider now the second way, and with that, Schleiermacher's struggle with the deeper theological problem of the study of theology. Here we have Schleier-macher responding not just to the conflict-of-the-faculties literature, but to the standard fourfold scheme of theological encyclopedia, typified in the course of study submitted by the Halle faculty in 1805. I have argued that the fourfold scheme originated more as a historical accumulation and sifting than from a rigorous intellectual derivation. It bears the marks both of the way and method of authority of Catholic and Protestant orthodoxy and the new historical consciousness of the eighteenth century.

Schleiermacher organizes theology into three disciplines. This departure from the fourfold pattern goes beyond a merely formal classification to an entirely new concept of theology's subject matter and the way it offers itself to specialized inquiry and teaching. We have seen that the fourfold pattern organizes theology itself into three "theoretical" disciplines which contrast to a fourth applied or practical discipline. The cornerstone of the three theoretical disciplines is Scripture (exegetical theology). In the Protestant form, the authority for everything else lies here, hence traditional notions of inspiration, canon, and a discrete period of revelation are all presupposed. Dogmatics is a systematizing of this authority and divides into various enterprises of discourse such as polemics, symbolics, and so forth. Church history is a third discipline, although no single rationale presides over the consensus that it should be there.

The scheme represents the shift from theology as knowledge itself to theology as the objective reference of knowledge, the doctrinal truths provided by revelation. The very heart of the scheme is that these truths are theology's subject matter whose definitive, authoritative historical bearer is Scripture, and, some would add, the confessional translation and organization of Scripture. It is just theology in this sense that historical consciousness and the critical methods of the Enlightenment challenged. The authors of the theological encyclopedias of the initial period presupposed these methods, but their attention was so much on organizing theological disciplines and their *literatures* for pedagogical purposes that the effect of these methods on theology itself was obscured. The fourfold pattern was the result.

There is no text in Schleiermacher which contains an explicit criticism of the fourfold pattern or which scrutinizes each discipline in that pattern. We can construct Schleiermacher's criticism from his own substituted disciplines in the *Brief Outline*, from his lectures and writings on these disciplines, and from his use and view of Scripture, confessions, and dogmatics in his *Glaubenslehre*.[38] The standard four disciplines would appear to have the following problems, given Schleiermacher's modification of them. Is Bible or Scripture a discipline? In the pre-encyclopedia period it is not itself a science but a source, an authority for the sapiential knowledge which theology itself is. In addition, it names a literature, the Old and New Testaments. While that literature fences off an *area of texts*, it does not itself coincide with a science or discipline. Insofar as a discipline is involved, it is one having the character of historical interpretation, but that is applicable to a much broader area of texts than simply the Bible. In other words, if the literature of the Bible is approached historically and its texts are not regarded as a priori authorities, then the resulting interpretation of the Bible is not a separate science with a methodology utterly different from the historical interpretation of other texts.

Once Scripture ceases to be an a priori authority, dogmatics in the traditional sense of a reduction of Scripture to major loci of doctrine and a discovery of their systematic interconnections disappears. Although he retains the term, Schleiermacher replaces dogmatics with an account of the constitutive contents and experience of a historical community of faith. Since both the interpretation of Scripture and "dogmatics" utilize historical method, there is no church history in the sense of a discipline separated from Scripture studies and dogmatics. In the fourfold scheme practical theology was a kind of addendum—the application of theoretical sciences to pastoral tasks, something occurring outside theology proper, the discipline concerned to articulate the divine truths. This attempted reconstruction of the critique implied by Schleiermacher's modified version of these disciplines is offered in order to show that his threefold pattern is an intended substitute for the reigning fourfold encyclopedia. He thus replaces the traditional doctrinal truths with a different subject matter, one which abolishes the theological disciplines of the fourfold pattern.

On what basis does Schleiermacher propose three disciplines of theology? We recall that "theology" names a positive science, hence its unity lies in its capacity to educate the leadership of a living community. This sets the criterion for determining the divisions of that positive science, namely, the cognitions (education) needed by church leaders in the guidance and governance of that community. According to Schleiermacher these cognitions fall into the three branches of practical, historical, and philosophical theology. We shall take these up in reverse order in order to uncover the *material* unity of the three disciplines.

One whole set of cognitions needed by the church's leadership has a direct relevance for the tasks of that leadership.[39] At this point we must be careful to avoid the present-day functionalist mind-set as a framework in which to interpret Schleiermacher. He is careful not to propose a discipline which itself determines the tasks of ministry or which is simply preoccupied with the technical operations, the how-tos, of those tasks. Instead, he calls for a normative discipline which critically apprehends the *rules* for carrying out the tasks of ministry.[40] In other words, there are ways of fulfilling these tasks (preaching, pastoral care, church education, administration) which disrupt, endanger, and violate the nature of the community of faith, and other ways which promote its vigor and health. Theology, then, needs a discipline which assesses the activities, procedures, and operations of the church's ministry. Without such a discipline, the tasks of ministry would be pursued under criteria which are indifferent to the health of the church. This discipline is *practical theology*. As a normative discipline, it does have a subject matter (the rules for the activities of ministry), hence practical theology is not simply a cluster term for a group of skills courses. Further, as a normative discipline, it is *theoria*, but a *theoria* directly related to the praxis of the church's leadership.

Under what criteria will these rules be determined? How does one judge what is and is not conducive to the health of the faith community? At this point the need for a different set of cognitions becomes apparent and, with that, a second theological discipline. What the leadership needs to know in order to appraise the procedures of ministry is . . . "Christianity."[41] Schleiermacher uses the term *Christianity* in its widest sense. It refers to the historical phenomenon of a determinate community of faith and therefore includes the origins, history, and present situation of that community. And we can know

what violates and what promotes the community of faith only by knowing what that community of faith is.

Schleiermacher calls the discipline which yields this knowledge of
"Christianity" *historical theology*. In one sense it is comprised of many
disciplines, since there are many literatures, epochs, and aspects to
be studied. On the other hand, all of these disciplines employ historical method, and all contribute to a historical knowledge of Christianity. In this sense historical theology is one discipline. Clearly,
Schleiermacher sees "Christianity" or the idea of Christianity to be in
some sense normative for the proper exercise of the ministry.[42] This
does not mean all the historical content and data uncovered about
Christianity have an authority a priori. Rather, Christianity names a
historical community of faith in which redemption occurs, and the
promotion of that occurrence is what sets the tasks of the leadership
or ministry of the church. Inevitably, then, the idea of Christianity
has a normative status for practical theology, hence the *knowledge* of
Christianity is indispensable. Within historical theology, Schleiermacher proposes the three traditional "theoretical" disciplines: exegesis, church history, and dogmatics. Each in its own way contributes
to a knowledge of the idea of Christianity and in its own way is a kind
of historical discernment and interpretation.

At this point a number of questions press themselves upon us. Is
a knowledge of "Christianity" mediated by a variety of historical investigations a sufficient criterion for the appraisals of practical theology? The minister with such knowledge would have a comprehensive
historical grasp of "Christianity," but such a Christianity would be a
mere aggregate of a million details. Further, such knowledge has a
neutral-descriptive character and does not necessarily embrace a vision
of the importance, reality, and truth of Christianity. For these reasons,
historical theology does not sufficiently provide the knowledge necessary for the exercise of the tasks of ministry, but must draw on
another set of cognitions and another discipline. The determination of
rules for the tasks of ministry does need a historical knowledge of
Christianity, but that knowledge will do little good if it is simply in
the form of a million details. Needed is some vision or insight into the
distinctive essence of Christianity.

Now "distinctive essence" can be construed as simply a synthesis
of the details, a common strand running through all the periods and

types of Christianity. In this language of "essence" (*Wesen*), Schleiermacher introduces the issue of the reality, the truth, the value of Christianity; that is, the reality and truth of faith in this particular historical form. To really understand the reality of this faith is first to grasp Christianity's *genre*, which in Schleiermacher's view is piety or religiousness. This is Schleiermacher's way of relating Christianity to a fundamental ontological structure and requirement of the human being. "Distinctive essence" also evokes the task of discerning the essentially distinctive piety in question. For Schleiermacher this piety occurs in a community of redemption mediated through Jesus Christ. Because the distinctive essence embodies the correlation between the determinate redemption of Christianity and the general structures and needs of the human being as such, Schleiermacher calls this discipline "philosophical theology."[43] It is the discipline which is preoccupied with that about Christianity which in truth and in reality corresponds to the human spirit. To articulate this is both to persuade others of this truth and to sort out within the historical phenomenon the distortions of that truth. In other words, philosophical theology includes apologetics and polemics.

We return now to the question of the material unity of theology. The teleological unity, we recall, is established by the educational and cognitive requirements of a church's leadership. However, present in all three divisions of theology, either as criterion appealed to or as a directly thematized subject of inquiry, is *the essence of Christianity*. This is Schleiermacher's substitute for the doctrines or divine truths which unify the three theoretical disciplines of the fourfold pattern. It is the presence of this motif, the essence of Christianity, which prevents practical theology from being a mere technology of skills and historical theology from being a mere collection of historical details. By means of this motif, Schleiermacher can give full rein to historical investigations at every level and yet not reduce theology to history. Also by means of this motif, Schleiermacher can reject a theory-practice encyclopedia and can argue that no division of theology is merely theory or merely practice.

Note what has happened in this encyclopedic proposal. Hitherto, the idea and problem of an encyclopedia of a science has been essentially ambiguous. It can mean the problem of grasping the essential tasks and divisions which the *subject matter* of the science puts forth (thus, geometry divides into both solid and plane geometry) or the problem of the divisions which the *pedagogy* or teaching of that science requires. By assigning theology to the positive sciences whose unity is given by cognitions required by a praxis, Schleiermacher proposes an encyclopedia in the second sense of a course of study. While there is a unity of subject matter running through the three disciplines, that does not itself determine what those disciplines are.

Presupposed here is the altered meaning of the term *theology*, which is a term parallel to medicine and law for an aggregate of sciences which contribute to the education of a special leadership. Gone are both theology as itself knowledge or wisdom (a *habitus*) and a single Aristotelian discipline. Its very definition is set by clergy education, and this eliminates in advance attempts to define theology or make sense of theology in settings outside education. We must acknowledge, however, that another definition of theology is also at work in the *Brief Outline*. Viewed from the standpoint of the material unity, theology means a knowledge of the distinctive essence of Christianity manifest in its reality and truth. This definition is, however, implied but not articulated in the work. To the degree that it is there, Schleiermacher's *Brief Outline* offers two different understandings of theology, one determined by the clerical paradigm, the other by the essence of Christianity. In the post-Schleiermacher period, one of these insights, the essence of Christianity, was reflected in the definition of theology as the science of the (Christian) religion, but this ceased to function in the twentieth century. The other, the clerical paradigm, became virtually universal in the understanding of the structure and course of theological study.

NOTES

1. Only two encyclopedias were available to the English-speaking world prior to 1870. They are Tholuck's 1842–3 Halle lectures translated for the American journal *Bibliotheca sacra* under the title "Theological Encyclopedia and Methodology" (1844); and the Farrer translation of Schleiermacher's *Kurze Darstellung des theologisches Studiums* (1811) in 1850.

2. For this reason, the works of theological encyclopedia do not always have the usual "encyclopedia and methodology" title, but frequently retain the older phrase from the post-Reformation literature, "the study of theology,"

and sometimes the expressions "introduction to theology" and "theological propaedeutic."

3. The literary entity in which these issues and problems were formulated was not restricted to the theological encyclopedia. Kant, Fichte, and Schelling wrote important essays on the general problem of the university disciplines and the place of theology therein. Semler's writings were extensive and influential. Also important as criticisms of extreme Enlightenment views were Herder's *Briefe das Studium der Theologie betreffend* (1780). See his *Sämmtliche Werke* (Stuttgart and Tübingen, 1829), vols. 13 and 14.

4. Mursinna, *Primae lineae encyclopediae theologicae* (Halle, 1764). 2d edition, 1784.

5. N.H. Gundling, *Die Geschichte der Übrigen Wissenschaften fürnehmlich der Gottesgelahrtheit* (Bremen, 1742), chap. 1.

6. For example, C.M. Pfaff's *Introductio in historiam theologiae literarum* (Tübingen, 1724), organizes the major sections according to authors.

7. This particular theory/practice distinction occurs in the framework of seventeenth-century Aristotelian notions and the debates over *theologia* as a *habitus*. Reflecting these debates on whether *theologia* is a prudence, wisdom, or science, he assigns disciplines of wisdom and prudence to the practical side and disciplines of instrumentality and principles to the theoretical side.

8. Gundling, *Übrigen Wissenschaften*, p. 342.

9. Thus, Walch (1753), Mosheim (1756), Krug (1796), Thum (1797), Tittmann (1798), Bellermann (1803) all incorporate the twofold theory-practice division of theological sciences.

10. Mosheim, *Kurze Anweisung die Gottesgelahrtheit.* (Helmstadt: Weigand, 1763). This work is a posthumous publication of Mosheim's lectures on the subject.

11. In Bellermann we find this explicitly expressed in the division between the objective sense of theology (its content) and the subjective sense (insight, knowing). See F.F. Bellermann, *Der Theolog- oder encyklopädische Zusammenstellung des wissenswürdigsten und neuesten im Gebiete der theologischen Wissenschaften* (Erfurt: Henning, 1803), pp. 1ff.

12. For instance, Pfaff, *Introductio in historiam theologiae literarum*, bk. 5.

13. The appropriation of the term *practical theology* (sometimes *applied theology*) as the inclusive expression for the pedagogies and disciplines of ministry becomes common in the eighteenth century and after. Thus, J.A. Nösselt, *Anweisung zur Bildung angehender Theologen* (Halle: 1786), vol. 3, pt. 3; W. Krug, *Versuch einer systemat. Enzyklopädie der Wissenschaften* (1796); D.G.S. Planck, *Grundriss der theologischen Encyklopädie* (Göttingen: 1813; updating of a 1794 publication).

14. Johann Georg Walch, *Einleitung in die theologische Wissenschaften* (Jena: Güth, 1753), chap. 7.

15. J.A. Nösselt, *Anweisung zur Bildung angehender Theologen* (1771), vol. 3, pt. 3.

16. Martin Kähler argues that the *loci* method originated in the need to render into textbook form the commentaries on Romans done by the Reformers. Thus Melanchthon's first edition of the *Loci communes* (1521) is really an arrangement of themes from Romans. By the time of the second edition, however, the work had become widely used as a textbook, hence Melanchthon expanded it to cover all the important themes of doctrine. From this "first Protestant dogmatics" come the many dogmatics written by Lutheran and Reformed theologians of the sixteenth and seventeenth centuries (Kähler, *Geschichte der Protestantische Dogmatik im 19. Jahrhundert* [Munich: Chr. Kaiser, 1962], pp. 18ff.).

17. It was Semler, the critic of orthodox theology and the Enlightenment historian, who insisted on the independence of the study of Scripture from dogmatics.

18. Buddeus, Walch, and Mursinna all press this view. According to Mursinna, church history covers two major periods: from Adam to Moses, and from Moses to Christ (*Primae linae encyclopediae theologiae*, p. 1704). The second period includes, however, the total Christian epoch down to the present.

19. Francke saw church history as a peripheral study but justified it as an aid to piety. See E. Peschke, *Studien zur Theologie August Hermann Franckes* (Berlin, 1966), pt. 4. This moral or pietist rationale for the study of church history is widespread in the eighteenth century. Buddeus, Walch, Mosheim, Nösselt, and Thum all have some version of it.

20. This justification of church history is present in Walch, Nösselt, and Thum.

21. Mosheim, sometimes called the father of modern church history because of his work, *Institutiones historiae ecclesiasticae antiquioris* (1737), calls it a "laborious and expensive science," a detailed knowledge of which is not necessary for pastors (*Kurze Anweisung*, pp. 177–8). Francke thought of it as peripheral. Rambach omits it altogether from the scheme of studies. Thum sees it as linking biblical studies with dogmatics. Krug lists church history in the propaedeutic part of the theoretical theological sciences.

22. Karl F. Bahrdt's *Über das theologische Studium auf Universitäten* (Berlin, 1785) was probably the most extreme Enlightenment-oriented work on the subject in this period.

23. According to Pannenberg, Ficino is one of the first to identify true religion as the subject matter of theology, a proposal to be adopted by Zwingli and Calvin (*Theology and the Philosophy of Science* [Philadelphia: Westminster Press, 1976], p. 307, n.). The post-Enlightenment proposal of religion or Christian religion as theology's subject matter would mean something quite different, namely, a historical phenomenon to be studied by historical methods.

24. Mosheim, *Kurze Anweisung*; Bahrdt, *Über das theologische Studium*.

25. Kant, *Der Streit der Fakultäten* (1798). This work appeared in three parts throughout the 1790s. See *Werke*, ed. Rozenkranz, vol. 10. Translated

by M.J. Gregor in *Immanuel Kant: The Conflict of Faculties* (N.Y.L. Abaris, 1979). Fichte, *Deducirter Plan einer zu Berlin zu errichtenden hohern Lehranstadt* (1807). Schelling, *Vorlesungen über die Methode des akademischen Studium* (1803). See *Gesammelte Werke*, 14 vols. (Stuttgart: J.G. Cotta, 1856–61), vol. 10. Translated by E.S. Morgan as *On University Studies* (Athens, Ohio: Ohio University Press, 1966). Schleiermacher, *Gelegentliche Gedanken über Universitäten in deutschem Sinn* (Berlin, 1808). See *Sämmtliche Werke* 3, chap. 1 (Leipzig, 1911).

26. Actually, each of the three articles comprising this monograph reflects a different situation. The essay on the conflict of the philosophy and theology faculties is written in a situation of censorship on the part of the state, challenging the freedom of the philosophy faculty to work strictly under the principle of reason. Kant argues that it is the one faculty that has a responsibility to do this and therefore the task of grounding the authorities taken for granted by theology falls to philosophy.

27. Thus, he speaks of the eternal (theology), civil (law), and physical (medicine) well-being of the human being (Gregor, *Immanuel Kant*, p. 31).

28. According to his argument there is a science, *law*, whose objective counterpart is the *ideal* aspect of the absolute; a science of nature, *medicine*, which reflects the *real* aspect of the absolute; and a science, *theology*, in which the two aspects coincide.

29. According to Hermann and Lautner, the "conflict of the faculties" originated in a dispute between the philosophy and theology faculties of Göttingen in 1793. Professor Reinhardt of the philosophy faculty announced a course in church history which was promptly opposed by the theology faculty, which based its case on the city statutes. The philosophy faculty supported Reinhardt on the grounds that church history as part of general history had nothing to do with theology. This posed the question which Schleiermacher was soon to take up: what then actually is theology? His answer is that all the theological disciplines can be construed as simply secular sciences except as they have to do with education for leaders who will exercise church guidance (W. Hermann and G. Lautner, *Theologiestudium: Entwurf einer Reform* [Munich: Chr. Kaiser, 1965], p. 60).

30. Fichte, *Deducirter Plan*, p. 130.

31. The German title is *Kurze Darstellung des theologischen Studiums zum Behuf Einleitender Vorlesungen* (Berlin, 1811). A second edition was published in 1830, and a critical edition was issued by H. Scholz in 1910, republished in 1961. The work has been twice translated into English: by William Farrer (Edinburgh, 1850); and by Terrence Tice (Richmond: John Knox Press, 1966), under the title *Brief Outline on the Study of Theology*.

32. See Heinrich Scholz, "Einleitung," the introduction to Scholz's critical edition of the *Kurze Darstellung*, p. xv.

33. "Gedanken über Universitäten." See Schleiermacher's *Werke*, ed. O. Braun, 4 vols., vol. 4.

34. Karl Barth attributes this motif of the state sponsorship of the (theo-

logical) faculty simply to Schelling's influence on Schleiermacher. In fact it is a common motif and presupposition of all four of these turn-of-the-century essays. Cf. *Die Theologie Schleiermachers*, ed. D. Ritschl (Zurich: TVZ, 1978), pp. 250ff.

35. The term *positive theology* has had a variety of meanings. A simplified historical account uncovers three quite different meanings. In late medieval scholasticism, it served as an alternative to scholastic theology. *Positive* theology meant theology (knowledge) occurring from authority, in which the content is simply established on its given principles. *Scholastic* theology referred to the emphasis on dialectical method and demonstration associated with high scholastic theology (Yves M.J. Congar, *A History of Theology* [Garden City: Doubleday & Co., 1968], chap. 5, D). A similar distinction arose in the seventeenth-century Lutheran theologians (Calixt) between school or academic theology (with focus on detail, learning) and ecclesiastical or positive theology which took up the main points of the Christian religion (W. Pannenberg, *Theology and the Philosophy of Science*, trans. F. McDonagh [Philadelphia: Westminster Press, 1976], p. 242). A second and quite different meaning occurs in the Enlightenment, where positive religion contrasts to natural religion. Here, positive connotes religion which is institutional, public, traditional, even precritical. Schleiermacher proposes a third usage yet. He retains the connotation of determinacy in his use of positive, but empties the term of its pejorative connotations and argues for the validity of the determinate (positive) nature of faith. In addition, he speaks of theology as a positive science, not only because of its determinacy, but because it pertains to the education of a specific leadership needed for an important aspect of culture, namely, religion.

36. "Gedanken über Universitäten," *Werke*, ed. Braun, vol. 4, p. 319.

37. Hereafter, this expression, *clerical paradigm*, will be used to refer to the prevailing (post-Schleiermacher) Protestant way of understanding the unity of theological education. According to this paradigm, the disparate fields and courses are connected by their capacity to prepare the student for future clergy responsibilities. Although this paradigm will be questioned as an adequate approach to theological education's unity, the author wishes to avoid the impression that this is a questioning of either the validity of clergy education itself or of the validity of education for specific activities and skills.

38. Schleiermacher's teaching and writing covered all branches of the fourfold pattern: New Testament studies, theological ethics, church history, dogmatics, practical theology.

39. Schleiermacher, *Brief Outline*, trans. Tice, pp. 25, 258–59, 267–71.

40. *Ibid.*, p. 263.

41. *Ibid.*, pp. 26, 259–60.

42. *Ibid.*, p. 70.

43. *Ibid.*, pp. 24, 32–40.

5

The Triumph of
the Fourfold Pattern

The term *theological encyclopedia* is perhaps an unfortunate way of expressing the problem of the structure of theology viewed as a discipline and course of studies. Only two American authors, John McClintoch and R.F. Weidner, used it to entitle works of this sort.[1] Others preferred to speak of the study of theology or theological propaedeutics. Complaints about the term are not uncommon in the history of the literature.[2] Because the term never was widely used in the United States and because most of the literature of the encyclopedia movement has long been lost to public view, one might get the impression that Schleiermacher was both the founder and the concluder of theological encyclopedia. We have already seen that he was by no means the founder, that he himself inherited a literature and a set of issues going back to the middle of the eighteenth century. It is equally clear that theological encyclopedia did not conclude with him, that in fact the major period of the literature began with him.

This chapter will attempt to trace what happened to "the study of theology" after Schleiermacher and what effect that had on theological education in the United States. It must be repeated that this is not a straightforward historical study either in the sense of a history of theological encyclopedia or a history of theological education. The method is to use the literature to expose the major types of proposals and their presuppositions. Even though the term, the concept, and the literature of nineteenth-century theological encyclopedia are not at present widely known and used, the fallout of the movement had an enormous effect on theological education in this country, and that effect continues into the present. Without uncovering this legacy, it would be difficult if not impossible to offer cogent criticisms and proposals pertinent to the reform of theological education today.

1. Theological Encyclopedia After Schleiermacher

The literature of theological encyclopedia originated, as we have seen, in the modern (post-Enlightenment) university of Germany. This is to be expected, both because these universities first developed the concept of "science" in the modern sense and because it had been standard practice in those theological faculties to introduce theology through a comprehensive survey of its disciplines and literatures.

For fifty or so years after Schleiermacher's *Brief Outline* of 1811, Germany continued to be the center of the theological encyclopedia movement. Occasional works appeared in other European countries from the 1830s on, and in the last third of the century a significant literature appeared in the English-speaking countries.[3] This post-Schleiermacher literature continued for about a century, ending with World War I. The period is less one of new discoveries of encyclopedic schemes than a consolidation of what had begun earlier. The concept of theological encyclopedia is now intact and self-consciously embraced. There is, in other words, a theological discipline which inquires into the structure of theology itself.

This discipline, most agree, has two main problems: the position of theology among the other sciences, and the relation of disciplines within theology to each other.[4] Most authors affirm that theological encyclopedia is transconfessional. That is to say, its subject matter is not limited to a branch of Christendom, but is "Christianity" itself. Yet there are disagreements about the nature and task of theological encyclopedia. According to those approaches which make pedagogy central, the encyclopedia is an introductory manual of divinity studies which presents the literature, history, even accomplishments of the branches of theology. A way of organizing the branches is proposed, but the schematism is regarded as self-evident and something to be established. Another kind of work sees theological encyclopedia as one aspect of theology itself, and as such faced with a tough theological problem: how to derive and justify the "sciences" of theology.

Strangely, in spite of the rich and varied history of theology in the nineteenth century, this literature remains amazingly uniform. At first glance there seem to be two major periods of publication, the first centering on the 1820s and 1830s, the second from the 1870s through the end of the century.[5] What gives the total period this appearance is a twenty-five-year dry spell of publication occurring in midcentury.[6] Yet there is little discernible difference between the introductions published in the early and late periods. Instead of different types of encyclopedias falling into major periods, we have a dominant and a subordinate strand continuing more or less throughout the period: the Hagenbach type and the Schleiermacher type.

The thesis of this chapter is that the pre-Schleiermacher fourfold pattern became virtually universal for Protestant schools throughout the nineteenth century and for theological education in Europe and America. The difference between the Schleiermacher pattern and the fourfold pattern will remain obscure insofar as the issue is restricted to Schleiermacher's historical influence or to a comparison of formal schemes. Schleiermacher influenced authors of both types, including the most influential work of the fourfold type, Hagenbach's publication of 1833.[7] As to formal schemes of arrangement, the fourfold (afterwards called the Hagenbach type) pattern can be disguised as a threefold scheme simply by placing two of the divisions under one heading.

2. Nineteenth-Century Modifications of the Fourfold Pattern

It is clear that the fourfold pattern originated and became dominant before Schleiermacher. It continued in Schleiermacher's contemporaries, such as Ehrhardt and J.C. Ch. Schmidt, who published encyclopedic introductions about the same time as the *Brief Outline*. And it continued in the first works that may have been influenced by the *Brief Outline*.[8] A survey of the Protestant publications distributed over the rest of the century discloses some version of the fourfold pattern to be overwhelmingly present. The eighteenth-century twofold scheme of theory and practice finds occasional representation.[9] For the most part, the nineteenth century drops this language of theory and practice to organize theological sciences. Present only sporadically

✓ Summary

Theologia

throughout the century is an organization of theology of the Schleier-macher type. It ranges from Rosenkranz and the Roman Catholic theologian Staudenmeier in the 1830s to Dorner at the end of the century.[10]

Five main features characterize the Schleiermacher type of pattern:

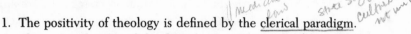

1. The positivity of theology is defined by the clerical paradigm.
2. The material unity of the disciplines is Christianity, historically conceived.
3. The whole enterprise is grounded in a fundamental theology which so formulates the essence of Christianity that its "validity" and "reality" are apparent (philosophical theology).
4. Historical consciousness and method pervade all the branches of study, including dogmatics.
5. A material content (rules of church guidance) integrally related to the essence of Christianity helps define practical theology.

Needless to say, not all of the works labeled the Schleiermacher type retain all of these features. Since the Schleiermacher scheme was not the dominant pattern of European theological schools, it was not exported to the United States. Instead, the Hagenbach type was the legacy of American theological education. Yet, what was transported was not simply the eighteenth-century fourfold pattern, but a modified nineteenth-century version of such. The task then is to describe the Hagenbach type, tracing its career in the nineteenth and twentieth centuries and its transplantation to the United States. Two issues or questions may be of assistance in expounding the nineteenth-century form of the fourfold or Hagenbach pattern: How was the unity of the pattern conceived? And what effect did this have on the particular disciplines?

The question of the unity of theological study faces us again with "theology." We recall that Schleiermacher offered two not completely consistent ways of understanding the unity of theological study: a teleology or goal of an educated church leadership and an historical-theological content, the essence of Christianity. With some modifications and even disagreements, the nineteenth-century encyclopedias continued both of these motifs as ways of understanding the unity of

[handwritten margin note: Feuerbach?]

theological studies. However, theology itself was defined by means of the historical-theological approach. The nineteenth-century authors agreed that theology was a science, thus they continued the Kantian contrast between religion and theology. Furthermore, some of them explicitly rejected the older view that theology was a *habitus,* a cognitive disposition whose contents were "God and divine things."[11] Theology is not itself religion, but a science, a scholarly enterprise directed at religion. Christian theology is the science of the Christian religion. With very few exceptions this is the standard definition of theology in the encyclopedic introductions throughout the nineteenth century.[12] The definition sounds clear and precise, but it obscures the essential ambiguity of the nineteenth-century introductions on the nature of theology.

Two problems attend this "science of Christianity" solution to the unity of theological studies. First, while the authors tend to agree that a science is a scholarly discipline whose systematizing of data yields cognitions, it is clear that the four areas of the fourfold pattern are not part of a single science in this sense. This problem reflects a departure from the Schleiermacher type of encyclopedia, where science is defined as "positive science" in Schleiermacher's revised meaning of "positive," a science pertinent to a particular societal community, area of needs, and leadership. Accordingly, for Schleiermacher only one of the three areas directly concerns and historically describes "Christianity": historical theology. But how a normative enterprise like systematic theology and a practical enterprise like practical theology are, with church history and Bible, parts of a single scholarly enterprise studying Christianity is not at all clear. Partly responsible for this problem is the second one: an ambiguity concerning what it means to say "Christianity" or the "Christian religion" is theology's object. The more conservative introductions, like Clarisse and Hofmann, retained the older normative meaning of Christianity as "true religion." The more liberal introductions, like Rosenkranz, Cave, or Drummond, assumed Christianity to be a complex of historical data. What then is theology? Is it a straightforward, strict, historical science whose object is a historical entity, one of the religions of the world? Is it a normative science whose object is the revealed *doctrine* residing in the Christian religion?

The nineteenth-century attempt to unify theological study by the theme *science of Christianity* is further complicated by the widespread retention of the second Schleiermacherian motif, the clerical paradigm. Here theology is not defined by a subject matter, but by a pedagogical goal, the training of clergy. Many of the encyclopedias explicitly and self-consciously take over this solution from Schleiermacher.[13] Some, sensing the incompatibility between the subject-matter oriented definition of theology and the teleological, clerical paradigm where theology is an aggregate of disciplines, articulate this distinction and reject or qualify the clerical paradigm. Räbiger thus says, "In opposition to this external mode of procedure, in order truly to accomplish its task, it has to show that those branches with which it has to do are connected with one another by an inner bond, and that, in accordance with an inner relationship, they are to be joined to one another in homogeneous groups."[14]

However they disagree over the nature of theology, these discussions are occurring in pedagogically oriented writings which serve as introductions to a course of studies for future clergy. They all propose as the culminating branch of theology, practical theology, a cluster of courses which explicitly address the minister's obligations in church leadership. In other words, Schleiermacher's "positive theology" solution to the unity of studies, the clerical paradigm, is operative in all the nineteenth-century introductions, whatever their specific definition of theology. We have then, in the nineteenth century, a continuation of both of Schleiermacher's ways of understanding theology's unity. Some of the authors are aware of this double-sided approach to theology and simply advocate it.[15]

In summary, the prevailing view of the nineteenth-century introductions is that theology is a science (a systematizing of data yielding knowledge) of the Christian religion for the special purpose of educating the leadership of the church.

It was argued above that the material solution to the unity of theology—theology as the science of Christianity—was general and ambiguous because of the different ways the solution could be construed. This confusion was further perpetuated by other developments in the nineteenth century, particularly what happened to the theological disciplines themselves. They had been identified as "sciences" in the eighteenth century, yet it was still typical for a single professor (like Schleiermacher) to cover many of these sciences in teaching and publications. But the direction of development was toward specialization, toward scholars whose research and teaching was restricted to one of the four areas or even to a field within one of them. A distinct history of scholarly undertaking marked each of the theological sciences. Each one gathered the sociological accoutrements of a science: the research-oriented journals, the professional society, the graduate program in that science alone, the delimitation of research projects within the bounds (the language, methods, literatures) of that science, the nationwide or worldwide collegium of scholars in that science.

Further, the development toward specialized sciences within theology altered the *meaning* of each of the four branches of theology. In the pre-encyclopedia period, specified undertakings (e.g., *theologica exegetica*) were abstractions from a single "knowledge," and the basis of the abstraction was a certain literature pertinent to that knowledge. In the eighteenth and much of the nineteenth centuries, theological "sciences" were distinguished both as aspects of an overall science of Christianity and as sciences pertinent to clergy education. With specialization, each science developed the critical apparatus it needed, its languages, satellite secular sciences, technical methods. The result was that each of the four theological sciences itself became an aggregate, a general area of scholarship within which were "sciences." This is especially apparent in church history, systematic theology, and practical theology.

I noted earlier the absence of consensus concerning the rationale for church history's inclusion among the theological sciences. A similar indecisiveness characterized the nineteenth-century introductions concerning the rationale and even subject matter of church history.[16] Yet there was at least some inclination in the earlier period to propose a theological subject matter for church history. Tholuck, accordingly, defines the third area (historical theology) as "the narrative of the changes through which the church of Christ has passed on earth." The ideal to which these changes are compared is the kingdom of God. Church history tries to show "the extent to which the Christian church, at different periods of her existence, has approximated to this state of ideal perfection."[17] This is a version of the eighteenth-century affirmation that church history is the story of God's saving work.[18] But as church history itself became specialized—by periods, by the contrast of history of doctrine and history of the institution, by branches and groups of Christendom, and by themes (ethics, worship, monasticism, etc.)—the *theological* aspect of the subject matter was lost. Church history came to be an aggregate of specialties comparable to American history or Russian history.[19]

Practical theology underwent a similar transition. One might properly argue that practical theology never was a single, unified theological science since, from its eighteenth-century beginning as "applied theology," it always was a collection of studies pertinent to the discrete tasks of ministry. Schleiermacher, however, had proposed a way in which these tasks could be subject to a single discipline by making its subject matter rules for determining the proper procedures for exercising ministerial tasks. Lobegott Lange continues this approach when he derives three major disciplines of practical theology (catechetics, homiletics, liturgics) from three dimensions of the church's social duration. The church, he says, endures by means of doctrines, holy customs, and the teaching office, and the rules for exercising this are the object of a discipline, practical theology.[20] However, the nineteenth-century introductions abandon this Schleiermacherian attempt to identify a theological subject matter for practical theology. The Hagenbach and Pelt proposal that practical theology is a theory for practice is already a step away from Schleiermacher since it omits the very thing which would connect the ministry and church practice with Christianity, namely, the ascertaining of how the nature of Christianity itself sets forth requirements, principles, "rules," which preside over the church's activities. The transition is completed when we hear of practical theology being described as a "technics" or as "the science and art of the various functions of the Christian Ministry."[21] Once *functions* of ministry comprise the unity of practical theology, that term becomes an aggregate of disciplines of the functions, each one with its specialists, auxiliary sciences, and so forth.

The effects of specialization on both biblical and systematic theological areas are parallel. The history of systematic theology in the nineteenth and twentieth centuries testifies to a constant struggle for a content, a subject matter, a method.[22] Hence, the specialties which systematic theologians adopt (this or that philosophy, philosopher, literature, language, historical period, secular discipline) indicate a discipline behind these specialties only in a very abstract sense.

The biblical field may seem to be the branch of studies most untouched by the forces of dispersion. It has a literary unity, a collection, a canon which sets the tasks of scholarship. Yet "Bible" names not a discipline but a collected literature. Is there a "science" of that collection? We usually do not speak of the "science" of the Pali Canon of Buddhism or the "science" of the Talmud, although clearly scholarly work using these collections does take place. In the pre-encyclopedia period, "biblical" or exegetical theology would not be thought of as a discrete science, but rather as the study of the writings where God's revealed Word was found. Late nineteenth- and twentieth-century specialists in the biblical area tend not to think of their subject matter that way—as revelation occurring in and with the texts of their specialty. More typical is the attempt to define the discipline or science not by the collection but by the historical phenomenon: the religion of Israel or the origins of Christianity. This is a viable solution from one point of view, but it results in dispersing what seems to be one science into the various scholarly enterprises which "the religion of Israel" evokes. However, if the specialists in these fields think of these ancient religions and their collections as having a certain contemporary importance, a treasure to be mined by modern hermeneutical methods, that importance is clearly not the *subject matter* and unity of the field, the thing about which the professional societies, research projects, and the like have gathered.

It is time now to consider the overall features of the nineteenth-century version of the fourfold or Hagenbach pattern, especially as they compare with the Schleiermacher type. The most general feature of the nineteenth-century introductions is that they have more a pedagogical than a theological character. The organization of fields which they articulate is already in place, institutionally fixed in the examination system in Germany. As such, it is self-evident to the authors. Hence, few of these introductions offer a tightly argued theological justification for the proposed pattern.[23] In one respect the fourfold schemes of the nineteenth century do not depart from the Schleiermacher type. They all occur under what we have called the clerical paradigm. Even though some of the authors explicitly criticize the concept of theology as a mere aggregate of sciences, most of these introductions assume that theology's setting is the education of ministers. Without exception, practical theology means for them a cluster of studies pertinent to ministerial tasks, capping a series of sequential theological studies.

The fourfold pattern departs from the Schleiermacher type in the following ways. First, the definition of theology as the science of Christian religion is, as we have seen, ambiguous. In the Schleiermacher type, "Christianity" is in some sense a norm, but its normativeness is not discerned apart from a rigorous program of grasping what is "essential" and an apologetic program of relating it to (human) reality. The fourfold type has no such discipline (philosophical theology), hence "Christianity" is simply a theme with which the various sciences have to do. And this aggregate character of the "object" or subject matter of theology has pervasive consequences.

Second, the fourfold pattern, unlike the Schleiermacher type, retained the eighteenth-century separation of biblical and historical theology. One can properly argue that they should be separated because the collection of writings called Scripture has a very different function in theology from that of subsequent Christian literatures. Schleiermacher himself knew this, of course, yet placed the inquiry into Israel's faith, early Christianity, the history of the church, and even dogmatics together under historical theology, because he saw all of them as parts of a historical attempt to fathom and provide detailed knowledge of the essence of Christianity. Once Scripture is separated into its own compartment, not only is the historical mode of understanding theology undercut (the Schleiermacher type), but the way is opened to the older biblicism and supernaturalism.

Third, most of the authors of the nineteenth-century encyclopedias were not proponents of the old Protestant orthodoxies, but represented in some fashion the post-Enlightenment commitment to historical method. Hence, their separation of biblical and historical fields resulted in the loss of the essence-of-Christianity material unity and normative reference; on the other hand, they did not return to a simple biblicism, but retained historical methods in each of the four theological sciences. The result was, as we have already seen, the promotion of each science or discipline as an independent scholarly enterprise. The fourfold pattern, lacking any material unity of subject matter and norm, is responsible for one of the main elements taken for granted in present-day theological education: the independence and autonomy of the department areas, disciplines of the theological school. And because this promotes these areas as independent clusters of scholarship, it alienates them from both personal life and the church. Originating here is the situation which developed in the twentieth century, the return of theory and practice as the way to interpret theological study.

Finally, because of the ambiguity of the material unity of theological study (theology as the science of Christianity), and because "theology" did not function as something to which each discipline was subject, the way was paved for what happened in the twentieth century. This is the loss of the material unity of theological study, leaving only the clerical paradigm as the basis for defining theology and the rationale for its disciplines. As will be argued later, this had far-reaching consequences, not only for theological education, but for the teaching of religion in universities and for church education.

3. The Demise of the Encyclopedic Issue in the Twentieth Century

In continuing the attempt to unravel the presuppositional strands of theological education in the United States, we may now track what happened to the Hagenbach pattern after its migration to the American continent and what effect it had on theological education.

In Europe (Germany), the post-Schleiermacher encyclopedic literature lasted, as a distinct genre, about 150 years, from the middle of the eighteenth century to World War I. To the knowledge of the present author, no encyclopedia of the Hagenbach type—the large, bibliographical-historical introduction to theology, organized into the major disciplines—was published in Europe after 1918.[24] It would be too strong to say that the issue of the unity and organization of theological study was totally absent after World War I. However, it is only sporadically taken up. A number of works, almost all European, have been published on "the study of theology" in the first seven decades of the twentieth century.[25] In addition to this genre of writing, there are proposals, primarily by European theologians in occasional articles and in introductions to theology and systematic theologies, concerning the pattern of theological disciplines.[26] These primarily European monographs on the study of theology are not really typical. The literary genre which seems to replace the old introductions is the multiauthor symposium.[27] In these works representatives of each branch of study, frequently from the same faculty, discuss the present state, importance, unity, and recent gains of their discipline. With rare exceptions these works do not offer any rationale for the existence of these branches of study or of their mutual relation, hence this genre of literature tends to presuppose whatever organization of fields is in force at the time.[28]

In addition to these symposia and European study-of-theology works there is an extensive literature in the twentieth century on "theological education." This includes both the German literature, especially concentrated in the 1960s on the reform of theological study, and the many publications in the United States on the history, institutions, curricula, and pedagogy of the theological schools. These literatures resemble the symposia and many of the study-of-theology works in one respect. They assume that the basic pattern of study is intact and valid.[29] In summary, the genre of literature called "theological encyclopedia" ends prior to World War I. The issue of a *ratio studiorum* is only rarely posed in the six decades which follow. Replacing that literature and issue are the descriptions-of-disciplines collections, occasional works on the study of theology, and extensive publications on various aspects of theological education.

4. The Fourfold Pattern in North American Theological Education

We have seen that the *problem* and literature of theological encyclopedia originated in the "modern" German university of the eighteenth century and that throughout the nineteenth century it remained centered in Europe. The reasons for its absence in the United States are evident. The context of theological education in North America had little resemblance to the German university with its foundational faculty of philosophy and its higher faculties of theology, medicine, and law. Even when the more informal apprentice-type education was replaced by the denominational seminary at the beginning of the nineteenth century, there was no survey of theological sciences which, as in Germany, introduced the course of studies. Accordingly, the United States did not produce a "study-of-theology" literature like that of the sixteenth and seventeenth centuries in Europe, even though ministers like Cotton Mather were acquainted with it. Instead of works on the study of theology or theological encyclopedia, we have in the United States works, usually modest in length, designed to counsel and advise students and ministers in the conduct of ministry. This genre of literature originates, it seems, in English puritanism, and Richard Baxter's *The Reformed Pastor* of 1655 is one of its more important instances.[30] It continued throughout the nineteenth century as the typical American Protestant work on the ministry and ministerial study.[31]

In this situation prior to the rise of distinct theological sciences, there is not as yet a problem of the pattern of theological study, nor can there be a theological encyclopedic literature. But theological encyclopedia did eventually come to the United States. The conditions of its doing so were described briefly in chapter 1. Ministerial education developed from the level of the log college to that of the post-college institution, the denominational seminary, with a several-year-long course of studies and a small group of faculty members. Yet something else had to happen before there could be receptivity to the European (encyclopedic) introductions. The modern, European ideal of specialized scholarship and specialized disciplines had to be applied to theology. This ideal took hold in the United States under the impact of the Germanization of American theological education.

The Germanization of American theological education was at work almost as soon as the first seminaries were founded. The key figures appear to be Moses Stuart of Yale and Andover; Nevin of Princeton, Western and Mercersburg; Edward Robinson and Edward Amassa Park, both of Andover; and Phillip Schaff of Mercersburg.[32] Robinson studied in Germany in the late 1820s, less than twenty years after the founding of Andover, and when he returned he pursued an aggressive agenda of acquainting American churches and pastors with German scholarship in his role as founding editor of the *Biblical Repository*.[33] Park and others studied in Germany with Tholuck, and Park, as the first editor of the journal *Bibliotheca sacra* (1844), also pursued a policy of urging the seminaries to imitate German scholarship and its model of theological education.[34] Phillip Schaff came to Mercersburg in the year of the founding of *Bibliotheca sacra* (1844) and he contributed to that journal's Germanizing agenda in a programmatic article published in 1847.[35] Members of the Princeton Seminary faculty (Charles Hodge, B.B. Warfield) likewise studied in Germany in this and subsequent periods. The result of all this was that the early seminary movement in America did adopt, in part at least, the German ideal of theological study comprised of areas of scholarship. The late-nineteenth-century emergence of graduate schools made no small contribution to this model. The outcome was that the typical theological faculty of the seminary was comprised of specialists in particular disciplines, and the course of study was a path through designated theological sciences. Once that concept of theological study was in place, American theological education could entertain the problem of the organization of theological disciplines.

We cannot say, however, that the adoption of the German ideal of divinity scholarship chronologically preceded the arrrival of the Hagenbach pattern of studies in the United States. The same people who were mediating that ideal were simultaneously communicating the encyclopedic pattern in which the theological sciences were organized. Thus part 4 of Robinson's article of 1831 contained a full description of the fourfold pattern. And the first volume of Park's *Bibliotheca sacra* (1844) contained a translation of Tholuck's Halle lectures (1842–43) on theological encyclopedia. This seems to be the first occurrence in English of one of the German introductions and fourfold pattern. In 1850 Schleiermacher's *Brief Outline* was translated in England. And in the 1850s the man who was eventually to become founding president of Drew Seminary began work on the first American theological encyclopedia, which was published in 1873.[36]

Thus began the rather brief period in North American theological education when works of this type were being published and made available. The 1880s and 1890s appear to be the "age of theological encyclopedia" in the United States.[37] This is not to say that a large corpus of publications appeared at that time. Even though the seminaries had appropriated some basic features of the European approach, they typically lacked the pedagogical institution that stood behind the German-type encyclopedia, the survey of the theological sciences course. English-language encyclopedias were few in number. They mediated to the United States the reigning fourfold pattern. This had been described, as we saw, in the 1831 edition of the *Biblical Repository* and had been extensively set forth in Tholuck's translated lectures in 1844. From McClintoch to World War I, the American and English introductions, as we would expect, all offer the fourfold pattern or minor variations on it. Through the mediation of the German approach to theological education and with it the European encyclopedic problem and literature, the fourfold pattern comes to American Protestant seminaries fairly soon after their beginning in the nineteenth century.[38]

Furthermore, the fourfold pattern survived the period of theological encyclopedia literature and continued as the standard way of classifying theological disciplines in the twentieth century. This is clearly indicated by a recent study of seminary and divinity school catalogues.[39] Although there are occasional attempts to think of theological studies along other lines than the inherited fourfold pattern, it appears to be not only the dominant scheme, but a scheme with even more institutional reinforcement now than it had in the nineteenth century. Two very powerful social forces are at work in this reinforcement. The first is that the graduate schools themselves have been organized along the lines of the fourfold pattern or of specialties within that pattern such as ethics, various periods or regions of church history, or Old and New Testaments. Some of these programs are part of universities for which the unity of the graduate program in religion cannot be grounded in the inherited Christian, clergy-oriented encyclopedia of disciplines. These schools have begun to organize their studies through categories which suggest a departure from the fourfold pattern. In fact, the result is a disguised form of the fourfold pattern to which studies in world religions are added. The second major force follows from the expertise begun in the graduate school. It is the social institutionalization of the scholarly specialties which creates a community of specialists, stages regular conferences, sponsors long-term research projects, sets lines of identity and loyalty, and fixes the categorical world in which all this takes place. The fourfold pattern with its layers of presuppositions may or may not be intellectually self-evident today. But it remains in force as the major way in which theological study is classified and conceived.

One of the theses that has been pressed in this essay is that the history of the fourfold pattern is a history of the decline of one of Schleiermacher's two motifs (the essence of Christianity) and the ascendancy of the other (the clerical paradigm). More specifically, the nineteenth century saw "theology" as a "science of Christianity," but because of its ambiguity and the increasing independence of the disciplines, that concept gradually disappeared as a way of understanding the material unity of the theological disciplines. The few twentieth-century attempts to formulate the unity of the disciplines (Barth, Jüngel, Ebeling, etc.) make no reference to this motif. It may not be too strong to say that twentieth-century theological schools in the United States simply have no material or substantial concept of the unity of the theological disciplines. What this leaves is the external-teleological approach, the clerical paradigm, as the one and only way of understanding that unity. In other words, the only thing which studies of Scripture, theology, history, and pastoral care have in common is their contribution to the preparation of the clergy for its tasks.

This was a new historical development, and it evoked a new historical response in theological education: the organization of seminary pedagogy into graduate-school specialties, each with its social and subject matter allegiance. This was already happening close to the end of the theological encyclopedia period and it evoked an early, programmatic call to a new situational approach to ministry studies by William Rainey Harper in 1899.[40]

This combination of the victory of the clerical paradigm as *the* unity of theological studies and a curriculum comprised of graduate-school specialties constituted a new historical situation. The primary feature of this situation was the experienced tension between commitment to both the scholarly ideal (the academic studies) and the requirements set by the modern world in preparing clergy for specific tasks. The problem behind this experienced tension was this. The victorious clerical paradigm had vanquished the material unity of theological studies.

The disciplines of the fourfold pattern remained, but without material unity. Their mode of presence in the theological school was as independent fiefdoms of scholarship. However, it was just this material unity (Christianity) which gave these disciplines their normativeness and importance and therefore enabled them to function in relation to the ministry. In other words, the two Schleiermacher motifs, retained in an ambiguous way in the nineteenth-century encyclopedias, were correlative. Once the material unity was lost and the disciplines became independent, they were no longer self-evidently contributory to the ministry. They were perceived and experienced as technical and "academic" studies. It was this which evoked the new response, and, ironically, that response was a new promotion of the clerical paradigm, resulting in the functionalist form of that paradigm: the attempt to make discrete, public, and congregational tasks of the ministry the rationale and unity of theological studies. More specifically, this means that the areas and disciplines of theological study either directly deal with those tasks or find their justification in dealing with those tasks. We are talking here about the third, "professionalist" period of theological education in the United States and also the third practical know-how stage in the career of *theologia* described in the first two chapters.[41]

The response to what was perceived as the theological curriculum's irrelevance to the ministry did amount to self-conscious modifications on the part of theological schools. Thus were promoted many new areas of ministry studies with their attendant satellite disciplines, new pedagogical methods such as case studies, proposals for field-based education such as *Intermet* in Washington, D.C., complex and sophisticated programs of supervision, new doctoral programs in practical theology areas, post-master-of-divinity continuing education degrees and institutes. Accompanying all this was a new image and slogan, "the minister as professional," and also a return to the mind-set (if not the language) of theory and practice.[42] According to this mind-set and sounding like a return to the eighteenth century, three of the disciplines with their subdisciplines (Bible, church history, systematic theology) were the "academic" or theory disciplines, and the ministry disciplines were the practical disciplines. These modifications occurring in the functionalist or professionalist form of the clerical paradigm were clearly not a true "reform" of theological education. The reason is twofold. First, the modifications presupposed the basic institutionality of theological education in the United States, the post-college three-year program. Second, they uncritically passed over and ignored the inherited, deep structure or pattern of theological study and its strata presuppositions.

NOTES

1. John McClintoch, *Lectures on Theological Encyclopedia and Methodology* (New York: Nelson and Phillips, 1873); R.F. Weidner, *Theological Encyclopedia and Methodology* (New York: Fleming H. Revell, 1898). Other works appearing in the United States with "encyclopedia" in the title are translations of German works: Tholuck's lectures of 1842–43 translated in the 1844 edition of *Bibliotheca sacra,* and the Crooks and Hurst translation of Hagenbach (1884). A translation of Räbiger's *Theological Encyclopedia* was published in England in the same year.

2. Hagenbach thinks the term has a bad name because of association with Diderot's encyclopedia and therefore connotes a free thinker (Karl R. Hagenbach, *Theological Encyclopedia and Methodology,* ed. and trans. G.R. Crooks and J.F. Hurst [New York: Hunt and Eaton, 1884], p. 8). See also Richard Rothe, *Theologische Encyclopädie* (Wittenberg: Koelling, 1880), p. 8; Eduard Vaucher, *Essaie de méthodologie des sciences théologiques* (Paris: Jules Claye, 1878), introduction. Vaucher prefers the term *methodology.*

3. From Holland come the following: J. Clarisse, *Encyclopedia theologicae epitome* (1832); P.H. Groot, *Encyclopedia theologi christiani* (1844); J. Doedes, *Encyclopedie der christilijke theologie* (1876); and A. Kuyper, *Encyclopaedie der heilige godgeleerdheit,* 3 vols. (1894). The French works are H.W. Kienlen, *Encyclopédie des sciences de la théologie chrétienne* (1842); Godet, "L'Organisme de la science théologique," *Bulletin théologique* (1863); Vaucher, *Méthodologie des sciences théologiques;* E. Martin, *La Science du Christianisme* (1882); and A. Gretillat (Switzerland), *Exposé de théologie systématique,* vol. 1, *Propédeutique* (1885). Sweden contributes H. Reuterdahl, *Inledning till theologien* (1837). From Hungary comes Revesz, *Theologia tudomanyok encyclopaediaja es methodologiaja* (1857). Many of these works had second editions. The only one to find its way into English translation is Kuyper, vol. 2. The Godet work is an influential article which evoked a response from Pronier. The works by Martin and Vaucher are doctoral dissertations.

4. While some call the first "general encyclopedia" and the second "special encyclopedia," others use these terms differently. Thus, "general encyclope-

dia" means the grasp of all sciences in relation to each other, while "special encyclopedia" means the inquiry into the organization of sciences within a specific science like medicine, law, or theology.

5. The decade between 1829 and 1839 may be the most intense period of theological encyclopedia publication in the century. Including both Roman Catholic and Protestant works, about thirty publications appeared in that period, most of them in Germany. Between Schleiermacher's 1811 monograph and this period, four theological encyclopedias appeared: D.G.S. Franke, *Theologische Encyklopädie* (1819); C.F. Staüdlin, *Lehrbuch der Encyclopädie, Methodologie, und Geschichte der theologischen Wissenschaften* (1821); L. Bertholdt, *Theologische Wissenschaftskunde*, 2 vols. (1821–2); and A.F.F. Karg, *Encyclopaedia theologia et methodologia* (1822).

6. We can only hypothesize the reasons for this virtual absence of publication of encyclopedic introductions to theology in this period. Although publications were few, *lectures* on the subject continued, by J.Ch.K. von Hofmann and R. Rothe, for instance. It was not a productive period for theological works in general, both because of political events of 1848 and after, and because conservatism and repristination (thus, Hengstenberg) had set in. Further, Hagenbach's encyclopedia had become the standard one, with eight editions appearing between 1845 and 1870.

7. Karl R. Hagenbach, *Encyklopädie und Methodologie der theologischen Wissenschaften* (Basel, 1833). This work went through twelve editions through 1889, the later ones being much enlarged over the first edition. Hagenbach was a Basel church historian, known for a seven-volume church history and for identifying the "mediating theology" of which he was a representative. The encyclopedia was translated into English with an enlarged bibliography by Crooks and Hurst in 1884.

8. D.G.S. Franke (1819), Staüdlin (1821), and Bertholdt (1821–2) (see n. 5 above.) Bertholdt's scheme is complex, distinguishing both preparatory and auxiliary sciences from theological sciences proper. However, the theological sciences divide into fundamental sciences, in which we find the usual three theoretical sciences, and practical sciences.

9. In Germany, see J.T.L. Danz, *Encyklopädie und Methodologie der theologischen Wissenschaften* (Weimar, 1832) and I.A. Dorner, *Grundriss der Encyclopädie der Theologie* (Berlin, 1901). Danz's version is that the theoretical disciplines concern the *sources* of knowledge of Christian faith while the practical disciplines concern ways and means of making faith effective to others. In addition, two of the French theologians offer a theory-practice scheme: Godet and Gretillat.

10. Excluding the Roman Catholic literature, there appear to be about ten authors who continue a Schleiermacher-type encyclopedia in the nineteenth century. Others, to be sure, have a threefold arrangement which is only a disguised form of the fourfold type. The Schleiermacher type includes the following, listed in chronological order: K. Rosenkranz, *Encyklopädie der*

theologische Wissenschaften (1831); Reuterdahl, *Inledning till theologen;* Zyro, "Versuch einer Revision der christliche theologischen Encyklopädie," *Theologische Studium und Kritikum* (1837); Kienlen, *Théologie chrétienne;* A.F.L. Pelt, *Theologische Encyklopädie* (1843); Rothe, *Theologische Encyclopädie;* J.Ch.K. von Hofmann, *Encyclopädie der Theologie* (1879); Alfred Cave, *Introduction to Theology* (1886); Dorner, *Grundriss der Encyclopädie der Theologie* (1901).

11. Thus, Francke, *Theologische Encyclopädie,* pp. 20–21. Pelt claims that the Enlightenment had discredited theology as knowledge of God and divine things *(Theologische Encyclopädie,* p. 28). Hagenbach explicitly sided with what he called the "modern" view of theology as an "aggregate of the knowledge which bears upon the life of the church" (Crooks and Hurst, eds., *Theological Encyclopedia,* p. 63). There were, of course, theologians in the nineteenth century, orthodox Lutheran and Reformed, who retained the *habitus* view. Thus, Abraham Kuyper, *Principles of Sacred Theology* (1894), vol. 2, pp. 298ff. Kuyper seems to be the only author of nineteenth-century theological encyclopedia who explicitly articulates the *habitus* view of theology. The *habitus* view is clearly propounded by the Lutheran theologian Francis Pieper in his dogmatics *(Christian Dogmatics* [St. Louis: Concordia, 1950], vol. 1, p. 9).

12. Pannenberg's statement that "from the seventeenth century onwards, and especially the nineteenth, religion became the fundamental theme of theology" *(Theology and the Philosophy of Science,* trans. F. McDonagh [London: Darton, Longman & Todd, 1976], p. 307) is confusing. In the seventeenth century, theology itself is a practical *knowledge* whose object is what God reveals for salvation, in other words, true religion. In the nineteenth century, theology is a scholarly discipline whose object is a historical entity, religion, or the Christian religion.

13. Thus, Hagenbach, J.P. Lange, Rothe, Staüdlin, and Heinrici. Lange's work is *Gundriss der theologische Encyklopädie* (1877), and Heinrici's is *Theologische Encyklopädie* (1893).

14. Räbiger, *Encyclopedia of Theology* (Edinburgh: T. & T. Clark, 1884–5) p. 165. Harless, Hofmann, Lange, and even Tholuck all criticize the teleological, external way of seeing theology's unity.

15. Thus, Pelt, Vaucher, Rothe, and Heinrici all claim theology to be the science of the Christian religion and at the same time a *Kunsttheorie* pertinent to the ministry. Heinrici, for instance, says that the content of theology is the essence, origin, development and present condition of the Christian religion and also calls the theology faculty "positive" because it serves the interests of the church (Heinrici, *Theologische Encyklopädie,* pp. 4–10).

16. One major issue of the subject matter of church history was the place of the history of dogma. Most authors assigned history of dogma to church history. Thus, Hagenbach, Tholuck, McClintoch, Zöckler, and Drummond all see history of dogma as a church historical discipline: Tholuck, "Theological

Encyclopedia and Methodology," trans. E.A. Park, *Bibliotheca sacra*, vol. 1 (1844); McClintoch, *Theological Encyclopedia and Methodology*, Otto Zöckler, ed., *Handbuch der theologische Wissenschaften in encyklopädischer Darstellung*, 4 vols. (1889).

17. Tholuck, "Theological Encyclopedia," p. 569.

18. For Mursinna, church history is a history of the *church*, which means true religion, especially divided into the two covenants, the old and the new (*Primae lineae encyclopaediae theologicae* [1764]). Thum describes church history as a natural follow-up of exegetical theology, a study of what happened to the divinely-founded religion and its society of believers over the eighteen hundred years subsequent to the apostolic period (*Theologische Encyklopädie und Methodologie* [1797]).

19. This transition of church history away from a theological discipline is described incisively in David W. Lotz's inaugural lecture at Union Seminary ("The Crisis in American Church Historiography," *Union Seminary Quarterly Review*, Winter, 1978). See also the article Lotz cites: Albert Outler, "Theodosius' Horse," *Church History* (1965).

20. L. Lange, *Anleitung zum Studium der christlichen Theologie* (1840). Hagenbach, likewise, attempts to stay with Schleiermacher; thus he proposes that practical theology is, like the other three disciplines, a *theory*, although he acknowledges it is a theory in an unusual sense, since it is "the theory which qualifies for the practice of an art" (Crooks and Hurst, *Theological Encyclopedia*, pp. 472–3).

21. Dorner, *Encyklopädie der Theologie;* Phillip Schaff, *Theological Propaedeutic* (New York: Charles Scribner's Sons, 1892), p. 448. See also Tholuck, "Theological Encyclopedia," p. 726.

22. Van A. Harvey's seminal essay, "The Alienated Theologian," in *The Future of Philosophical Theology*, ed. Robert A. Evans (Philadelphia: Westminster Press, 1982) is a superb account of this problem.

23. What justifications there are tend to occur at a fairly superficial level. Thus, Alfred Cave argues for a science of *sources*, of truth considerations, and of application (*Introduction to Theology*, #11). Räbiger's derivation is clearly a theological one. After observing that the Christian religious idea appeared in a person, Jesus Christ, who was necessary for a community which realized the "universally human principle of life," he then could propose four aspects of the development of this idea and community: origins, subsequent history, the Spirit thematized in an ideal way, and practical application (*Encyclopedia of Theology*, vol. 1). Ernest Martin derives the divisions from an analysis of the act of faith and its conditions (*Introduction à l'étude de la théologie protestante* [1883], pp. 16–19).

It is Martin Kähler who offers one of the most persuasive and serious rationales for the fourfold pattern, although we find this not in a theological encyclopedia, but in his *Die Wissenschaft der christlichen Lehre* (1883), "Einleitung," 1. (2.). He sees theological encyclopedia—at least in its formal aspect—as a theological, not just pedagogical, inquiry. Hence, it must begin with a determination of theology's object, which is God as salvifically revealed in Christ. This is what sets the cognitive requirements for theology, the first being the history of that revelation as manifest in Scripture. Yet faith and response to revelation are not simply a response to what is manifest in an ancient period of history. It has a contemporaneous, confessional aspect in which the totality with which faith is concerned is confessed. And this is Kähler's way of saying that the knowledge which attends faith has a doctrinal element. Between the original manifestation of revelation (Scripture) and contemporary acknowledgment is the history of the church, and this is a history of interpreting the meaning and distinctiveness of the original occurrence. Therefore, knowledge of this history is indispensable to anyone who would formulate and confess the faith in the present. Furthermore, Christian self-knowledge perpetually tests its own *present* status in the light of doctrine and history, its effectiveness as an external power. And this testing involves principles, rules, laws. Thus, like Schleiermacher, Kähler sees a substantial subject matter in the fourth area, practical theology.

24. A third edition of Paul Wernle's *Einführung in das theologische Studium* (Tübingen, 1908) was published in 1920. Kuyper's vol. 2 was reissued in English translation in 1980.

25. Sporadic attempts to struggle with the problem of theological encyclopedia occur in the twentieth century, especially in Germany: Pannenberg, *Theology and the Philosophy of Science;* F. Mildenberger, *Theorie der Theologie: Enzyklopädie als Methodenlehre* (Stuttgart: Walver, 1972); Karl Rahner, *Zur Reform des Theologiestudiums* (Frieburg: Herder, 1969); L.J. van Hold, *Encyclopaedie der Theologie* (Assen, 1938); G. van der Leeuw, *Inleiding tot de Theologie* (Amsterdam, 1935); H. Van Oyen, *Inleiding tot de Theologische studie* (1946); R. Latourelle, *Theology: Science of Salvation* (1969).

26. See P. Althaus, *Die Christliche Wahrheit: Lehrbuch der Dogmatik* (1949), vol. 1, pp. 7–18; E. Jüngel, "Das Verhältnis der theologischen Disziplinen untereinander," in Jüngel, K. Rahner, and M. Seitz, *Die Praktische Theologie zwischen Wissenschaft und Praxis* (1968); G. Ebeling, "Discussion Theses for a Course of Introductory Lectures on the Study of Theology," in *Word and Faith* (Philadelphia: Fortress Press, 1963); Pannenberg, *Theology and the Philosophy of Science:* and A. Grabner-Heider, *Theorie der Theologie als Wissenschaft* (1974).

Karl Barth offers a very brief proposal that theology, concerned as it is with the foundation, aim, and content of the language of the church, divides into biblical, practical, and dogmatic theology (*Church Dogmatics*, trans. G.T. Thomson), I, 1, p. 3. Grabner-Heider attempts to formulate theology as a science through an appropriation of Anglo-Saxon analytic philosophy and proposes a variation of the fourfold pattern. Pannenberg's scheme is likewise a variation on the fourfold pattern, to which he adds a "theology of religion." Jüngel's proposal, perhaps the most carefully argued of all of them, tries to derive the fourfold pattern from dimensions of the Word of God; thus, the Word of God as text, tradition, event, and truth.

Ebeling's article very much resembles Jüngel's. Rejecting the conglomerate view of theology as a mere aggregate of sciences, he states that the *event* of the Word of God is the unity of theology. Like Jüngel, he finds an ingenious way of defending the fourfold pattern. The Word of God is present in a decisive, normative *past* proclamation and a *present* proclamation. The past dimension of proclamation requires Old Testament, New Testament, and church historical studies. The present requires systematic-normative and practical studies. The scheme sounds like a phenomenology of dimensions of proclamation (proclamation as provisional, conclusive, subsequent, in process). Ebeling's book-length study, although it calls itself an "encyclopedic orientation," makes no schematic proposal, but restricts itself to description of the various disciplines (*Studium der Theologie: Eine enzyklopädische Orientierung* [1975]).

One of the most recent works to offer a major encyclopedic proposal is David Tracy's *The Analogical Imagination: Christian Theology and the Culture of Pluralism* (New York: Crossroad, 1981). See especially chap. 2.

27. G.B. Smith, ed., *A Guide to the Study of the Christian Religion* (1916); Yale Divinity School Faculty, *Education for Christian Service* (1922); K.E. Kirk, ed., *The Study of Theology* (1939); H. Frick, ed., *Einführung in das Studium der evangelische Theologie* (1947); W. Baetke et al., *Grundriss des Theologiestudiums* (1948); Martin Doerne, ed. *Grundriss des Theologiestudiums*, 3 vols. (1948); R. Bohren, ed., *Einführung in das Studium der evangelisches Theologie* (1964); H.E. Short, ed., *Education for the Christian Ministry* (1953); E. Neuhäusler and E. Gossmann, eds., *Was ist Theologie?* (1966); Paul Ramsey, ed., *Religion* (1965); Daniel Jenkins, ed., *The Scope of Theology* (1965); H. Siemers and Hans-Richard Reuter, eds., *Theologie als Wissenschaft in der Gesellschaft* (1970); G. Picht and E. Rudolph, eds., *Theologie—Was ist Das?* (1977).

28. One clear exception is the introductory essay to the volume of essays published by the faculty of Princeton Seminary on the school's 100th anniversary, *Biblical and Theological Studies* (1912). The essay, "Theological Encyclopedia," by Francis L. Patton does argue for a rather distinctive classification of theological disciplines. Patton is critical of both Schleiermacher and Hagenbach schemes and argues that "knowledge of God" is the one unifying theme of theological study. Accordingly, the three branches of study are natural knowledge of God, revealed knowledge of God, and the ecclesiastical extension and interpretation of both. The essays which follow are not accounts of various theological disciplines, but are specific examples of scholarship by the members of the faculty. Needless to say, Patton's scheme has little relation to the actual way that faculty is organized, as this is reflected in the other essays of the volume.

29. Thus the recommendations of the "mixed commission" for the reform

of theological education in Germany leaves untouched the Hagenbach pattern of studies. The division assumed there is the fourfold division, with the biblical area divided into Old and New Testament fields. See Hans-Erich Hess, ed., *Reform der theologischen Ausbildung* (1967), pp. 78–79.

30. The works which initially influenced the American colonies were published in England. The most important of these advice-to-pastors works are Richard Bernard, *The Faithful Shepherd* (1607); George Herbert, *The Country Parson* (1652); Henry Dodwell (the Elder), *Advice on Theological Studies* (1691); John Mason, *Student and Pastor* (1755). Written especially for the New England situation were the following. Thomas Bray's *Bibliotheca parochialis* (1697), written for Maryland Episcopal clergy, was a strong plea for the founding of pastor's libraries throughout the colonies. Having more the character of study-of-theology books because of their bibliographic origination were two widely used eighteenth-century works. Samuel Willard's *Brief Directions to a Young Scholar* (1735) was written shortly after 1700, and Cotton Mather's *Manuductio ad ministerium* (1726) was later published in London in an English translation under the title, *Cotton Mather's Student and Teacher* (1781).

31. In the nineteenth century we find E. Bickersteth, *The Christian Student* (1830); John Brown, *Christian Pastor's Manual* (1837); E. Pond, *Young Pastor's Guide* (1844); and Washington Gladden, *The Christian Pastor and The Working Church* (1898).

32. Moses Stuart was teaching German biblical criticism (Rosenmüller, DeWette) before 1825, and introduced the issue of the conflict between modern and biblical cosmologies. Nevin was introduced to this literature by Stuart but was especially influenced by the German historian, Neander, and with this background collaborated with Schaff at Mercersburg in introducing German scholarship to this country.

33. See Robinson's essay in the very first issue, "Theological Education in Germany," *Biblical Repository*, vol. 1, no. 1 (1831).

34. The *Biblical Repository* was founded and edited by Edward Robinson of Andover. Its first volume was issued in 1831 and it contained in four parts a lengthy account of "theological education in Germany" written by Robinson, who had studied there in the late 1820s. While Robinson has his criticisms of the German system, he also appreciates that about the system which promotes rigorous scholarship, and he sets this out in detail. By 1844, when *Bibliotheca sacra* was founded, Edward Amassa Park of Andover had also been to Germany, studying under Tholuck, and he published in the first volume of *Bibliotheca sacra* a translation of Tholuck's lectures at Halle on "theological encyclopedia and methodology," offering America the first glimpse of what was, by this time, a large literature of this type. Furthermore, in the same volume, Park and others submitted a long and eloquent criticism of theological education in the United States and a plea for the teaching of "theological science." The article is entitled "Thoughts on the State of Theological Science and Education in our Country," *Bibliotheca sacra*, vol. I (1844). It begins with a

question posed by German theologians: "Why have not the Americans some theological science?" The article urges American theological schools to adopt what in fact are the major marks of the German system: a division of labor among teachers, more candor and criticism, more reference to foreign authors. They plead for fewer seminaries and larger faculties made up of specialists. Hodge functioned similarly at Princeton. In 1847 Phillip Schaff wrote an article for *Bibliotheca sacra*, "German Literature in America," summarizing the many resources and movements of Germany at the time. Further, in 1857 he published a book-length study and apologetic for the German system and was himself at Mercersburg practically a reincarnation of a German professor (Schaff, *Germany: Its Universities, Theology, and Religion* [Philadelphia, 1857]).

35. "German Literature in America," *Bibliotheca sacra* (1847). Schaff had been educated in Germany at Tübingen, Halle, and Berlin, and was Tholuck's assistant. He had heard many of the famous German scholars of the day lecture (Schelling, Dorner, Baur, even the very conservative Hengstenberg). He and Nevin engaged in literary debates with German mediating theologians like Dorner. Schaff's American career was that of a research-oriented German scholar.

36. McClintoch, *Lectures on Theological Encyclopedia.*

37. Between McClintoch's work (1873) and the end of World War I, seven theological encyclopedias appeared in the United States and four in England. Three of these were translations of well-known European works: Hagenbach, Räbiger, and volume 2 of Kuyper. McClintoch's work had some continuing effect, since two Drew faculty members, George R. Crooks and John F. Hurst, translated and adapted Hagenbach in 1884. The translation of Räbiger by John MacPherson, *Encyclopedia of Theology*, appeared in the same year. Two English theologians published encyclopedias in the mid-1880s: James Drummond of Manchester New College, *Introduction to the Study of Theology* (London: Macmillan, 1884), and Alfred Cave of Hackney College, *An Introduction to Theology.*

In the United States, translation of Hagenbach was the stimulus for a number of subsequent writings. The first to follow was the Lutheran, R. F. Weidner, *Theological Encyclopedia and Methodology.* After Weidner came the following: R. V. Foster, *Introduction to the Study of Theology* (1889); Schaff, *Theological Propaedeutic*; W. N. Clarke, *The Circle of Theology: An Introduction to Theological Study* (1897); the translation of vol. 2 and part of vol. 1 of Abraham Kuyper's three-volume *Encyclopedia of Sacred Theology: Its Principles* (New York: Charles Scribner's Sons, 1898)—reissued by Baker Book House in 1980 under a new title, *Principles of Sacred Theology*; and Henry C. Sheldon, *Theological Encyclopedia* (Cincinnati and New York: Eaton and Mains, 1911). In England, E. D. Davis wrote *Theological Encyclopedia* (London, 1905).

38. A full study of the history of seminary curricula in the United States

remains to be done. The most complete study to date remains Robert L. Kelly, *Theological Education in America* (New York: George H. Doran, 1924). See especially chaps. 3 and 4. According to Kelly, Harvard by 1830 had five professors, and their announced offerings in that year constitute virtually the fourfold pattern. They cover Old Testament, New Testament, Christian theology, pastoral care and homiletics, and German language and literature. This is the fourfold pattern minus church history. In 1839 Andover's announced program, distributed over three years, covers work in Bible (language and exegesis of both Testaments), Christian theology, history of Christian doctrine, and rhetoric and homiletics. Kelly studied the 1870 curricular offerings of seven major seminaries and the pattern is fairly clearly the fourfold pattern. The changes that occur in the 1895 and 1921 curricula of these same schools are primarily a reduction of language study and the adding of newer course areas which are either subdivisions of the fourfold pattern (e.g., ethics) or new fields of practical theology.

39. The study was done by Anna Case Winters, an assistant to this project. It surveyed recent catalogues (1979 and 1980) of fifty-four North American Protestant theological schools, two Greek Orthodox, and ten Roman Catholic seminaries. All fifty-four of the major Presbyterian, Methodist, Episcopalian, Christian (Disciples), United Church of Christ, and Lutheran schools were included and forty-eight of them organized their courses either according to a straightforward fourfold pattern or with slight modifications of that pattern. The modifications were formal and schematic. That is, Bible and history, or systematics and church history, would be placed together, or the biblical field would be divided into Old and New Testament areas. The most frequent variation (sixteen schools) obtained a threefold pattern by putting history and theology together. Most of the exceptions to the fourfold pattern occurred because of more detailed distributions of the areas of study, e.g., making ethics a separate field, or several areas of practical theology separate fields. Of interest was the fact that almost all of the Roman Catholic schools also classified their offerings within the fourfold scheme.

40. William Rainey Harper, "Shall the Theological Curriculum Be Modified and How?" *American Journal of Theology* (1899).

41. See chapter 1, pp. 6–12 for a discussion of the period of professionalism.

42. In our study of recent catalogues, the language of theory and practice was only rarely used, either in the schematic descriptions of areas or in the general rationales for them. The most widespread type of rationale given in these catalogues suggested a bridging of the ancient (the sources, the tradition) with the contemporary (the culture, the churches). Present here is the tone, if not the language, of theory and practice.

PART 2

ISSUES
AND ELEMENTS FOR
A REFORM-ORIENTED CONVERSATION

6

A Critique of
the Fourfold Pattern

1. The Fourfold Pattern and the Clerical Paradigm
in Contemporary Theological Education

summary

According to this analysis, the major elements structuring the North
American approach to theological education are the continued dominance of the fourfold pattern, the absence of a material unity of studies,
a functionalist version of the clerical paradigm as that unity, and a
theory-practice mind-set. These historically accumulated characteristics have deeply shaped both the churches and the theological schools.
Six features of this shaping are especially prominent.

The first feature is especially related to the functionalist form of the
clerical paradigm. It is simply that the *problem* which functionalism
and the professionalist approach would alleviate is, ironically, inten-
sified. This is to say, the alienation between theological studies and
the needs and tasks of the church's leadership is promoted, not reduced, by the functionalist attempt to make the tasks of ministry themselves the criteria, subject matter, and end of theological study. The
reason is that the public tasks and responsibilities of clergy (preaching,
counseling, managing, organizing, teaching, evangelizing) represent
altogether only a formal, sociological description of a minister or priest.
They pertain to the social duration of the Christian community as it
would be *sociologically* described. Passed over is the Christian community in its essential, defining, ecclesial aspect of being a redemptive
community, with a leadership whose tasks center in the corporate and
individual occurrence of redemption.

In other words, the education of a leadership for a redemptive community cannot be *defined* by reference to the public tasks and acts by

127

which the community endures (a formal approach), but rather by the requirements set by the nature of that community as redemptive. Defining ministry by its community tasks ignores the community's own redemptive nature, its received tradition, its truth convictions. The very thing that makes theological education important to and related to the church and to the church's leadership, which calls for the various public tasks and sets criteria for their exercise, is absent. Accordingly, the more the external tasks themselves are focused on as the one and only *telos* of theological education, the less the minister becomes qualified to carry them out. This is why the functionalist form of the clerical paradigm promotes and worsens the problem with which it is concerned.[1]

A second feature pertains to specific branches of theological study. As long as these branches had some material unity (i.e., "Christianity," the Christian religion, revelation), they might retain their theological character and their interdependence. Once that unity is replaced by a reference to professional functions, the rationale for each discipline is not its *theological* character, its relation to Christianity or Christian faith, but its contribution to the training of professionals. This external, teleological reference to the training of ministers is not what makes these branches disciplines; it merely unifies them all in a single ped- agogical enterprise. This means that each area, insofar as it is a region of scholarship, is responsible for its own unity and subject matter. Once the overall theological reference is eliminated, what defines each discipline is the particular object or realm of objects which evokes its particular methods. Accordingly, a literature, the collection of Israel's written heritage, forms the parameters of "Old Testament." The events, institutions, and literatures of the church are the unity of church history.

In addition, most post-Enlightenment theological schools adopt to a certain degree the critical principle and the importance of going with the evidence wherever it leads. Therefore, in the nineteenth century the relation between theology and the larger circle of sciences was formulated not simply as a part-to-whole problem, as in the Middle Ages, but as the relation between discrete theological sciences and the satellite or auxiliary disciplines each one needed. In fact, it is the auxiliary disciplines which provide the scholarly apparatus for the theological disciplines and which give them the character of "sciences." Thus, we have linguistics, archaeology, history, ancient chronology, hermeneutics, rhetoric, sociology, psychology, and various philosophies. The satellite disciplines likewise contribute to the definition of each theological area, the result being that each area, while retaining its justification as part of theological study from the clerical paradigm, is defined by a designated subject matter, frequently a literature, correlated with methods drawn from auxiliary, secular disciplines.[2]

The struggle of the so-called normative or constructive disciplines like systematic theology and theological ethics to find and formulate their subject is well-known. Lacking a self-evident literature or historical period to function as the parameter of the discipline, they especially symptomize the losses incurred from the demise of the way of authority. Accordingly, they are clear instances of theological undertakings controlled by their auxiliary disciplines. Theology and ethics thus search for that which will give them scholarly status, and to this end easily transpose themselves into the categorical worlds of history of thought, social science, or philosophy. The practical fields reflect a similar tendency, but for different reasons. Once the shift from the Schleiermacher to the Hagenbach definition of practical theology occurred, from a theological subject matter to a technics of ministry, practical theology as such disappeared. That is, it became, like "theology," a generic term for a cluster of separate pedagogical endeavors. Lacking a reference to a necessary theological subject matter, each area became defined as the application of a satellite discipline (rhetoric, psychology, management, pedagogy) to a task of ministry. And the central, defining thing, making it a "discipline," became the appropriated auxiliary discipline.

This and the next two consequences are effects of the twentieth-century form of the clerical paradigm, a unifying of theological studies by making their end and aim the tasks of a professionally-defined ministry. This paradigm binds "theology" by definition to a postcollege institution of professional education. The very definition of theology as a discipline, set of disciplines, or knowledge resulting therefrom, is tightly correlated with education needed by the professional leadership of the religious community. If it is "knowledge," it is knowledge needed by that leadership. Its initial setting, then, is an institution in which that leadership is educated. Its final setting is an institution (the church, the congregation) in which that leadership is exercised and that knowledge is put to use.

We have here a later chapter in a story which began before Schleiermacher but which was formulated by Schleiermacher as a solution to the problem of affirming theology as a valid faculty of the German university. This "clericalization" of theology is so much the air we breathe that it is very difficult to imagine a time when it was any other way. In chapter 2, the case was made that theology at one time meant a disposition and knowledge which resembled wisdom, and as such had no clerical restriction. It was simply the sapiential knowledge which attended Christian life. This is not to say that a lengthy and rigorous clergy education was lacking. It does mean that that education as the "study of theology" was thought of as an education in something which attended Christian life as such, something shared in by non-clergy. Clergy then are "masters of divine knowledge which they are to teach others."[3] In the clerical paradigm, "theology" is not something attendant on Christian existence but something clergy need in order to function as leaders of the church community. In the functionalist form of that paradigm, the leadership itself is defined by an assortment of discrete tasks, and theology is a theory or a theory of practice about those tasks.

Prominent are three rather pervasive results of this clericalization of theology. The first is the unfortunate way it has influenced the interpretation of Christian or church education in both Protestant churches and their seminaries. The negative premise of this approach is that education in the churches, whatever it is, cannot be "the study of theology." This is necessarily the case insofar as the study of theology *means* a pedagogy for ministerial education. We must acknowledge that the education movement in Protestant churches has had its benefits. Both the *religious* education movement of the earlier part of the century and its neo-orthodox critics and imitators of the 1940s and 1950s repudiated the old catechetics associated with the learning and transmission of doctrine. The result was not so much a single, clear consensus about a field or discipline but a teaching area (in seminaries) which has two major and relatively unrelated subject matters. The one addresses an inescapable aspect of the modern Protestant minister's work, the church school program, which is historically related to but not identical with the Sunday school. Graduate degrees in Christian education, and one type of course work present in seminaries, have as their unity and subject matter the *administration* of a church education program. Specialists in Christian education in this sense are themselves neither teachers nor theologians, but are trained as educational administrators. The other subject matter results from the attempted correction of catechetics, indoctrinalization, and objectified learning. Here we have a set of courses whose unity is the psychology of nurture, frequently organized around human stages of growth.[4] In many Protestant schools, the education field has come to be the residing place of what used to be ascetic, spiritual, or mystical theology, the place where formation issues are presented.

In question here is neither the legitimacy of educational administration nor the psychology of the process of faith. However, it is the case that the Protestant churches have not yet seriously considered the viability of theological education as *church* education. Hence, the minister as theological educator is not an idea which disposes and guides present-day church education. If a church did embrace the ideal of a theological education for its constituency, it would have to incorporate into its educational program something of the structure of theology itself. The fourfold pattern is, of course, the traditional view of that structure, but it is present in church education only in the most sporadic and occasional ways. What produced this state of affairs—the church's repudiation of the study of theology—is not the Christian educators of the seminaries, nor the anti-catechetics polemics of earlier times, but simply the triumph and narrowing of the clerical paradigm. The laity cannot be *theologically* educated because theology *means* a cluster of studies pertinent to the church's leadership. As long as this mind-set prevails, theological education must remain an enterprise of seminaries, not churches.

Another consequence of the restriction of theology by the clerical paradigm is the interpretation of *practice* in the theological school.[5] Criticisms of theological schools on questions of practice are now widespread. Questions have been raised by black, feminist, and South American liberation theology.[6] With the exception of the feminist statement in the Cornwall study, the liberation theology criticisms tend to pertain to "theology" in a more general and conventional sense and not to theological study and its conception and pattern.[7] In addition, extensive criticisms of theological education have characterized the widespread functionalist-professional approach of the last generation.[8] Needless to say, these criticisms occur within the narrowed form of the clerical paradigm. Since both liberation theology and functionalists are concerned with "practice," this theme has been in the forefront of recent American thinking about theological education. Practice is reflected in the concern for culture, spirituality, oppression and liberation, therapeutic, case-studies, experience, field-based education. Everyone, it seems, is *for* "practice."

In my view, practice in its widest and most significant sense is systematically eliminated from the structure of theological study by the fourfold pattern and the clerical paradigm. Prior to the theological encyclopedia movement and in the time when the genre of theology was a *habitus*, a sapiential knowledge, practice was built into theology by definition. The reason was that this disposition of sapiential knowledge was a constitutive feature of Christian life in the world. A step away from this was taken when the distinction arose between scholastic and mystical theology, or between speculative and positive theology.[9] A second step was taken toward making practice external to theology when *theologia* became an aggregate of four disciplines in which three are theory and the fourth is practice as *ministerial* responsibility.[10] Theology, therefore, not only is narrowed to the pedagogy of clergy education; *practical* theology means the aspect of clerical pedagogy addressed to the leadership practice of the clergy.

Does this cause the total disappearance from theological study of practice in the sense of the life, existence, and behavior of the believer or the faith community in the world? In the earlier and broader sense of the clerical paradigm, this reference is indirectly present. The reason is that the area of practical theology occurs under the substantial criteria of the essence of Christianity. Clerical practice as proclamation or teaching is directed to the cultural and worldly life of the believer. In the narrowed, functionalist sense, the world reference is virtually eliminated because clerical practice is defined by the technical problem of carrying out discrete, public tasks. This does not mean that all reference to world and individual transformation is absent from the theological school. It is sporadically present in all disciplines, and is a structural element in black studies and feminist theologies. But the only way practice is present in the structure of theological study itself is in the narrowed form of the clerical paradigm. In other words, twentieth-century theological education represents a clericalization of practice. And this too appears to have far-reaching effects on the way practice is interpreted and pursued by the churches. It is also responsible for the widespread phenomenon that students in theological schools experience their education as something alienated from praxis, that is, from issues of personal existence and social justice.

The clerical paradigm appears to be one of the historical forces at work in the American exclusion of "theology" from the university. The history of this exclusion is the history of a transition from an earlier period when theology was taken for granted in American higher education to the present period where it is regarded as a sectarian intruder. For most of the nineteenth century (to 1875), the typical American post-high-school educational institution was the denominational college. In that institution, the teaching of religion was the teaching of the Christian religion. And when graduate programs began to furnish teachers of religion, the organization of courses followed the graduate-school specialties, which meant the fourfold pattern minus practical theology.[11] The college teacher of religion was a specialist in one of these areas (or sub-areas), but usually taught over the whole spectrum. Well-known are the events of recent decades in which many denominational colleges either folded or separated from their denominational roots, and in which the majority of the bachelor degree population shifted to the larger private and state universities. The resulting changes in the teaching of religion (when it was taught at all) occurred in two stages. Since the graduate schools and their specialties had not changed, the fourfold pattern (biblical, historical, systematic, theological) continued to set the parameters for disciplines, teaching specialties, and courses. However, the teacher began to function less as a denominational representative or an advocate of a (Christian) faith and more as an independent scholar. In this stage the *area* or discipline of the Christian encyclopedia still functioned, even though little credence was given to its rationale (the fourfold pattern).

In the second, recent stage, that of "religious studies," the arbitrariness of organizing the study of religion through the Christian encyclopedia is realized. And while "Christian studies" or some aspect thereof is retained, "theology" is not. The visible reason for this seems to be that religious studies as a legitimate area of *Geisteswissenschaft* and humanities has a valid claim to scholarly work on sources; this does not, however, include "theology." At work here are the continuing historical effects of the clericalization of theology. Insofar as theology is a generic term for preparatory studies for the Christian ministry, it seems to have no place in the university circle of sciences. On the other hand, if theology means a mode of reflection, understanding, insight attached to a determinate religion, the teaching of it no more violates the university's commitment to universal truth than the teaching of Buddhist meditation or the insights and modes of understanding evoked by romantic poetry. But this parallel is obscured by the prevailing clericalization of theology. In the clerical paradigm, "theology" is for ministers (the leadership of a faith community), not human beings, students, or laity.

The final effect of the fourfold pattern and its paradigm, perhaps the most serious one, is best expressed in the negative. As long as theological study resides in the fourfold pattern, certain other disciplines or areas of study cannot lay claim to any necessary place in theology. They must remain occasional, dispensable, invisible; the course of theological study can be thought about and pursued without them. As we have seen, one of the areas prevented from thematization is praxis in the sense of world transformation.[12] Three other regions of study are also viable candidates for thematic representation in theology. In the period when theology was one thing, either *habitus* or discipline, central to this sapiential knowledge or demonstrative discipline was the use of "reason." How faith was related to reason—the universally valid insight and formulation of the world, being, reality, and universal truth—posed a central and indispensable issue to theology and therefore to the study of theology. In our day, that question is cast less in terms of "reason" than in terms of the sciences. How is faith and its world, its truth, its reality related to the world as set forth in human, social, and natural sciences? This question is not totally absent in current theological study, but it does not pervade the very structure of that study. One can study without dealing with it. The reason is that, in the fourfold pattern, theology means an aggregate of studies of disciplines, and the question of faith and science is isolated as a subquestion, an occasional and rare course or part of a course, in the totality of studies. This gives the totality of theological studies a certain insulation, a certain provinciality, in spite of the persisting declared intentions to make faith relevant, to relate faith and culture, etc.

The question of faith and world (science, reality, reason) can be construed primarily as an objective, cosmological, or metaphysical question, and as such it resembles that part of the older approaches called natural theology and apologetics. It can also be construed as the attempt to uncover those dimensions of the human being which found, anticipate, desire, require redemption, apart from which redemption is utterly heteronomous and alien. Here we have the new apologetics, "fundamental theology," correlation theology, transcendental method. If there is any validity to this issue, it would seem that it too deserves major thematization, not isolation as a subissue of the fourfold pattern.

A third region of questions which has only recently received renewed attention is that of religion and world religions. Taken one way, the question of religion can be the issue just treated, the question of fundamental theology. However, many questions and issues are posed by the very existence of other historical forms of salvation with their histories and claims to truth and reality. This theme had occasional expression in some of the post-Schleiermacher theological encyclopedias.[13] But it can occupy no major place in the fourfold pattern. Accordingly, the issues of faith and reality (science), of fundamental anthropology, of world religions all continue to have the status of dispensable special-interest subjects and cannot rise to thematic status as long as the fourfold pattern is taken for granted.

2. The Formal Character of the Fourfold Pattern

We move now to a critical assessment of the fourfold pattern. It will be argued here that this pattern is largely a formalistic approach to theological study, and, to the extent that it is, it carries with it no theological rationale. At the same time, the pattern has a material theological element which is a *source-to-application* concept. That is, the teleology of the pattern is from the academic study of literature which bears the church tradition (the theory) to its application to life and situations. A critique of the fourfold pattern as a formalism will be given in the present chapter, and the next chapter will take up the source-to-application element.

To clarify the thesis that the fourfold pattern, especially in its twentieth-century version, is formalistic, consideration should be given to one of the ambiguities in the concept of "theological encyclopedia." Theological encyclopedia can be construed as a primarily *pedagogical*, *curricular* problem and enterprise. The encyclopedia pattern can refer simply to a way of organizing courses in a curriculum of clergy education. The question then is: Under what general regions of subject matter should the course offerings occur? Theological encyclopedia means, on the other hand, the theological problem of the genre and unity of theology, and if that genre and unity is in any sense a "discipline," what is its immanent strucure (its subdisciplines) and what propaedeutic and auxiliary disciplines does it require? This distinction is made here in order to establish that encyclopedia in the first sense of curricular pattern, isolated from the second sense of discerning the structure of the discipline, is formalistic.[14] As a merely curricular scheme, it will mean an arrangement of areas of study (courses) under general rubrics. For the total scheme to be valid, the rubrics (e.g., Christian ethics, Christian education) must be clearly established. The present thesis is that the twentieth-century fourfold pattern is largely a curricular scheme.

The formal character of this pattern is evident in the historical transitions that have been described. Prior to the encyclopedia movement and literature, theology was *one* thing, a *habitus* and science of God, which meant God revealed in Scripture. It was self-evident, then, that knowledge of God meant knowledge of Scripture, its texts, and of the texts thematically gathered into doctrines. And if that revelation were to be proclaimed, interpreted clearly in such "means of grace" as preaching, that too could be a part of "the study of theology." When theology in this one sense eroded into "sciences," each science began to lose its material, substantial connection with the others. Preaching and catechizing are viewed not as "means of grace," but as discrete tasks of ministry correlated to needs of congregations. Church history is no longer the study of the history of God's continued activity in the community of salvation or historical knowledge for the sake of refuting heresy and defending the church's antiquity, but a cluster of historical disciplines each unified by a selected aspect of Christian history. Systematic theology is not an ordering of the revealed texts, but a clarifying or vindicating of themes of faith under general philosophical criteria. Such is the transition from a materially conceived study of theology to the dispersed disciplines of the fourfold pattern. This pattern itself is formal for the following two reasons.

The first reason is that the fourfold pattern is a general, curricular pattern which occurs over and above actual theological convictions. Three ways of materially filling in the pattern are especially evident. The pattern can be, first of all, a vehicle for traditional, precritical modes of thought. In this conservative version, the biblical area teaches the deposit of revelation in the canonical and authoritative texts; systematic theology formulates this deposit thematically; and practical theology attends to its application in the life of the church. This conservative version is rare and untypical of the literature (the introductions) of the encyclopedic movement. For the most part, that literature took for granted the historical-critical mind-set of the Enlightenment. Its version of the three curricular phases was determined by its view that theology was a science of the Christian religion. Thus there were the historical sciences of Christianity, a normative science of the truth of Christianity, and applied sciences of the ministry. This liberal way of interpreting the fourfold pattern was clearly a compromise between certain assumptions in the traditional view and the Schleiermacher type.

Since the fourfold pattern is only rarely a subject of consideration in North American theological education, the issue at stake between these various ways of filling in the formal, catalogue-like pattern with a conservative or liberal interpretation are rarely voiced. The result is that some schools and faculties which embody critical, historical approaches retain, at the same time, precritical language and categories. This especially occurs by means of exploiting the ambiguity of the concept of *canon* of Scripture. The issues at stake between precritical and postcritical approaches to the Bible are obscured by two contemporary redefinitions of canon. In the first, canon is a merely historical concept, a term for an ancient collection. In the second, canon is expanded into a symbol for any and all ways of retaining the biblical writings in the church. In the first, canon is an historical fact none would dispute. In the second, canon is simply Scripture as it functions in a faith community.

What these redefinitions obscure is the concept of canon itself as it originated and functioned in an ancient and precritical framework of authority. According to the precritical approach (e.g., orthodox Catholicism and Protestantism), the text, rightly interpreted, is itself an authoritative depiction of historical, doctrinal, and moral truth. Canon in the traditional and—this author would say—precise sense carries this theological freight of meaning. This conviction lays the groundwork for an approach to theological study founded on the divinely given two-testament collection and its authoritative texts. A historical-critical approach cannot avoid some distinction between what is true, authoritative, and real, and the content of the canonical texts. The nineteenth-century encyclopedias realized this fact; hence their proposal that the Christian religion is the subject of theology. That proposal does not survive. At the same time, the retention of traditional language (canon, Old and New Testament, dogmatics) suggests, falsely, that contemporary theological schools promote an uncritical orthodoxy. In fact, pedagogy and the organization of studies occur as parts of the academy's inherited tradition and as structures in its institutions. They tend not to occur as theological issues subjected to open debate. Accordingly, the intellectual struggle necessary for the resolving of many of these ambiguities is not part of the academy's everyday conduct of its affairs.

There is some coherence attending each of these approaches. However, with a few exceptions, neither the conservative nor the liberal way of filling in the fourfold pattern is operative in contemporary theological schools. Most of these schools have abandoned the deposit-of-revelation approach, yet most of them have not taken up the nineteenth-century concept of a science of the Christian religion. The historical-critical consciousness of modernity is sufficiently pervasive to discredit the conservative approach. And the dispersion of biblical and historical areas into subspecialties of scholarship prevents these faculty members from arranging themselves under an overall rubric of "Christianity." How then are these areas with their courses and their scholarly undertakings justified?

The justification, when attempted at all, occurs usually not by assignment to a place in an argued encyclopedic scheme, but by an appeal to the values inherent in the particular specialty or discipline. Studying Paul, Jeremiah, Augustine, the Oxford movement, moral agency, and ecclesiology yields certain human benefits. As disciplines, these studies are ways of uncovering the insights of those figures or moments of tradition which any generation of human beings can profitably share. In other words, the justification proceeds along the lines, not of a theological, but of a general humanistic argument. It is the sort of rationale one hears for various studies within liberal arts: a documentation of the benefits obtained from reading Cicero, modern American poetry, Sigmund Freud. This general humanistic approach is, then, the third way of filling in and interpreting the meaning of the formal scheme. If this description is accurate, it means that a theological rationale is offered neither for the fourfold pattern itself nor for the discrete scholarly enterprises which occur in conjunction with it.

The second reason why the fourfold pattern is formalistic and not an expression of any substantial theological conviction is its further dispersion into subspecialties. At issue here is the sense in which the fourfold pattern is comprised of independent disciplines. Bernard Lonergan has refined the rather vague concept of a discipline by an analysis of *ways of distinguishing specialties*.[15] He offers a typology of three approaches to classification: disciplines distinguished according to *data* (e.g., law, prophets, wisdom specialties in Old Testament studies); disciplines distinguished by *subject*; and disciplines distinguished by *successive stages*. This analysis does illuminate ways of classifying subspecialties of disciplines, but not disciplines themselves. Disciplines themselves fall into two general types: those whose unity is that of some *region of being* or reality and those whose unity is an *activity* or undertaking.[16] Perception is the guiding metaphor behind the regional disciplines; activity behind the functional disciplines.

Disciplines as specialties of science or scholarship are abstractions for cognitive purposes from the total and concrete region or function. Accordingly, the major types of specialties or disciplines represent ways of carrying out the abstraction. Three such ways can be distinguished, one of which coincides with Lonergan's third classification. The first abstracting decision concerns the aspect of the region (or function) which is the object of interest, focus, or knowledge. It can be its mathematical structure, history, factual data, predictive projections, etc. The second is the designated method, as linguistic, archaeological, semiological, experimental, etc. Presumably there is correspondence between the abstracted aspect and the method or methods. The third is abstraction by stages of investigation or understanding, hence there can be a building up, an accumulation of understanding.

This typology of disciplines prompts a question: In what sense is the fourfold pattern comprised of "disciplines" or specialties? In the nineteenth-century introductions, the first three areas (Bible, theology, church history) are conceived as regions of a larger historical region, Christianity. They differ from each other both by the aspect of Christianity considered (history, truth), and also by method used (historical, normative). The fourth discipline, practical theology, is a functionally unified concept, referring as it does to ministerial activity. In the twentieth century the region Christianity is abandoned as a way of conceiving the unity of the first three disciplines. If the clerical paradigm alone unifies all four, that would suggest that each of the areas is part of an overall *functional* undertaking (ministerial activity). However, it is not self-evident that each of these is a specialty of ministerial activity. It may be argued that homiletics or pastoral care are disciplines in that sense, but this is not self-evidently the case with church history or systematic theology. One can only conclude that the four areas organize neither an overall region nor overall function or activity. They are not subgroupings of either a comprehensive discipline or a function. Nor is there a single reality which provides them their subject matter or method. The result is that each area is subject only to the discrete data, usually of a historical character, which evoke its inquiries. That being the case, the four areas are names for an aggregate of (usually historically oriented) scholarly specialties.

A sign that this has in fact happened is that each area possesses ways of abstracting aspects of the region and different corresponding methods. Church history can mean history of exegesis (Ebeling), history of the ecclesiastical institution, a history of theology and doctrine. That it means one or the other depends on what historiographies dominated the graduate school and the transmission of the specialty, and not on theological determination of the overall region within a theological encyclopedia undertaking. This is why the areas of the fourfold pattern name not disciplines, but clusters of subspecialties.

In summary, the reasons for the formal and nontheological nature of the fourfold pattern are: (1) the pattern is a general pattern whose material meaning requires filling in, but the only filling that now occurs is through the general humanistic hermeneutics promoted by each area; and (2) the pattern names clusters of subspecialties. In other words, the fourfold pattern is not now a genuine, theologically based pattern but a school-catalogue phenomenon, a way of organizing courses. Accordingly, it is more accurate to label the divisions of the fourfold pattern catalogue fields than disciplines.

3. The Effects of Fragmentation on the Catalogue Fields

The initial section of this chapter described certain historical outcomes of the fourfold pattern. It argued that the pattern is now largely a formal, catalogue matter, an expected concomitant of the dispersal of theology into independent disciplines. We now pursue the archaeological inquiry to the level of the current fate and condition of these relatively autonomous catalogue fields. This essay has questioned the prevailing assumption that the fourfold pattern is made up of clearly conceived sciences (scholarly specialties) whose teaching representatives share an overall consensus about the object and method of the science. With this perspective, we may briefly review the major "catalogue fields" of the theological school. There is, of course, a risk in doing so. In the framework, mentality, and even sociology of the scholarly guilds, any one person is an outsider to most of them, and outsiders are unqualified by definition to comment on the state of disciplines other than their own. The present author can only acknowledge this lack of qualification on his part. Technically speaking, he will not be commenting on the "state of the discipline" in the sense of identifying the horizon of needed research. Instead, he will attempt some generalizations about what seems to be the catalogue field's relation to some overall content which one might call theological. The thesis to be argued is that these fields, for the most part, are, in their dispersion, separated from and not subject to that content, and that this has created problems for the fields in their efforts to be disciplines. Such a generalization, however, cannot be a fair account of specific authors or published works which do successfully make connections with the larger subject, theology.[17]

The historical archaeology of part 1 included an account of a time when "theology" was a single thing. And although it did evoke various "studies," these were not conceived of as scholarly disciplines. I have tried to show that the encyclopedic movement did think of its divisions of study as disciplines. The question I am raising now is whether the fourfold pattern is intact in this sense, whether the four (or five, etc.) areas of study—Bible, church history, dogmatics, practical theology—name disciplines. It was argued previously that these divisions are themselves names for clusters of courses, studies, specialties, not unified scholarly disciplines, and to the degree that this is the case we live now in a post-encyclopedia and post-fourfold-pattern situation. *Theologia*, in other words, has dispersed not only into the independent sciences of the fourfold pattern, but into a great many subspecialties which have lost contact with the disciplines of the pattern itself. For this reason the divisions may be called "catalogue fields" rather than disciplines, that is, rubrics for exhibiting courses to students.

Many historical forces have collaborated in this dispersion. The most basic one is the vast transformation which modernity worked on both Catholic and Protestant orthodoxy. Both communions assumed the method of authority, a mode of thought in which authorities (texts of Scripture and of church tradition) functioned *as* or in place of critical and evidential ways of establishing claims. A deposit of divinely revealed truths carried in ancient texts was the one ground of the one thing, theology. This one thing, theology, could lend itself to different usages and purposes: exhibiting truth, defending its truth, controverting heterodoxy's falsity, etc. If we did try to translate the present catalogue fields back into these terms, we would find them all collapsing into aspects of the one thing, the exhibition of truths of revelation grounded in the textual deposit.

Between this precritical period and now, a sea change has occurred, and its initial effect is a radical alteration of the nature of the theological and churchly activities to which the studies of *theologia* pertained. Exhibiting and defending the faith, living the Christian life, caring for souls, preaching, evangelizing *mean* something different after the demise of classical orthodoxy. To this transformation of the life and interpretation of faith itself was added the concept and agenda of "scholarship" in the sense of the modern German university, transforming the old aspects of *theologia* into independent, critical, and scholarly enterprises. The two together are responsible for an idea and mindset which we now take for granted: the attempt on the part of systematic theologians, ethicists, biblical scholars, and practical theologians to maintain their field as scholarly disciplines. The task is herculean. *Theologia* and the traditional versions of dogmatics, preaching, etc., are no longer with us. No relatively uniform mode of thought or even interpretation of what Christian faith is has replaced it. The result is that the catalogue fields are marked by the following features.

First, the compromised and indecisive character of the fourfold pattern continues in the catalogue fields. This seems due to the fact that the demise of the house of authority is only partially acknowledged. Whether we are talking about ethics, systematic theology, or pastoral care, the absence of any clear consensus about how one makes or grounds judgments theologically lends a certain obscurity to these fields at the point in which they might claim to be theological fields. The obscurity is due in part to the general lack of consensus about theological procedures and in part to the mixture of precritical modes of thought with elements of modernity.

Homiletics is a case in point. Since preaching remains an important liturgical activity, it continues to be central to ministerial preparation. The character of preaching, the problem of formulating the sermon, at least in Protestantism, was at one time fairly clear. It was the problem of grasping and transferring the truths of a discrete and selected text of Scripture into a rhetorical unit in which these truths could be received and applied by the hearers. Behind this notion is the whole conceptual apparatus of the Protestant method of authority: canon, discrete authoritative texts, deposit of revelation, etc. With the exception of those traditions and their schools which self-consciously retain that apparatus, most present-day theological schools have abandoned it. At the same time, the problem of preaching is still formulated as the problem of discovering how to effect the proper transfer from the biblical texts to the rhetorical unit. Contemporary homiletics introduces a more historical-critical way of dealing with the text and more up-to-date hermeneutics, rhetoric, and approaches to language. But this interpretation of preaching assumes as intact a text-to-situation view of preaching whose grounds have long been undermined. This approach rests on the assumption that each text of Scripture is an a priori authority which can be "applied" simply by means of interpretation, without passing through any theological appraisal.

Second, there is a certain sense in which the various catalogue fields appear to be disciplines, scholarly enterprises. What gives them that appearance is that certain *literatures*, with their concepts, interpretive requirements, histories, and the like, provide the touchstone of these fields. There are literatures of systematic theology, church administration, moral analysis, and early Christianity. Now there is surely a distinction between a region or function of reality itself and the literatures in which the interpretation of reality is deposited. Accordingly, there can be a relation to the literature of a field which focuses not on the literature as an end in itself but through the literature on the fact, reality, subject matter, event. Concern with a literature can, in other words, attend a scholarly discipline. If, however, the region of reality or function is itself problematic or has receded from view, then the subject matter, object, and even method begin to coincide with the literature itself.

This development may be termed a "phenomenalism," because the primary defining reality of the discipline has been replaced by the second-order phenomenal literary carrier. For instance, a phenomenal approach in systematic theology would define theology's subject matter as the *writings* of theologians. If in fact the primary region or function is obscure, literature in itself cannot establish a field except in the *phenomenal* sense of an existing literature, and any literature can be the object of scholarly investigation. In addition, literatures do correspond to an object or region insofar as they record or are evidence for historical matters: events, period, ideas, stories, controversies, etc. The second symptom of the break-up of the traditional disciplines of the fourfold pattern is, then, that discrete literatures or ever more discrete historical regions have come to define the catalogue fields rather than the aspects of *theologia*, faith or Christianity. Faculty specialists tend to be specialists in literature, not just as they are distributed over the fourfold pattern, but in more specific subdisciplines and their auxiliary sciences. Theological ethics, accordingly, does not seem to be itself a scholarly discipline, but a rubric under which various kinds of literature are studied. Particular representatives may, of course, have a clear vision of that field, its contours, objects, methods, but no one such vision seems determinative of the field.

Third, the catalogue fields as clusters of subspecialties appear to have no common norms by which they are *theological* disciplines. We would expect this given the demise of the way of authority and the absence of a widespread alternative. Lacking such norms, these subdisciplines of the catalogue fields are not subject to whatever defines a mode of thought or inquiry as theological. There is, of course, a general inclination on the part of many representatives of these fields to see the field as "theological." This can mean anything from the field's pertinence to the task of ministry (the clerical paradigm) to its coherence with Scripture. But the loss of clear connection to any unitary sense of theology means that the norms or criteria for judgment in the subspecialties tend to be general norms of scholarship. Accordingly, most of the subspecialties can agree that their work should be clear, precise, coherent, subject to evidence, etc. As to less formal norms, these tend to be supplied by the auxiliary discipline appropriated by the subspecialty. In the absence of a working connection with theology, the auxiliary discipline becomes that which makes the subspecialty "scholarly" and thus provides criteria for work. For this reason, the catalogue fields as clusters of subspecialties are vulnerable to translation into their appropriated auxiliary sciences: homiletics into modern language study, pastoral care into therapeutic psychology; ethics into social science or philosophical ethics, systematic theology into some appropriated philosophical system and method, church history into secular history of religious institutions.

Fourth, these comments about common problems between the catalogue fields should not obscure the fact that each area faces different kinds of problems and this in turn makes them "clusters" of subdisciplines in different senses. Some catalogue areas (Old Testament, New Testament, American church history, etc.) are unified by historical periods or the literatures thereof. These literatures create subspecialties of a particular corpus (wisdom, patristics). Thus, in these areas the disciplines remain fairly intact in the sense of humanistic studies. In the so-called practical fields, the subdisciplines are not literatures but areas, tasks, skills of church leadership. As such these are not disciplines, but they attempt to locate and interrelate disciplines pertinent for the task. The so-called normative areas (theology, ethics) are particularly vulnerable to current confusions about (theological) norms, hence they tend to break up into either *agenda* subspecialties (Christian social ethics, philosophy of religion, theological language, method) or *literature* and *historical movement* subspecialties (Reformation, nineteenth century, a major figure, a philosophical movement). The combination of some literature or period with an agenda specialty is the normative areas' version of a cluster. All of these catalogue areas have, for the most part, lost their theological character, but for different reasons and in different senses: by reason of merely literary-historical focus, or by amalgamating skill-oriented disciplines, or by very restricted agenda adoption.

In conclusion, the four catalogue fields of the fourfold pattern do not necessarily constitute four clearly conceived scholarly disciplines as the nineteenth-century encyclopedia movement would have it. They are rather rubrics under which pedagogical efforts occur and within which work subspecialties of various sorts. The gains of this development are clear. It has opened the various enterprises of teaching and interpretation to the full spectrum of resources and sciences available in the modern world. The losses are serious, prompted as they are by the severance of connection with *that which makes a theological education theological.*

NOTES

1. The functionalist-professionalist form of the clerical paradigm has not only promoted this alienation, but has had what appear to be unfortunate effects on the theological schools in the last generation. A certain clergy piety appears to fix the ethos of some schools. The focus of clergy piety is not on

personal formation or societal oppression and justice but on the minister and his or her congregation. It exists in a social world in which the minister's obligations toward the congregation set the criteria for reality, authentic life, even Christianity. Clergy piety may be responsible for that part of the seminary's ethos which appears to be anti-intellectual. It is reported, though not established, that the center of Protestant religious scholarship has shifted in the last generation from the seminaries to the colleges and universities. The generalization here is that seminary faculties, in many cases, are not communities of scholars in as determined and rigorous a sense as before, that many faculty members interiorized the pervasive societal and churchly consensus that technical academic work is elitist and irrelevant. These notions are proffered here not as facts but as suspicions, surmises to be further explored.

2. This isolation of theological disciplines is present, it seems, regardless of how conservative or liberal the school. In the biblical field, the more conservative approach would see the object of the discipline as a collection (of Old and New Testaments), the literature itself. The liberal approach would see the object as the historical entity behind the literature, the religion of Israel, the origins of Christianity. Even though the collection-of-texts approach sounds more traditional, suggesting the canon principle, it occurs in the twentieth-century pattern of study as a discrete discipline isolated from any overall theological subject matter.

3. Thomas Bray, *Bibliotheca parochialis* (1697). This is found in T. Bray, *His Life and Selected Works Relating to Maryland*, ed. B.C. Steiner (1901), p. 95. Samuel Willard likewise sees this identity between what the minister learns in theological study and what non-clergy are to learn and know. The reason is that what ministers are appointed to teach is simply "knowledge of God," instruction in the Kingdom of God (*Brief Directions to a Young Scholar* [Boston, 1735], preface).

4. Anna Case Winters did a study for this project of the offerings in the area of church education of thirty-four American seminaries. This study suggests that there is little consensus in the seminaries as to either the importance or the nature of education. In about twenty percent of schools it had little or no representation at all. In about twenty percent there were extensive offerings. In addition to the basic course such as "pastor as educator," or "foundations of . . . ," the recurring subjects were administration, curricular design, teaching methods, developmental psychology. The two main types of overall approach were psychological formation (nurture, discipleship, development), and administration of church education.

5. For a more detailed prosecution of this thesis, see the author's essay, "Theology and Practice outside the Clerical Paradigm," slated to appear in a volume of essays on practical theology edited by Don Browning.

6. See, for instance, the dissertation by Terry Harter, "A Critique of North American Protestant Theological Education from the Perspectives of Ivan Illich and Paulo Freire" (Boston, 1980); and The Cornwall Collective, *Your*

Daughters Shall Prophesy: A Feminist Alternative (New York: Pilgrim Press, 1981).

7. The first essay in the Cornwall study, "Toward a Feminist Understanding of Theological Education," does describe the general approach and model of theological education as a university model, with little integration except that which is given by students themselves, and with faculty "trapped into the self-perpetuating disciplines of the traditional curriculum" (p. 3). Its recommendations are limited, however, to pedagogical processes and do not pertain to a new curricular structure or overall pattern of study.

8. Typical of this literature is the volume of essays edited by Charles R. Feilding, *Education for Ministry* (Dayton: AATS, 1966).

9. Yves M.J. Congar, *A History of Theology* (Garden City, N.Y.: Doubleday & Co., 1968), chap. 5, D.

10. In the post-Schleiermacher introductions, the standard disciplines listed under practical theology were five: homiletics, catechetics, church law (polity), pastoral care, and liturgy. Additions and deviations from this list are rare in the literature. They occur as the occasional listing of missions, evangelistics, even apologetics and polemics. If the field is itself organized, it is always by means of Schleiermacher's distinction between disciplines concerned with church *guidance* and those concerned with church *governance*.

11. The practical theology areas of study were not entirely absent from the denominational college's offerings. Hence, we find Christian education, missions, evangelization occasionally offered.

12. If there is any sign at all of a qualification of the fourfold pattern in the theological schools, it may be here. Some schools are now creating an area of studies, distinct from ministry studies, having to do with society, culture, and the like. For instance, we find "Christianity and Culture" (Emory), "Human Nature and Culture" (Eden, Yale), "Ethics, Society, and Culture" (Howard), "Church and Society" (ITC), "Persons, Society, and Culture" (Iliff), "Christianity and Culture" (Phillips).

13. Thus James Drummond (1884); Alfred Cave (1886); W.N. Clarke (1887); Davies (1905); and Wernle (1908). Francis Patton also urges the study of world religions as part of rational theology ("Theological Encyclopedia," in *Biblical and Theological Studies* [New York: Charles Scribner's Sons, 1912], p. 8).

14. This language of formalist (curricular) and theological senses of encyclopedia should not be confused with the standard distinction present throughout the introductions between "formal" and "material" encyclopedia. This distinction itself did not always mean the same thing. For some authors, formal encyclopedia referred to theological schemes or patterns of the disciplines while a material encyclopedia summarized their literatures and results. In this sense, Schleiermacher's *Brief Outline* is formal and Hagenbach is material. Others thought of formal patterns as simply proposed schemes unattended by a theological attempt to derive them or justify them, and material encyclopedias as theologically founded. In this sense, Schleiermacher and Kähler

offer material approaches since they are products of rigorous theological argumentation, subjecting the scheme to the actual nature and requirements of faith and its criteria.

15. Bernard Lonergan, *Method in Theology* (New York: Herder and Herder, 1972,), pp. 125ff.

16. "Region" is a spatial metaphor indicating subject matters which are manifest to distinguishable types of experience. Reality as past (history), the planetary surface, and the poetry of Yeats are all "regions" of objects whose distinctive features are manifest to different modes of experience.

17. For informative historical and contemporary interpretations of the major disciplines, the following works are especially useful: W. Pannenberg, *Theology and the Philosophy of Science*, trans. F. McDonagh (London: Darton, Longman, & Todd, 1976), chap. 6; G. Ebeling, *The Study of Theology*, trans. D.A. Priebe (Philadelphia: Fortress Press, 1978); Georg Picht and E. Rudolph, eds., *Theologie—Was ist Das?* (Stuttgart: Kreuz Verlag, 1977); R. Bohren, ed., *Einführung in das Studium der evangelische Theologie* (Munich: Chr. Kaiser, 1964); Paul Ramsey, ed., *Religion* (Englewood Cliffs, N.J.: Prentice-Hall, 1965).

7

The Recovery
of *Theologia*

The historical archaeology, the criticisms, and the constructive argument of this essay are all concerned primarily with clergy or seminary education. These final chapters will offer some suggestions which are intended to be of sufficient ecumenical character to be pertinent to theological schools of different denominations and even different branches of Christendom. These suggestions explore ways of surmounting the accumulation of problems and incoherencies which constitute present-day theological education.

This exploration presupposes the historical archaeology of part 1. The thesis of that analysis was that the transition of theological study into North American theological education carried with it the European solution to the problem of the unity of theological study and its accompanying loss of *theologia*. This loss has had far-reaching and unfortunate consequences for the education of ministers. The loss is not an absolute one. Some remnants of sapiential knowledge and even theology as a discipline persist, but as specialties and discrete elements in the theological school. *Theologia* no longer forms part of a theological school's conception of its course of study, and the result is a loss of unifying subject matter and criteria for the various catalogue areas. This absence of criteria and subject matter tends to rob the catalogue areas of their potentialities to be theological disciplines and turns them over to the control of their auxiliary sciences. As a result, theological education becomes an amalgam of academic specialization and culture adaptation. The central theme of this essay is the recovery of what would restore unity and criteria to theological education, namely *theologia*, or theological understanding.

1. A Basic Distinction: *Paideia* and the Course of Studies

The historical archaeology offered in part 1 has given what may appear to be inordinate attention to the theological encyclopedia movement and its literature. Does this imply that "the problem of theological education" *is* the problem of discerning a new and more adequate encyclopedia, a pattern of organizing theological sciences? It is clear that it is not. A theological school could reorganize its course of studies in any one of dozens of ways, including the Schleiermacherian three-fold pattern, and this reorganization would not itself constitute a res-toration of *theologia* to theological education.

At this point a distinction must be made which the theological en-cyclopedia movement did not make between two aspects of the en-cyclopedia problem: the *theological* problem of discerning the divi-sions (sciences) of theology and the *pedagogical* problem of proposing a course of studies. In the nineteenth-century encyclopedic move-ment, "sciences" (regions of scholarly-cognitive undertakings) and "studies" coincide. The result of this coinciding is that "the study of theology" is experienced in seminaries as an exposure to a plurality of scholarly or skill-oriented disciplines. This essay has attempted to show that the fourfold pattern is in fact not a coherent account of a single theological science. The fact that its unity is teleological and clerical suggests that this pattern is fundamentally a pedagogical arrangement. However, in the encyclopedia period it was expounded as a course of studies, the areas of which were "sciences." We now come to the most serious criticism of the theological encyclopedia movement. Is it the case that the "sciences" which constitute a single, comprehensive the-ological science coincide with the divisions of a course of theological studies?[1]

A certain understanding of the nature of education grounds this assumed coincidence. It is the post-Enlightenment view that educa-tion is both learning and socialization in the discrete undertakings of scholarship. Education means a communication of the many regions in which scholars and scientists divide up the cognitive universe. Ab-sent from this view is the ancient Greek ideal of culture *(paideia)*, according to which education is the "culturing" of a human being in *areté* or virtue. The question which guided this approach was simply: What type of education leads to *areté*?[2] The education whose center is *theologia* is an ecclesial counterpart to *paideia*, focusing as it does, not on *areté*, but on a sapiential knowledge engendered by grace and divine self-disclosure. The view that education (the course of studies) means the exposure to sciences or realms of scholarship tends to promote a technological view of education. Education as mere scholarly learning is not a process affecting and shaping the human being under an ideal, but a grasping of the methods and contents of a plurality of regions of scholarship. The loss, then, of *theologia* to theological study resembles the older loss of education as *paideia*.

Once we abandon the assumption that the *divisions* of theological science and the *disciplines* of a course of studies coincide, a new way of formulating the so-called problem of theological education becomes possible. If we fail to make this distinction, the problem of reforming theological education is simply an encyclopedic problem, and its major task is the determination of the subspecialties of theological science. But if theology as science (or understanding) and theology as a course of studies do not coincide, the proposing of a course of studies cannot itself be simply the task of discerning theological sciences.

We can make headway toward an alternative only if we first resolve the ambiguities resident in both "theology" and "course of studies." Theology in its primary meaning and as we are using it is a personal and existential wisdom or understanding. As such it is not tied to any specific course of studies such as clergy education. As such it sets its own requirements for studies, knowledge, and disciplines depending on the context in which it occurs. Insofar as clergy education is theological, a *paideia* of theological understanding, it must discern and incorporate those requirements. Hence, one indispensable task in the overall construction of clergy education is the discernment of the structure and requirements of *theologia*. "Course of theological study" is, likewise, ambiguous and cannot be reduced to clergy education. Courses of theological study which incorporate *theologia* are possible and appropriate in both university education and in church education. The concern here is, in fact, clergy education, and it too makes its own demands and sets its own requirements. Discerning the requirements of a pedagogy which is distinctively for the church's leadership is itself a special task and not synonymous with the discernment of the structure of *theologia*. Furthermore, both theological understanding and the distinctive requirements of clergy education mutually influence each other. That is, the church's leadership may require a special kind of education precisely because its task is, centrally, to facilitate theological understanding, and the theological understanding it requires may be of a special sort because of that leadership task.

Although it has been argued here that theological schools must discern the requirements set both by theologia and by the leader's special context, there is no suggestion that the "disciplines" which have been so central to theological education should be abandoned.[3] The virtual explosion of areas of scholarship in theological schools since the Enlightenment has resulted in new worlds of understanding and knowledge in the interpretation of religion. To ask whether these fields can organize the course of study is not to discredit the fields as such. But what role do they play in a course of clerical study? The present thesis is that only a discernment of the requirements of both theological understanding and of a clerical pedagogy will determine the disciplines needed in the course of study. This thesis has a negative aspect. Limiting the task of determining and classifying disciplines to considerations of the requirements of *theologia* and the requirements of clergy education implies that these disciplines do not organize a single comprehensive *science* called theology.

 In fact, there does not appear to be a single theological science in the modern sense of a comprehensive, ordered inquiry aimed at a designated region of being and classifiable into subsciences. The closest modern resemblance to such a science is a comprehensive *historical* inquiry into the Christian religion. This undertaking does, it seems, parallel other humanistic, historical disciplines. It does focus on a designated phenomenon, employs a generally specifiable method, and it can be divided into specific scholarly specialties. This historical discipline is clearly neither *theologia* itself nor a comprehensive science which organizes the whole plethora of post-Enlightenment disciplines of theological education.[4] The medieval scholastic notion of theology as a science simply claims demonstrative status for certain methods employed by the *habitus*, theological knowledge. In that sense, theology is not a comprehensive science embracing subdis-

ciplines. When the disciplines did arise in the Enlightenment universities, they did not organize a science of theology except in the above-
mentioned sense of a historical science of Christianity. What remains,
then, is either theological understanding (and disciplines propaedeutic
to that) or special theological pedagogies (ministry, church, university)
and disciplines propaedeutic to them.

A summary of the tasks necessary to the construction of a course of
studies for church leadership is now in order:

1. The requirements of this specific pedagogy must be discerned
   and set forth. These include both a theology of ministry itself
   and a description of the institutions and cultural situations in
   which it will occur.
2. A second task is a descriptive account of *theologia*, of theological
   understanding, the ecclesial counterpart to and specification of
   paideia.
3. Theological understanding does not occur magically, automatically, or above history and culture. Informed by tradition, it
   depends necessarily on disciplines which ground both historical
   knowledge and theological judgment. This being the case, a third
   task is to propose the disciplines which are propaedeutic to theological understanding.
4. The pedagogical requirements special to ministry will need to be
   described, and with them the disciplines propaedeutic to those
   requirements. It would be perilous to see ministerial pedagogical
   requirements as utterly separated from sapiential knowledge
   (theology). These requirements will reflect a synthesis of that
   knowledge and the situation(s) of ministry, the distinctive tasks
   involved in the facilitation of theological understanding.
5. On the basis of tasks 1–4, a course of study would be proposed
   whose subject matter is theological understanding *(theologia)* as
   it is exercised in the institutionality and situation of ministry.

This fivefold description of tasks confronting the reform of clergy
education indicates that the problem of theological education is not a
problem of a single encyclopedic organization of disciplines. Instead,
several kinds of organizations are involved. This is inevitable to the

degree that both theological understanding and distinctive ministerial pedagogy are involved. What follows is not a proposed course of studies. It does begin the tasks described in steps 2, 3, and 4. Hence, it offers an account of both theological understanding and the special requirements of ministry pedagogy sufficient to illustrate an approach to clergy education which overcomes the present imperialism of the specialties by restoring *theologia* to the course of studies.

The historical archaeology of part 1 traced the career of theology, identifying several fundamentally different meanings of the word. That career saw the displacement of *theologia*, a sapiential knowledge or understanding, by other meanings, a displacement which had fateful consequences for clergy and church education. The main thesis of this essay is that a significant reform of theological education which addresses its deepest problems must find a way to recover *theologia*. Without that recovery, theological education will continue to perpetuate its enslavement to specialties, its lack of subject matter and criteria, its functionalist and technological orientation. The argument now calls for some account of *theologia*. This account, though brief, will be threefold: a location of *theologia* in the geography of faith, a depiction of what survives the destructive effects of criticism on traditional forms of *theologia*, and a description of the "life" and dialectic of theological understanding. The genre in which all three of these expositions unite is *theologia*, the personal, sapiential knowledge (understanding) which can occur when faith opens itself to reflection and inquiry.

2. Toward a Geography of *Theologia*

By "geography" of *theologia* is meant simply an attempt to understand theology's place or location on the map of faith's situation. This geography may begin with the distinction basic to the whole structure between faith's prereflective insightfulness, which I shall call "beliefful knowing," and *theologia* or theological understanding. The distinction assumes that there is a certain insightfulness which characterizes faith itself. Faith describes the way in which the human being lives in and toward God and the world under the impact of redemption. As such, it is neither empty of content nor blind hypothesis but an opening onto the world. The imagery, existentiality, and corporate relations operative in redemption instigate this insightfulness. Inadequate, therefore, is any description of faith as blind and contentless until self-conscious inquiry renders it cognitive. Rather, there is a cognitivity which attends faith itself. This prereflective cognitivity or insightfulness should be distinguished from what happens to that insightfulness when it becomes self-conscious, when it subjects itself to deliberate processes of reflection and inquiry.[5] The result of activities of reflection and inquiry when they are successful is understanding. It is just this understanding which is here referred to as *theologia*.

To move to a second distinction, theological understanding is not one thing but many things. This is because it occurs in different social *matrices*, and each of these matrices has its own distinctive *mode* of understanding. Three especially are prominent, and some version of each one has attended the ecclesial community from the beginning. The first matrix (context) is the situation of the believer as such.[6] This situation is, of course, not simply one thing but many things. It varies from believer to believer, culture to culture, epoch to epoch. The understanding called for is what is needed in the specific situation. This is not to say there are no perennial elements in the situation of the believer. Candidates for such would be the built-in disposition of any human being to know, to grasp clearly, to understand, and also the understanding required when the redemption which faith experiences and serves is called forth by a corrupt and oppressive social system. These examples make it clear that habitual prereflective insight is not sufficient, that the particularities of individual and social existence require self-consciously obtained understanding. The *mode* of understanding which attends the situation of the believer is simply that which is required by the perennial features of that situation: personal self-insight, the grasp of the corrupted elements in the social situation, and the possibilities for redemption. Although the understanding of the believer may result from a self-conscious effort, this does not mean technical scholarship. It is the understanding required by the life of faith in the world. This mode of understanding is *reflection* or theological reflection.

A second matrix of theological understanding is the situation of leadership in the church. This leadership includes the priesthood of the Catholic communions, ministry in the Protestant communions, and responsibilities taken on by the laity. Its essence is the exercise of some special responsibility in and on behalf of the community of faith. The most general way of characterizing what all ecclesial leadership has in common is that it is activity through which the community of faith is gathered up to function as a redemptive community. Such leadership can occur primarily in and for the community of faith or in and for the world. This happens as the leader assists the community in mobilizing its traditioning, corporate memory, and care in acts which are proclamatory, sacramental, administrative, and nurturing. These acts of facilitation and mobilization call for a different mode of understanding from simply that which is operative in the believer, precisely because their aim is to assist the believer as he or she exists in the situation. Assisting the traditioning and corporate memory of the church will involve a level of interpretation which does not simply reproduce the believer's reflective life. The activity of proclamation will involve a distinctive mode of self-conscious theological under- standing because it aims to evoke the believer's understanding and action. No single term is available to us from tradition to describe this leadership mode of theological understanding. *Diaconal* understand- ing is descriptive but awkward.

The third matrix of theological understanding is that of inquiry and scholarship. It is occupied by what might be thought of as one kind of leadership, what the Middle Ages called the "doctors of the church." The social context which accompanies this matrix is usually, but not necessarily, the school. The task is the determination or uncovering of truth. What this determination specifically involves varies enor- mously from epoch to epoch, and especially varies from the time of the period of classical Catholic and Protestant theologies to recent centuries dominated by the natural, human, and social sciences. When *theologia* occurs in the form of self-conscious inquiry under scholarly or scientific requirements, it exists in a third mode of understanding, that of theological knowledge.

To understand these three matrices as exclusive would be an un- fortunate turn of the argument. While it is conceivable that scholarly inquiry occurs without a basis in faith itself, even inquiry into matters (usually of a historical character) pertaining to the Christian religion, it would be misleading to regard that isolation as typical. If a typology of *matrices and modes of theological understanding* is what is under discussion, then all three modes will contain dispositions which occur prereflectively in faith itself. Further, a focus on one of the modes—for instance, that of leadership—does not preempt other modes. The leader of the church as believer will pursue the reflective life of a believer, and the development of that reflective life will surely be part of the education of the leader of the church. In addition, the leader of the church may, because of particular situations of leadership, also pursue the third mode of inquiry and scholarship.[7]

This location of theology on the map of faith and its institutions may further extend the criticism that theological education occurs under the dominance of the clerical paradigm. Theology itself is a self-conscious level of understanding which the prereflective insightfulness of faith can and should obtain. Its restriction to one social matrix (e.g., the church's leadership) was a fateful development in the church. Unfortunately, the restriction was attended by a transformation of theology/knowledge into enterprises of scholarship, hence theological understanding is eliminated as a necessary or desirable ground for education in the tasks of ministry. This attempt to acknowledge modes and matrices of a *theologia* which attends the life of faith itself is more in the "democratic" and anti-elitist tradition of pietism than in the more restricted approach of the schools. Accordingly, a phenomenology, history, and even therapeutic of theology is not simply a matter of reviving theological *science*, one of its modes.[8]

3. *Theologia* Beyond the Way of Authority

It seems clearly evident that the original meaning of theology as *theologia*, sapiential knowledge (understanding), has not been operative in the church for many generations. It was banished from both clergy and church education. If that is the case, is not any attempt at a recovery of *theologia* doomed to failure? Historians might cognitively mine the past for its information, but they cannot raise the dead. Is not *theologia* like Stoic psychology or Roman *auctoritas*, a concept whose reality and power depends on the living framework in which it once occurred? It is at this point that the archaeology of the career of *theologia* may be misleading. The changes described in that narration are paradigm shifts and modifications of language which did radically affect the way church and clergy education were conceived. *Theologia* as the unity and subject matter of both church and clergy education was in fact exported from the paradigms which governed their interpretation. As a result the meaning of the term *theology* was radically narrowed.

Theologia did not, however, totally disappear from the community of faith or from its educative undertakings. To the degree that faith itself continues at all (some would argue that it has not), a certain prereflective insightfulness will attend it. Further, human beings rarely if ever exist in the world without reflective responses of some sort. Accordingly, even in the modern, highly secularized and pragmatic religious community, faith's prereflective dispositions find ways to rise into understanding: in reflections of believers, in acts of ministry such as preaching, in church schools and educative processes, in Christian feminism and black theology, in technical and scholarly inquiries. Theological understanding occurs in these matrices even though it is itself rarely thematized and pursued as such. As the argument goes, this understanding does not preside over the way we think of the unity and goals of clergy education. It is nevertheless present in that education, if for no other reason than that faith's prereflective insightfulness is pressed into reflection and self-conscious assessments, especially as it occurs in the matrix of church leadership. The task before us, then, is not so much to resuscitate the dead as to persuade the living to incorporate into their educational paradigms something which is in fact at work in their midst.

An older time would have expressed this issue as the relation between piety and intellect. *Theologia* as the insightfulness, the "knowledge" which attends faith in its concrete existence, is not identical with piety. Expressed in these terms, the argument is that theological education has assumed that its unity and subject matter had no relation to the sapiential knowledge which accompanies faith's concrete existence (piety). The flurry of activity going on these days about "formation" and "spirituality" is no doubt some sort of attempt at the restoration of piety. The Protestant form of these efforts is so far not highly credible. Because the aim has been to spiritualize the theological school's life and ethos but not its course of studies, the formation movement perpetuates the inherited separation of piety and intellect. Presupposed here is that spirituality pertains to a realm other than the subject matter and end of studies. All the schools could be spiritualized in this sense with no effect at all on the unity, pattern, and end of the studies themselves. Furthermore, formation and spirituality seem to be so viewed as to have little to do with faith's sapiential knowledge (*theologia*). This may be why it has been so easy to talk about and urge a formation which lacks spirituality's very essence, namely, discipline. This lack of a cognitive element and the discipline necessary to it may be the reason formation in the present-day sense exports intellect from piety.

The recovery of *theologia* is not automatically assured by this distinction between its present reality and its absence from educational paradigms. *Theologia* existed in the initial stage of its career (classical Catholicism and Protestantism) in a conceptual and institutional framework of authority. That framework defined the nature and bases of theological understanding. This suggests that the relation between the conceptual world of classical Christian orthodoxy and *theologia* is one of interdependence. Accordingly, the demise of the former surely carries with it the discrediting of the latter. In the conceptual world of orthodoxy, theological understanding is faith's actual knowledge of God and the things of God. Monasticism and Protestant pietism viewed it as a knowledge whose final and highest instance was the beatific vision. Hence, *theology* was that personal-existential knowledge which was obtained in stages of spiritual or mystical discipline or through the means of grace. Scholasticism viewed *theologia* as a demonstrative knowledge (*scientia*), which included both a meta-theological, rational demonstration of divine being and theological demonstrations of conclusions from posited authorities. Both lines saw theological understanding grounded in a *depositum* of revelation, the authoritative texts of Scripture and tradition. The question this raises is whether *theologia* can be disengaged from that framework, whether it can have a postorthodox form.

The underlying issue here is whether *faith itself* can have a postorthodox form. In the author's view, classical orthodoxy and its method is one among many possible historical conceptual habitations in which faith can reside. Faith is not necessarily tied to the way in which the classical period of Christendom construed the authority of Scripture and tradition. If this is the case, faith's insightfulness or belief-ful knowing can reside in and use other conceptualities in a historical career which adopts various modes of understanding (reflection, scholarship). Thus theological understanding can occur in contemporary and postorthodox forms of Catholic and Protestant Christianity and in revisionist theological frameworks. Furthermore, both monastic and scholastic approaches to theology in the classical period have their counterparts today. The sapiential knowledge which we are calling theological understanding does have a personal-existential dimension. The reason is that theological understanding is born of faith and serves the agenda of faith, which is living in the world attuned in some way to the disclosure and presence of the sacred. Second, this sapiential knowledge is not indifferent to or independent of the cognitions which occur when it appropriates the tools of scholarship. It makes different uses of these conditions depending on its matrix and mode. This use of scholarship is the modern counterpart of the older use of reason in both natural theology and the study of the authoritative texts. For these reasons, *theologia* is a perennial possibility for faith as it occurs in its various social contexts. It is not, therefore, simply a correlate of the orthodox conceptuality.

4. The Structure and Dialectic of Theological Understanding

Theological understanding is not a theory or invention, something wafted into existence by the theologian's magic wand. It names a dimension of the life of faith itself, the understanding required of faith as it exists in various life contexts. But there has been a low level of awareness of this dimension in the encyclopedic period and after because the life and structure of theological understanding have gotten tied up with clergy education. There are interpretations of theological understanding implied in these literatures. The entelechy of the fourfold pattern, proceeding as it does from Scripture through history and theology to the practice of ministry, implies a source-to-application model. In this view, theological understanding describes a move from a disclosed knowledge made possible by acquaintance with the *de-*

positum of revelation to the application of that knowledge. A modern variant of that model occurs in hermeneutic theology insofar as it formulates theological understanding as a dialectic going-on between *texts* and understanding. The pedagogy built on this mode is reflected in the study-of-theology literatures of the sixteenth and seventeenth centuries, the later theological encyclopedia writings, and most current approaches to theological curricula.

The primary problem with the model is not simply its close relation to precritical approaches to faith and theology, but the fact that theory and practice do not separate in that way in theological understanding. There simply is no beginning moment of mere knowledge and received revelation from which assessments, situations, sifted and selected concerns, historical corruptions have been emptied. One suspects, therefore, that the model arose in the first place under the pressure of synthesizing theological understanding with the requirements of a course of study.

A second model of theological understanding is present in more recent generations of theological and church education. It is, in fact, the reverse of the traditional model since it proposes a situation-to-disciplines movement. The explicit examples of this approach are not so much direct accounts of theological understanding as pedagogical proposals; for instance, case-study methods and field-based education. Some versions of liberation theology, however, do self-consciously address theological understanding and not just a course of study. According to these views, theological understanding is born in a historical situation (of oppression) and is shaped by that situation. Disciplines, theory, knowledge are all ordered toward the praxis, and the route is from praxis to appropriated science, not vice versa.

Both models share at least two convictions. Both divide theory and practice, assigning each one to some place in the process or event of understanding. And both are relevance models. That is, relevance to the situation sifts, measures, and disposes the "theory." Both models tend to be closely tied to a pedagogical structure and do not arise from a direct account of theological understanding as such. And it is the pedagogical element with its tendency to distribute elements (theory, practice) over the moments of a course of study which prompts these models to obscure the dialectic of theological understanding.

A direct, though very brief, account of theological understanding will be attempted here. When we consider such a task, two quite different perspectives and approaches present themselves. The first focuses on the components, the structure, of theological understanding; the second on its life and dynamics. The first task, a morphology of *theologia*, is more formal and abstract because it treats theological understanding as if it were a single cognitive moment, an instant without duration. Viewed this way, *theologia* appears to have three immanent elements, and the absence of any one of them destroys its character as *theologia*. Since the understanding that is being referred to here is informed by the mythos and vision mediated through a specific historical community of faith, one component is the interpretive grasp of that mythos. Because this understanding is not simply an antiquarian preoccupation with tradition, but is concerned with that tradition because of the claim it lays upon us—its truth character—it is unavoidably an interpretation which at the same time is an assessment, an appraisal. And because this understanding occurs in and toward the present, it directs its appraised tradition at the situations in which it lives.[9] Knowledge of the mythos and tradition of the world of faith, the ascertaining of its truth, and the incorporation of both into the contemporary situation are the components of theological understanding viewed statically and structurally. If a pedagogy were taken from this analysis as it stands, it would retain the source-to-application model.

Theological understanding in actuality is not simply a timeless instant, a structure, but an activity, a life process. Because that process has the character of perpetual self-correction, theological understanding in actuality is a dialectic. What follows here is a very brief description of that dialectic, but a number of qualifications are called for. Not only does this description fall short of a full account of the dialectic itself, but it omits most of the issues which should be treated in such an account. It does not take up, for instance, the way faith and its insightfulness set preconditions for theological understanding. Hence, the things which give that understanding the character of doxology, world orientation, empathy, wonder, and the like are not considered.[10] In addition, this description is a general one. It is meant neither as definitive nor as a replacement for accounts of *theologia* which occur in the theologies of specific branches of Christendom.

We begin with what might turn out to be an axiom: the axiom of the primacy of the situation in which theological understanding occurs. Whatever is to be said about the independence and primacy of revelation in the order of knowledge and salvation, theological understanding is inevitably the understanding of an individual existing in an already disposed biographical, social, and historical situation. One aspect of that situation may be the enduring structures of nature, the fundamental ontology and existentiality of human being (Tillich), but these do not exhaust the situation. The situation is always also a concrete situation and moment in the individual's biographical life set in a social space and historical time. There is no other matrix of theological understanding than this concrete situation. All theological work, be it classically conciliar or parochial and individual, occurs from and in the concrete situation.

It is the situation in which occur events and states of affairs which constitute the individual's life and which evoke responses and interpretations. There is simply no way of conducting theology above the grid of life itself. The dialectic of theological understanding is set in motion here, by the matters which evoke response and interpretation. To speak of the primacy of the situation in this sense is to say nothing of its *status* in theological understanding, whether or not its primacy qualifies it as a criterion, whether its primacy is a prison which faith cannot transcend. Nor does this describe a merely "secular" moment at the beginning which is empty of reference to revelation and redemption. The reason is that the understanding in question is preceded by and grounded in faith and its predispositions.

The references and imagery of faith are present prereflectively in the initial move of theological understanding, but not as explicit, self-conscious themes. But as we struggle to interpret and assess the situation, these prereflective references demand a hearing. Generally speaking, this is because the human being is in the world in the posture and reality of faith; its reading of the situation prompts it to self-consciously draw on the references of faith as guides to the interpretation and assessment of the situation. "References of faith" means simply the realities of faith carried in the imagery and even doctrinalizations of the ecclesial community. The matrix and unity of these realities is ecclesiality itself, a universalized form of a redemptive community. The first movement, then, of the dialectic of theological understanding is a thematization of the faith-world, of ecclesiality, of faith's language, references, realities. This movement attends to the total mythos of Christian faith, i.e., the essence of Christianity, the primary symbols, the themes of proclamation, the dogmas of tradition. Most traditional forms of education in the church have in fact focused on this moment, for instance, the Sunday school and a medieval cathedral school. This is the moment which draws on, and takes into account, the historical and distinctive content of tradition.

It was said earlier that the primacy of the situation was the primacy of a *matrix*, a context, not the primacy of a norm, a criterion, an ideal. But it is just this normativeness which unfaith would grant to the situation—the absolute status of what must be appeased, adapted to, satisfied. The self-oriented agendas, the principle of satisfaction, prompts the human being to grant not merely ontological but criteriological primacy to the situation. And at this point, in a second moment of the dialectic, faith intervenes, in what recently has been called a hermeneutics of suspicion.[11] It repudiates the situation's claim to absoluteness (or the claims of elements in the situation) as it discerns its corruption and its relativity. In this second moment of theological understanding, the situation is refused normativeness and becomes a candidate for theological criticism. This is to say, it is viewed in relation to the transcendent, and therefore in both its creaturely and corrupted status. This moment of critique is exercised in a multiplicity of ways: as personal and autobiographical criticism, as ideological critique and the uncovering of injustice in the fabric of society. To use recent jargon, this second moment "raises the consciousness" to self-conscious awareness of the relativity and corruption of the situation.

If this dialectic stopped here, theological understanding would be simply the repudiation of one absolute criterion (the situation or its contents) on behalf of another, the historical tradition which disposes faith. The relative and corrupt cultural situation is contrasted to the absoluteness of tradition (Christianity, Scripture, dogma, primary symbols, etc.). The peril of simply adapting to a particular situation, thus granting it autonomy, is replaced by the peril of adapting a situation to a heteronomous authority. But the dispositions of faith itself

resist such an exchange. These dispositions are formed by a redemption which occurs in reference to the transcendent, the eternal, and
they carry with them what Tillich calls the "Protestant principle" and
what H. Richard Niebuhr calls radical monotheism.

Faith, accordingly, is prompted to refuse all absolutizations, all
claims that human, historical, interpretive matters elude relativity and
corruption. Hence, theological understanding would be incomplete,
even self-destructive, if it failed to apply a hermeneutics of suspicion
to its own tradition. For what in fact is that tradition? Even if it is
granted the status of revelation, divine disclosure, it is something
which occurred in the historical past. In other words, the tradition
and its imagery, primary symbols, and dogmas originated in former
concrete *situations*. In whatever sense it is divine work, it is clearly
also a human work. To grant it the status of the eternal itself is simply
one more idolatry. The third move, then, of theological dialectic is
distancing and criticism in relation to tradition itself—the attempt to
overcome the propensity to worship the norms. Again, to use modern
jargon, one moment of the dialectic is a raising of the consciousness
toward tradition itself. Only then are the elements in the tradition
which serve oppression, ideology and the legitimization of privilege
unmasked. Hence, the distancing we are talking about is informed not
only by the critical temper of the Enlightenment, but by the social
criticism of the nineteenth and twentieth centuries.

According to this account of the dialectical spiral of the theological
understanding, one set of moments elevates the content of the normative mythos (tradition) at work in faith itself. However, all that has
been said so far is that theological understanding embraces both a self-
conscious knowledge of that mythos and a self-conscious refusal to
regard it as absolute. At this point theological understanding is in the
ambivalent position of interpreting the mythos from two apparently
competing perspectives, the one insisting on the normativeness, the
other on its relativity of tradition. In this position the believer is not
ready simply to return to the situation through the mythos. Hence,
a fourth moment in the dialectic is called for which surmounts this
impasse and grasps the mythos in its enduring reality and its power.

Any of these moments covers a vast terrain of possible tasks, issues,
undertakings, and even sciences. This fourth moment, the determi-

nation of the normativeness of tradition, is no exception. What is discerned here is that about the persisting imagery, symbols, and doctrines of that mythos which expresses enduring truth. This truth pertains to more than simply the objective facticities of history or nature. As finally a truth about God and the presence of God, it has to do with what the world is and what human being is. Hence, one of the many specific tasks which would serve this moment in the dialectic is fundamental theology. This is not necessarily to claim that each moment in theological understanding is itself a discipline, a massive body of facts, data, and evidences. The point, rather, is that the dialectical reflection in which faith rises into understanding involves some grasp of the way in which the Christian mythos is a mirror of truth and reality. This truth and reality are inevitably present as the believer exists in the world in a self-conscious process of appraisal.

Theological understanding does not end with simply a relativizing critique of tradition. At that point nothing has yet happened to bring the assessed tradition into connection with the situation. Such an expression may be unfortunate. It sounds like a return to a theological pragmatism where the end of theological understanding is determined by a tradition whose autonomy was not really challenged in the third dialectical move. Medieval (neoplatonic and mystical) accounts of the believer's *itinerarium* decisively affirm the end and goal of that journey to be God and the vision of God. And yet few of them would formulate the matter in such a way as to obliterate creation. If the end is God, it is also God gracefully present among creatures working to fulfil ends which are theirs.[12] Accordingly, what theological understanding discerns is "the kingdom of God," *the situation* as God undergirds it, pervades it, disposes it, lures it to its best possibilities. In this view, God is not a mere means to serve the autonomous situation nor is the situation ignored for the sake of a vision of God. This is why one hesitates to speak about the "object" of theological understanding. That language invites us to draw into the foreground something discrete: faith, revelation, God, Christianity, and so forth. Yet any of these things can be *theologia's* object insofar as it functions as a generic term for the presence and activity of the sacred in the situation, the kingdom of God.

This final move of theological dialectic attempts to discern beyond the possibilities of corruption the place, legitimacy, beauty, redemptive possibilities, in short the theonomy, of the situation. And this is the case whether that situation be the individual's own concrete biographical life or a political situation of an oppressed people. Guiding this discernment is an assessed, de-absolutized tradition which has a disclosive character.

This discussion so far has focused on theological understanding as such. If the description is correct, the three components and the dialectic of this understanding would occur in some form in all the specific matrices. In the clerical paradigm, theology (minus theological understanding) is something for the clergy alone. In the view propounded here, theology is that dialectic of understanding which is evoked by faith's attempt to exist faithfully in its situations. Because it is not simply prereflective insightfulness but occurs at a self-conscious and even deliberative level, and because it is evoked by concrete situations and by the tradition of faith, "education" is appropriate to it. Under consideration here is the education required for the leader of the church, and this calls for an exploration of the form theological understanding takes in the exercise of that leadership.

It goes without saying that because the leaders of the church are also human beings and believers, they will experience and interpret ordinary life situations: illness, recessions, and threatening nuclear holocaust, personal grief, and so forth. Two levels of theological understanding, however, are pressed on the leader of the church which go beyond the demands of ordinary life situations. The first is set by the specific environment in which the leader works, the church itself. Concrete situations are still there to be interpreted, relativized, and so forth, but for the leader of the church many of these situations occur in and to the community of faith and its members. They include situations of the leader's special responsibilities: church maintenance, church crises, ecclesiastical politics, and so forth. The church leader lives in and toward these situations and works as believer and as leader to interpret them and to discern in them their dimensions of corruption and possibility. But there is a second and even deeper sense in which the church leader is called to exercise a distinctive level of theological appraisal. Here the exploration cannot avoid a theology of church leadership. The most general feature of church leadership is the facilitation of *theologia* itself. This does not mean that leadership's central focus is on the intellectual life. *Theologia*, we recall, is a sapiential (existential, personal) and praxis-oriented understanding, and as such it is the way faith rises to self-conscious dealing with the world. *Theologia* is salvation viewed as a self-conscious interpretive activity. Accordingly, the sacramental, administrative, proclamatory, and caring activities of leadership are ordered toward *theologia*. The church leader pursues these activities on both individual and corporate levels, mobilizing this praxis-oriented, sapiential understanding.

If this is true, the church leader must exercise a level and type of theological understanding necessary to that facilitation. This will mean, among other things, a knowledge of how particular corporate events and acts (preaching, counseling, etc.) happen in such a way that they evoke and deepen theological understanding. Obviously, such a knowledge involves critique of those same corporate acts insofar as they are simply moralizing, managing, or psychologizing. Since the church properly requires different kinds of leaders, each taking up special responsibilities in the community of faith, different aspects of the dialectic of understanding may be pertinent to their education. Some responsibilities will give priority to a critique and interpretation of a certain kind of situation, e.g., politics. Other responsibilities will focus more on the tradition itself and its interpretation.

The aim of this chapter was to explore the possibility of the restoration of theological understanding *(theologia)* to theological education. Because this understanding is both a *habitus* and a dialectical activity of faith as it exists responsibly in the world, the educative environment which contributes to the forming of this *habitus* has aims not unlike the *paideia* of classical Greece. If that is so, the reform of theological education cannot be centered merely in the encyclopedia question of the derivation of theological sciences. If reform takes place on the basis of a recovery of *theologia*, two issues must somehow be brought into relation to each other: the requirements of theological understanding as it occurs in the mode and matrix of church leadership, and the reconstruction of theological disciplines and pedagogical fields. Theological understanding—it has here been argued—can be restored to theological education because it is a perennial dimension of faith itself (not simply an antiquarian phenomenon) and because precritical ways of interpreting theology are not a priori to its existence and vitality. What remains is the question of what happens when the "sciences" of a theological course of study and a *paideia* of theological understanding are considered together.

NOTES

1. Most of the twentieth-century proposals for classifying theological study, science, or education are elusive on just this point. They rarely specify exactly what the classification pertains to. Even David Tracy's recent proposal to divide theology into three disciplines (fundamental, systematic, practical) is not completely clear as to what theology refers to—whether a course of studies, an overall unitary science, or a personal knowledge (*The Analogical Imagination* [New York: Crossroad, 1981], chap. 2).

2. Werner Jaeger, *Paideia: The Ideals of Greek Culture*, 3 vols. (New York: Oxford University Press, 1945), vol. 1, p. 286. Jaeger's study of *paideia* is surely the definitive account to date. According to him, *paideia* "was now connected with the highest *areté* possible to man: it was used to denote the sum total of all ideal perfections of mind and body—complete *kalokagathia*, a concept which was now consciously taken to include a genuine intellectual and spiritual culture." He calls *paideia* culture, not in the sense of an anthropological concept describing the character of a particular nation, but "the conscious ideal of human perfection" (p. 416).

3. The English word *discipline* is not without its ambiguities. It can refer simply to an area of pedagogy, a way of organizing various studies in such a way as to teach them, to create from them a unit of understanding or educational experience. In this essay, the term *catalogue fields* is used to communicate discipline in this sense. Second, it can refer to a "science," an ordered undertaking for the purpose of making a cognitive advance on some region of reality. In this proposal the total organization would fall into "disciplines" in the first sense. However, the question now being raised pertains to disciplines in the second sense: scholarly or scientific undertakings for the purpose of discrete and precise knowledge—historical, sociological, psychological, etc.

4. It may be that Bernard Lonergan's eight functional specialties of theology presuppose theology to be a comprehensive science in the sense being rejected here (*Method in Theology* [New York: Herder and Herder, 1972], pp. 125ff.). The eight specialties fall into two main groups, the first concerned with the recovery of tradition (research, interpretation, history, dialectic), the second concerned with the assessment of truth and theological judgment (foundations, doctrines, understandings, communication). That being the case, Lonergan's "specialties" do not name subdisciplines of a comprehensive sci-

ence, but disciplines propaedeutic to and moments immanent in theological understanding.

5. The author has attempted a fuller account of faith's cognitivity and its grounds in *Ecclesial Man: A Social Phenomenology of Faith and Reality* (Philadelphia: Fortress Press, 1975); and an account of theological reflection and inquiry in *Ecclesial Reflection: An Anatomy of Theological Method* (Philadelphia: Fortress Press, 1982).

6. A helpful account of this situation is Julian Hartt's essay, "The Situation of the Believer," in Paul Ramsey, ed., *Faith and Ethics* (New York: Harper & Brothers, 1957).

7. There is some correspondence between the three matrices of theological understanding and three levels of present-day educational undertaking. We have, accordingly, the Sunday school and "Christian education," seminary or so-called theological education, and the graduate school (Ph.D.) education. However, since *theologia*'s presence in the matrices is so minimal, the correspondence has little substance. *Theologia* in the mode of reflection occurring in the situation of the believer is not the way church programs of education understand their subject matter or goal. *Theologia* in the mode of theological understanding in ministry is not the way theological schools understand themselves. And graduate schools tend to be schools of scholarly endeavor without structural relation to the spectrum of theological understanding.

8. James Gustafson follows the proposal of Julian Hartt to say that theology is "a way of construing the world" and "an activity of the practical reason." Because it ties theology to modes of faith itself and not to the more elitist and specialized environment of the school, this approach parallels what is here being claimed for *theologia* (*Ethics from a Theocentric Perspective*, vol. 1, *Theology and Ethics* [Chicago: University of Chicago Press, 1981], pp. 158-59).

9. This threefold morphology of theological understanding is presented in elaborated form in the author's *Ecclesial Reflection*, chap. 8. It describes dimensions of "ecclesial reflection," which in the scheme offered here is theological understanding occurring in its primary and basic mode.

10. Karl Barth provides a rather comprehensive description of that which preconditions theological understanding (although that is not his language) in *Evangelical Theology: An Introduction* (New York: Holt, Rinehart & Winston, 1963).

11. Paul Ricoeur, "Philosophical Hermeneutics and Theological Hermeneutics: Ideology, Utopia and Faith," in *The Center for Hermeneutical Studies in Hellenistic and Modern Culture*, ed. E. Wuellner (Berkeley: Graduate Theological Union and University of California, 1975), 17th colloquy, p. 19. In addition to being a general element in all appropriation of meaning, Ricoeur calls it "the 'de-construction' of prejudgments which impede our letting the world of the text be."

12. One of the clearest and most profound struggles with this very problem is to be found in Jonathan Edwards's "A Dissertation Concerning the End for which God Created the World." The problem taken up here is how God can be the end of all things including God's own acts and at the same time pursue the ends of creatures.

Creatures pursue the ends of God,
not vice-versa!

8

Theologia in Clergy Education

This essay began with an account of the loss of *theologia* to theological education and culminated in a proposal for its restoration. This proposal argued that reforming the course of study of clergy education was not a single encyclopedic task. It must move on several fronts: the structure of theological understanding, the identification of disciplines (sciences), and the plotting of a course of study. Chapter 7 took up the first of these tasks, the description of theological understanding. The present chapter considers the second two tasks, the problem of disciplines and the course of studies. Its primary concern is the education of the leadership of the church. It does not, however, propose a *curriculum*, a particular sequence of courses, but attempts to discover the major components and criteria of that education on the assumption that *theologia* is its unity and subject matter.

1. The *Theologia* of Church Leadership

Because what is primarily in view is the education of the church's leadership, the proposal cannot avoid a general and ideal account of that leadership. Necessary, then, is the exercise of the dialectic of theological understanding toward ecclesial leadership. "Leadership" embraces a great variety of levels ranging from fully employed and ordained leaders (e.g., priests, ministers) to lay leaders who carry out selected and occasional responsibilities (e.g., church school teachers). Although the concern here is primarily with the education of clergy, everything proposed has some pertinence to the education of any church leader.

The "minister-as-professional" literature tends to permit church

[handwritten margin note top left: Yet what do these stories originate in? - in scripture]

leadership to be defined by a variety of tasks set for the minister by a parish or specialized ministry. This is clearly a nontheological approach to church leadership because it permits a set of negotiations or unstated expectations between minister and congregation to determine the leader's nature, task and responsibilities. Leadership, then, is defined by the exercise of these negotiated responsibilities. This approach is closely bound up with the view that the education of the church leader and the education of the believer have utterly different goals and subject matters. The (ordained) leader does things which the believer does not do (preach, administer sacraments, manage the organization, counsel) and must know things the believer need not know (church history, exegesis, pastoral psychology, and so forth).

[handwritten margin note: cf p 180]

This essay proffers a different relation between education in the church and (ordained) leadership education. *Theologia,* theological understanding, is the presupposed subject matter and goal of all education in the ecclesial community. Special educational requirements arise depending on the specific social matrix (e.g., ordained leadership) in which that understanding occurs. Such an approach calls for a theological rather than a nontheological account of the special educational criteria for the leadership matrix. Since believers as such invariably pursue a ministry in the world and not simply their own salvation, the idea of ministry is not strictly limited to church leadership. If Christian existence as such is characterized by self-conscious reflection (the dialectic of theological understanding) and ministry to particular situations, what is the task of the church leader? Simply put, that task is the mobilization of the ecclesial community to just those things, to theological understanding at the service of the believers' ministries. To put it differently, the church leader, lay or ordained, works to enable the church's ministries and the theological understanding(s) which they require.

Because the ecclesial community is itself, ideally speaking, a community of redemption whose effect on its environment is redemptive, the leader's work of mobilization and facilitation is centered in redemption. It is, finally, redemption which the believers' ministries serve, and it is redemption which is the aim of the dialectic of theological understanding. But redemption occurs in the ecclesial community in connection with the particular mythos and "gospel" of that community which (ideally) governs the way that community endures

[handwritten note at bottom: Redemption to the work of God. God's understanding that work.]

through time and over generations. Tradition and traditioning are, in other words, one dimension of the redemptive nature of the ecclesial community. If this is the case, the enabling work of the leadership will play a part in that traditioning. More specifically, some mediation of the tradition (the "gospel") is essential to what the leader does in the evoking, disciplining, and broadening of that *habitus* which we are calling theological understanding. There are, to be sure, many different paradigms for the enabling and mediating work of the church leader: evangelical/proclamatory, political/liberative, individual/contemplative, sacramental, and so forth. All of them have the character of enabling and are related to traditioning and to redemption beyond the faith community.

One other general feature of the enabling work of the leader is important to this proposal. Because the leader is in some way a mediator of tradition, and because theological understanding is a self-consciously exercised dialectic of consideration and appraisal, the enabling I am talking about is an enabling and mobilization of *interpretation*. Whatever we might say about faith's convictions, affections, its subterranean life, the believer exists in situations in the world in an interpretive way, because interpretation is part of all human responding. An interpretive (analytic, assessive, imaginative) element is a part of any action, activity, decision, posture, even policy. When faith's dispositions become self-conscious, interpretation will be involved. This is simply another way of describing theological understanding. And if interpretation is central to faith's existence and to its understanding, then the education of the church leader has especially to do with interpretation. This seems to be the case whatever specific task or responsibility is taken up in that education. Interpretation is occurring and also being evoked in preaching, church education, counseling, and the like.

2. The Effect of *Theologia* on the Course of Study

This essay culminates in the proposal that theological education needs to recover *theologia*, a recovery which will call forth a new course of studies and a new way of structuring catalogue fields. The problem is that the proposal to reinstate *theologia* in theological education is ambiguous. Does this imply that *theologia*, a *habitus* of faith itself, can be taught? Does it mean that *theologia* or theological understanding can itself be the subject matter of a course of studies, thus placing scholarly matters in the background? Does the recovery of *theologia* occur at the expense of the distinctive needs of clergy education? These questions converge into a single question: What would it mean for theological education to recover *theologia*? We have materials for some resolution of the ambiguity in the distinctions which have been forged in the course of the essay. What follows is a summary of these distinctions, a consideration of what the recovery of *theologia* means, and finally an attempt to clarify specific issues.

The overall entity with which we are concerned is theological education for the leadership of the church, hence a course of studies for that purpose. Three major elements must be distinguished within this overall program of study. The first is *theologia* or theological understanding both as a *habitus* of sapiential knowledge and as a dialectical activity. At this point we remind ourselves that our focus is on theological understanding in one of its modes, that of church leadership. The second element is pedagogy, education, and here must be distinguished education as a *paideia* promoting, forming, disciplining theological understanding, and education as the course of studies with its areas, courses, and methods. The third element is scholarship or the totality of sciences, both fundamental and auxiliary, available to the course of studies. The criticism of past and present theological education running throughout this essay is that the first element has been largely ignored and the second and third elements have been amalgamated. Accordingly, the problem of determining the course of studies was assumed to coincide with the problem of deriving theological sciences.

Two comments are in order concerning these three distinct elements. First, there are correlations among parts of these components as they occur in the overall enterprise of theological education. Therefore, because *theologia* is both a *habitus* and dialectical activity, the education which serves it has the character of *paideia*. Because this theological understanding is itself truth-oriented and critical, the education which serves it must inevitably co-opt learning, science, scholarship. And all three elements correlate in their level of occurrence precisely because they come together in an enterprise of clergy education. The second comment is that the language of divisions (areas, fields), subject matter, aim or end, and unit remains ambiguous until the element to which these pertain is designated. Hence, it is of little use to speak of the "subject matter" of theological education, since that can refer to the subject matter of the various sciences involved, of the courses of study, or even of *theologia* itself. The same holds for divisions. *Theologia,* the course of studies, and theological disciplines all can be divided or arranged into areas. Thus, to speak of the divisions of theological education itself is fruitless.

What then does it mean to call for a recovery of *theologia* in theological education? The answer occurs as we track various ways in which *theologia* pervades the total enterprise.

1. *Theologia* is present in the way education of the leadership of the church is conceived, namely, as a disciplining of the *habitus* and dialectic of theological understanding for the purpose of leadership tasks including the one task of facilitating theological understanding.
2. Because of 1, the *educational process* has the character of a *paideia,* a cultivation of theological understanding as these occur for the leader of the church.
3. The *course of studies* appropriates and incorporates the promotion of a *paideia* of theological understanding for leaders of the church as they exist in facilitative ways in envisaged situations.
4. Because theological understanding is a critical discerning whose exercise in leadership situations requires knowledge and disciplined procedures, the educational process and course of studies inevitably appropriate areas of knowledge and inquiry (*sciences*). In a course of studies, these "sciences" do not exist simply on their own, but in the context or environment of pedagogy.
5. As the aims of the course of studies converge with available areas of learning and methods of scholarship, *pedagogical fields* originate. The criteria for determining pedagogical fields in the course of studies are the scientific requirements of *theologia* as it exists in the mode and matrix of the leadership of the churches for the purposes of *paideia*.

To summarize, *theologia* is restored to the overall program of studies as that which evokes *paideia* as an element in the educational process, as that which permeates and guides what church leadership is called to do and be, as the criterion (in its connection with church leadership) for determining pertinent areas of inquiry and knowledge (sciences), and with them, areas of teaching.

In response to the initial question which exemplifed the ambiguity of the proposal, the following clarifications are offered.

Is theological understanding the *aim* or end of the course of study? Yes, *theologia* as it exists in the mode of church leadership is the aim.

Is theological understanding the *unity* of the course of study? In the sense developed above, it is the unity. That is, the course of study is prevented from being a compilation of autonomous sciences by the incorporation of sciences into fields of teaching which themselves are determined by the criteria of a *paideia* of theological understanding.

Is theological understanding the *subject matter* of the course of studies? No. A more precise use of the term refers to the discrete contents of specific areas or enterprises of teaching. For example, the events, persons, literatures, and movements of first-and second-century Palestine and Asia Minor are the subject matter of a course on the origin of Christianity. However, that subject matter can occur in a number of different ways of teaching and is subject to different overall aims of teaching. Accordingly, the origin of Christianity can be so taught that it contributes to a *paideia* of theological understanding.

Do the dimensions or aspects of theological understanding, either as *habitus* or dialectical activity, determine or coincide with the divisions of the course of study? No. The divisions of the course of study are areas of study which arise as "sciences" are appropriated by the *paideia* of theological understanding. These dimensions would, however, serve as criteria in the determining of areas of study.

Can *theologia* itself be taught? If this means that theological understanding originates only through pedagogical process, then *theologia* is not taught. Its origin, like that of faith, is complex. However, like faith, theological understanding forms in an environment. There is no more reason to exclude teaching from the forming of *theologia* than preaching or sacraments from the forming of faith. Teaching has a special role to play in the forming of theological understanding because of the cognitive, critical, and disciplined character of that understanding. It may be that the dialectical activity of theological understanding arises more through teaching than does the *habitus* of sapiential knowledge. Although both aspects may be formed in educational process, the dialectical activity may be a more explicit aim of that process.

Does *theologia* as the unity and aim of the course of studies exclude the clerical paradigm? Yes. According to the clerical paradigm, the unity and aim of theological education is a training for the exercise of clerical activities. Proposed here is an education which centers on a *paideia* of theological understanding. The clerical element is present as the mode and matrix of that understanding.

Does the incorporation of sciences or critical scholarship into a *paideia* of theological understanding compromise the autonomy and rigor of science? No. Inquiry serves various sorts of individual motivations (curiosity, prestige, power) and exists in pedagogical environments which have different agendas. The mere fact of motivation or environment should compromise the rigor of science only if the use of evidence is corrupted by the motivation. Although no human being or society appears to be above the corruption of evidence, there seems to be no reason to say that theological understanding is corruptive of the evidence principle for some a priori reason. In fact, if its orientation is to both truth and criticism in the radical sense of the dialectic of theological reason, a tampering with evidence only suspends that dialectic.

3. Three Criteria for Clergy Education

The previous section proposed three areas of pedagogy pertinent to clergy education. "Areas of pedagogy" may be a misleading phrase, since it suggests curriculum divisions. They can as well be called *criteria* which set distinctive aims of clergy education.

The Problem of General and Special Knowledge

The first criterion (area of pedagogy) is the *knowledge* with its attending postures, skills, and methods which is required by theological understanding. Expressed this way, the criterion is ambiguous because it obscures the important distinction between general scientific, historical, and humanistic knowledge and the areas of knowledge specially related to theological understanding.[1] The question of the sense in which the education of the leadership of the church builds upon a general education is a difficult and virtually ignored question. In present-day seminary education with its dispersed "sciences" and its technological professionalism, the question means the following: What preseminary studies are needed to enable the students to handle both "academic" theological studies and the studies which offer technologies of ministry? A *theologia*-centered approach places a different question: What general areas of knowledge and interpretive skills are necessary or helpful to leadership-oriented theological understanding?

The problem is made more severe by the lack of consensus in higher education itself as to what it means to be an educated person. In other words, church and leadership education cannot presuppose a culture-wide ideal of *paideia*. Furthermore, to the degree that clergy education is a mixture of independent academic fields and technologies of ministry, it has itself no notion of a general *paideia* behind its own course of studies. Even as it lacks criteria to measure its own dispersed disciplines as *theological*, so it lacks criteria by which to set general educational requirements. It may be plausibly argued that financial constraints make it impossible for the schools to consider the question of introducing an ideal of education into admission requirements. However that may be, leadership education centered in theological understanding does have a general educational propaedeutics. Whatever are the economics of admissions policies, some clear and decisive judgments on general education must be part of any reform of leadership education which projects the restoration of *theologia*.

A reform along these lines is surely a long-range and corporate task which cannot be even outlined in an occasional essay of this nature. The marshaling of proper criteria will be a necessary initial step. Three areas of pedagogy or criteria are pertinent: the knowledge and interpretation of ecclesiality, theological understanding in its various aspects and dialectic, and the leadership matrix and mode of theological understanding. All three play a part in determining the desired general education. It goes without saying that any graduate-level professional school wants students who are educated in the sense of exposure to a broad spectrum of studies in sciences and humanities. The pedagogical areas of a theological course of study set some very specific requirements, two of which may be explored here for illustration.

The very center and unity of the special knowledge required by theological understanding is a "knowledge" of *ecclesia*, the historical and corporate matrix of faith itself. Because *ecclesia* is a historical movement with an origin, history, tradition, mythos, and contemporary form, its interpretation involves not just the exegesis of ancient authoritative texts, but hermeneutical sifting of a historical complex. In other words, knowledge of *ecclesia* calls for hermeneutic skills of distinguishing levels of language, discerning comprehensive structures of symbols, combining critical distancing with existential appropriation. Skills such as these cannot and should not begin with graduate education, but need to form over a number of years and in the course of the process of education.

Second, theological understanding involves assessments, appraisals, judgments, directed both at the hermeneutically sifted tradition and at current situations. Chapter 7 argued that this appraisal was a necessary part of the discernment of the truths and realities with which faith has to do. Appraisal, therefore, must discern the way tradition and its symbols are connected to world (and human) structures, and this requires knowledge of those structures. World structures and operations are the very subject matter of the sciences, natural, social, and humanistic. For instance, the sociology of human community will be useful though not sufficient or autonomous in the understanding of the ecclesial community (ecclesiology). Fundamental ontology of human being will be operative in the discernment of what sin and evil do to human being. Hence, a working knowledge of the sciences and their mode of thinking, including philosophy, both linguistic and ontological, is indispensable to self-conscious and critical carrying out of theological reflection.[2]

In addition to general knowledge and interpretive skills, the appraisals, assessments, and imaginative constructions of theological understanding make use of areas of knowledge and interpretation specially correlated to that understanding. These special areas of knowledge exist as theological understanding reflects in and toward the situation on the basis of a particular historical faith, tradition, and mythos. Because the symbols resident in this particularity have universal import, they continue to be available as ways of interpreting and living in the ever-changing situations of the world. *Ecclesia* (ecclesial existence) names this historical particularity, and the dialectic of theological understanding requires a critical and historical knowledge of ecclesial existence. Without this rootage in ecclesiality, theological understanding loses its theological character and becomes an appraisal whose criteria coincide with the situation itself.

The knowledge we are talking about has primarily a historical character. This is unavoidably so if ecclesial existence is itself a historical entity, something which originated in history, which has a history, which occurs as a community in history. Are we saying, then, that "knowledge of the Christian religion" is the special knowledge theological understanding requires? This may in fact be the case, but not in the sense of a mere aggregate of historical studies, that is, "church history." Two features of the agenda of an education centered in *theologia* prevent this dispersion and call forth a distinctive historiography. First, there is a subject matter for the historical studies which is not simply a discrete strand of religion occurring in a historical time, like fourteenth-century mysticism or the Great Awakening in New England. These designated strands or events are as important to the medieval historian or the North American historian as to the theological historian. All history is about something. The point here is that an aggregate of these details or strands under a general category of national history does not capture the historical subject matter which guides and informs theological understanding. Theological understanding requires not so much a mass of historical details about the general past or even about the religious or Christian past as a portrait of ecclesial existence.[3]

Let us not forget at this point that what is under discussion is not simply sciences in themselves, each one competing for a place in clergy education. I have repudiated the nineteenth-century "encyclopedic" view that the divisions of clergy education are simply designated sciences. The argument here is that there is an area of pedagogy in clergy education which has a historical character. Its unity, subject matter, and major task are the discernment of ecclesiality. Discrete historical sciences (textual criticism, medieval philosophy, Calvin scholarship, etc.) will be operative in the undertaking, but they will not necessarily be themselves the units of teaching, nor will the sum total of them automatically be the subject matter which founds the dialectic of theological understanding.

A second feature of education centering in *theologia* which prevents the interpretation of its own tradition from being an aggregate of relatively unrelated historical studies arises from a criticism prompted by theological understanding itself. Any post-Enlightenment historical undertaking will be "critical" in the sense of an attempt to discern the mutual influences of all historical events and entities. But faith sees history not only as a network of reciprocally influencing events, but as a region of moral corruption. This corruption appears not simply in individuals but in nations, denominations, and institutions. This means that ecclesial existence itself occurs in connection with oppressions, ideologies, and absolutisms. One aspect of the historical portrayal of ecclesiality is, accordingly, a description of the church's own complicity in the ongoing drama of human evil. If the portrait of ecclesial existence is purged of this complicity, the theological understanding which it founds will make uncritical use of ideological and oppressive strands of the tradition. The resulting theological understanding is easily co-opted as a partner in that complicity.

The Teaching of Theological Understanding

What has been described so far is the knowledge and interpretive skills which theological understanding requires. Distinguished were the general knowledge on which all the areas of theological pedagogy rested and a special area, the historical portrayal and social critique of ecclesial existence. The description moves now to a second area of pedagogy, that of theological understanding itself.

The life of *theologia* is a dialectic of interpretation impelled by faith and its mythos occurring in and toward life's settings. It is faith's way of self-consciously and critically existing in the world. It has, accordingly, the general character of *appraisal*. In faith's rise to self-conscious understanding, the human being exists in the world in the mode of appraisal. This appraisal is neither a detached curiosity nor even the kind of truth orientation which would dominate its scholarly mode. Yet it is clear that the very nature of faith prompts a resistance to uncritical, passive, merely gullible postures toward its own tradition and toward situations. Faith's emotional qualities (passion, praise, awe, wonder, emphatic suffering, indignant anger, peacefulness) do not exclude but require appraisals. If this is the case, all theological education, the *paideia* of the community of faith, be it for church leader or believer, is centrally an education in *theologia* as an appraising, assessing activity.

To think of this appraisal as made up of "sciences" is a category mistake. On the other hand, faith's life of appraisal can and does call for a pedagogy. It can and does call for an education, formative process, and even efforts of scholarship. This educative process, the teaching of theological appraisal, requires that different aspects of dimensions of that understanding be isolated and brought to self-consciousness. What follows are some selected dimensions of theological appraisal and even specific types of appraisal which seem important enough to deserve attention in the teaching of *theologia*. Needless to say, all of these dimensions or types draw on the hermeneutically refined tradition previously described.

1. Appraisal must discern constitutive (ontological) features or ciphers of the human being's being and situation in the world, especially as they bear on the relation to the eternal and the need and possibility of salvation. This dimension is construed in many different ways: as a phenomenology of human "religiousness" (Schleiermacher), a phenomenology of lived and secular experience (Gilkey), as fundamental theology (Tracy), as the ontological correlate of primary symbols (Tillich), as the transcendental conditions of the knowledge of God (Rahner). This is the *inquietus* (restless) theme of the Augustinian tradition. A negative formulation may indicate what is at stake here. If the human being lacks what these various interpretations are attempting to describe, salvation becomes an alien, arbitrary, heteronomous violation. Affirmed here is not the human power of self-salvation, but the salvageability of the human being.

2. Theological appraisal inevitably must formulate the tradition in such a way that its enduring references are uncovered and

grasped as real and true. This goes beyond historical knowledge of ecclesial existence to the discernment of its truth, its disclosive character, its enduring illuminating power. In other words, theological appraisal is more than simply a recovery of the past, more than interpretation of ancient texts, more than exposition. It cannot avoid going beyond these important historical tasks to ask whether or not the texts, symbols, and narratives of the retrieved past have anything to do with reality. Do they disclose in any sense the way things are? Do they communicate anything about God, the world, or human being?

3. Appraisal discerns how the "truth" of ecclesial existence pertains to choices, styles, patterns, and obligations of individual human life. This discernment occurs under the criteria which preside over faith's translation into modes of life, behavior, and action. A more academic version of this theme focuses on how criteria are determined, how choices are made, how virtues are proposed, and so forth. Such are the themes of various schools of past and present moral theology and theological ethics. The personal, existential, and mystical tradition evokes from the individual a certain way of thinking, a disciplined contemplation. Likewise pertinent is the history of spirituality, Christian mysticism, and movements within Protestant pietism.

4. Finally, appraisal discerns the connection between the enduring truth of ecclesial existence and the public world. This "connection" may have the character of radical criticism of the public world or the uncovering of redemptive possibilities. Public world is the world of corporate, societal movements and institutions. It includes everything from the very comprehensive phenomenon of contemporary Western culture, a phenomenon which ranges from general, all-pervading features such as narcissism and nuclear technology, to such local and ephemeral social realities as organizations for leisure activities or ecology groups. If faith lives in the world in the mode of appraisal, then the social worlds which constitute its environment perpetually call forth that appraisal.

These four areas of discernment illustrate aspects of appraisal which can and should be specific subjects of the teaching of theological understanding. The aspects themselves are abstractions from the concrete life of appraisal and, although they are not sciences, they correlate with and may even call into existence specific scholarly inquiries or areas of inquiries. In addition to these dimensions of appraisal, there are areas of teaching which result from lifting out of faith's mythos some symbol or theme and relating it to theological understanding. For instance, the appraisal of tradition itself in its truth and reality occurs with reference to the transcendent. So do all theological appraisals. The relation of appraisal and the transcendent can be a proper way to form or evoke appraisal itself.

Theological Understanding in the Education of Church Leaders

Under discussion has been the teaching of *theologia* itself. A new educational dimension is added when theological understanding occurs in one of its modes and matrices, namely, the ordained or full-time *leadership* of the faith community. Any theological education centered in theological understanding will include knowledge and interpretation of ecclesial existence and thematic treatment of elements of that understanding. Accordingly, the education of the church's leadership will surely include these two themes. But what precisely will that education be since it *is* to be the education of church leaders? Highly problematic are two current, though not necessarily exclusive, ways of approaching this question. The first tacks the leadership element on to the academic curriculum under the rubric of "practical theology," setting the problem of how to bridge the academic to the practical. The second so identifies the course of education with education in specific clerical responsibilities as to discredit all merely "academic" elements. The problem may be formulated as follows: How is the total course of education carried out if its center, theological understanding, occurs in the matrix and mode of church leadership?

No response to this question will get very far without some theology of church leadership. An earlier section described leadership as the facilitation or enabling of theological understanding, which also means the mobilization of the community of faith as a redemptive community.

When this *theologia*-centered approach to church leadership is translated into an educational program, three themes appear to be unavoidable: the nature of ecclesiality itself, the essential activities and institutions of the ecclesial community, and, based on these first two themes, the essence, nature, and responsibilities of the church leader. It goes without saying that this programmatic and occasional essay cannot deal with these matters. Briefly stated, an account of ecclesiality attempts to grasp the very essence of the ecclesial community as a corporate, redemptive, historical presence. Further, it describes the way that community is the vehicle of redemption through its "traditioning," its retention of a mythos of redemption, its function as a social matrix of the actual occurrence of redemption, its role in world transformation.

Proclamatory, sacramental, and caring are the major activities of the ecclesial community as redemptive and which guide its "traditioning" through history.[4] The proclamatory activities describe the community's perpetual attestation to its own mythos, the interpretation of its tradition. Sacramental activities include not only the typical Protestant sacraments of divine presence in the church (baptism and Communion), but ritual and liturgical activities occurring in the dramas, perils, crises, and turning points of human life (marriage, burial, sickness, departures, and so forth). Caring activities are conducted not simply toward individual members of the community of faith (of pastoral care), but include the church's postures, agendas, and strategies toward all social corruption and oppression. None of these activities occur simply for the sake of the ecclesial community, but refer beyond that community to the world. Any adequate account of the nature and agenda of these activities would involve the exercise of the dialectic of theological understanding toward each one.

Only when there is some clarity as to the nature of ecclesiality itself and the character of its constitutive activities can there be a discernment of the actual role and responsibilities of the church's leadership. Although that leadership's general task and agenda is enabling and mobilization, this occurs through the proclamatory, sacramental, and caring activities. This way of determining the responsibilities of leadership is clearly different from two fairly widespread approaches. The more traditional one sees clerical responsibilities as correlates of the "means of grace," which are primarily preaching and the two Protestant sacraments. A more recent and functionalist approach simply permits the clergy-congregation negotiations, the job description, and current professional expectations to determine clergy responsibilities. What is being proposed here is that a theology of ecclesiality determine the responsibilities of church leadership and its constitutive activities. Only when that is accomplished are we prepared to take up the question of a *paideia*, that is, education in theological understanding for that leadership.

Described above is an approach to a theology of church leadership and to the question of how the responsibilities of the leader are determined. How would this approach determine the *education* of that leadership? The means-of-grace and functionalist ways of determining clergy responsibilities correspond to ways of conceiving clergy education. According to these approaches the major areas of responsibility are preaching, care of souls, education (catechetics), liturgy, and church polity. These in turn call forth areas of teaching and sciences corresponding to these areas.[5]

The encyclopedia literature assembles these "sciences" under the label *practical theology*. The modern functionalist approach expands these traditional teaching areas (disciplines) to include areas of expertise required for the efficient maintenance of the life and institution of the church. While it is assumed that each of these areas will somehow translate the *theoria* of the academic course into this expertise, the translation rarely if ever occurs. This is because the academic area itself is not a single subject matter or set of norms, but an aggregate of various scholarly undertakings. In fact, the areas of expertise tend to be controlled by the auxiliary discipline: management theory, linguistics, Rogerian psychology, and so forth. The "practical theology" of the encyclopedia movement is a curricular area marked off from the prepractical (theoretical) areas of study and unified by areas of pastoral expertise directed to the life of a congregation. Since the theoretical foundations are foundations for practical theology, the education of the church's leadership means in essence an education in various scholarly undertakings whose rationale is the undergirding of pastoral expertise.

This is, of course, the clerical paradigm, and it explains why the education of the believer is assumed to have nothing to do with either practical or academic theology.

How would the restoration of *theologia* push the theological education of church leadership beyond "practical theology?" A *theologia*-centered education directed to church leadership would have three distinctive features. First, the *sense* in which it is education in theological understanding would be determined by the level of theological understanding needed to mobilize that understanding in the ecclesial community. Assumed here is that all theological education, whether for believer or leader, is education in theological understanding. But if the leader's general task is itself the enabling of theological understanding, conceived not simply as the passing on of tradition but of evoking a situationally oriented dialectic of interpretation, the leader's own knowledge of the tradition must be extensive and her or his awareness of the features of the dialectic must be honed to a fine edge. This means more specifically that the church leader requires not just knowledge of the distinct areas of scholarship (e.g., medieval church history, the minor prophets), but of the comprehensive historical phenomenon, ecclesial existence. Further, the church leader needs sufficient self-consciousness about world structures, human ontology, and the reality-references of the tradition, to be able to evoke theological appraisal in the individual and corporate life of the church.

Second, because the church's leadership is facilitative of the church's redemptive activities, the education of that leadership will include a special thematization of ecclesial presence in the world. This means an education which conducts a theological appraisal of the ecclesial community, its institutions, its activities, and even its own leadership. In other words, the education of the leader involves a theology of leadership itself, which theology appraises both the nature and responsibilities of the church leader.

Third, the education of the leader is distinctive to the degree that it concerns specific areas of responsibility. Although this can mean simply a taking up of "practical theology" in the traditional sense, the proposal here departs from that in several ways. For one thing, it identifies the areas of leadership responsibility by means of a theology of ecclesial existence and the constitutive activities through which it is a world presence in a redemptive way. In addition, it directs the dialectic of theological understanding toward each of these areas and approaches the education in that area as education in the exercise of theological understanding.

An example is appropriate here. If preaching is identified as an area of leadership responsibility, the act and event of preaching is itself the situation (or an aspect thereof) in which reflection begins. The dialectic of *theologia* would in its negative move resist allowing the ecclesiastical-cultural situation of preaching to determine what preaching is. It would refuse absoluteness to that situation. It would attempt to recover the tradition, the mythos, and structure of ecclesial existence in relation to preaching, but would also refuse to grant absoluteness to that. It would have to engage in a hermeneutical, truth-oriented purging and sifting of the mythos before it could make preaching subject to it. Finally, it would attempt to discern what preaching is as an aspect of corporate redemptive activity. In the more traditional approach, the problem posed by preaching is how to bridge the (academically) exegetically purified authoritative text to the individual lives of the hearers. In the proposal made here, the problem is how to preach in such a way that theological appraisal is evoked from and conducted with the hearers, who are thereby mobilized toward a ministry in the world.

Finally, this proposal goes beyond "practical theology" because it rejects the traditional way of conceiving its unity. In that view, practical theology assembles areas of church leadership all of which contribute to the self-maintenance activities of a congregation. In that formulation, "ministry," not leadership, is the interpretive category and what is ministered *to* is the congregation. The activities of the leader as minister occur in and are directed to the church. However it was originally, it is now an essentially economic formulation of church leadership, since leadership responsibilities are identified and agreed upon in the negotiations between minister and congregation. But if all believers minister, and if ministry, even if born in the interrelations of the community, is directed outward, then the areas of leadership responsibility are not exhausted by the maintenance requirements (psychological, financial, growth, educational, and so forth) of the congregation. The areas which constitute leadership responsibility include world situations which evoke the redemptive ministry of ecclesial community. To think of the training of church leaders as training in congregation-directed activities alone defines "practice" as clergy activity in a congregation. What is under criticism here is not the congregation as such, but a notion of ministry whose final end is the congregation. Such a view self-evidently violates the very structure of *theologia*, the dialectic of understanding as situational. If that structure is retained, practice will not mean simply "professional activity," but the ministry of the congregation in the world. The areas of leadership responsibility are thus broadened from congregational-maintenance activities to areas of congregational mobilization in its ministry to the world. It is not being suggested that such things as preaching or pastoral care are eliminated by this broadening, but rather that distinctive areas of church leadership include the areas of world situationality to which the church's ministry is pertinent: politics, entertainment, education, and so forth.

Two clarifications are called for in these suggestions concerning the education of the church's leadership. The first indicates in a general way what the proposal is and is not. It is clearly not a curriculum proposal. The three major aspects treated in this chapter are not curricular divisions and represent no particular order of study. They are rather criteria and desiderata for what a course of study would include. Translating some of these suggestions into a course of study is a future undertaking. One or more of these criteria might in fact become a division of studies in a specific course of studies. Also appropriate might be courses which introduce the three criteria or desiderata outlined here: the (historical) knowledge of ecclesiality, the dialectic of theological understanding, and the theology of leadership.

As to what the proposal is, it can be summarized in several ways. It is an attempt to get beyond the difficulties which a theory-practice approach creates for clergy education. One of these difficulties is the autonomy granted to auxiliary disciplines once the "practice" area is severed from theological understanding. The proposal also attempts to reconcile the Enlightenment scholarly ideal with the true nature of

theologia as a *habitus* of understanding. As such it attempts to reconceive theological education as a *paideia* and not merely a scholarly
learning or learning for practice. Centered in theological understanding, the proposal attempts to make the problem of truth and reality
central to theological education, but resists reducing that problem to
historical-critical issues set by texts. It could also be said that this is
an attempt to solve the problem which scholarly *specialization* has
created for theological education by its elimination of *theologia*. Likewise, it could be described as an attempt to find an alternative to the
clerical paradigm as a way of conceiving the unity and subject matter
of the course of studies.

This introduces the issue which calls for a second clarification. The
special situation and responsibilities of church leaders set distinctive
requirements for their education. Hence the whole course of that
education, even the teaching of matters shared with other constituencies, may have a special character. Does this not return us to the
clerical paradigm? This paradigm, we recall, solves the problem of the
unity of the course of study teleologically, permitting that unity to be
established by the churchly responsibilities of the church leader. It
defines theology through that teleology, thereby excluding the believer
from *theologia*, and the later, functionalist version defines leadership
through an aggregate of discrete clerical tasks. It is clear that the
posing of an alternative to the clerical paradigm cannot be a course of
education indifferent to the demands of the leadership matrix and
mode of theology. The whole proposal is built on the distinction between the essential structure and dialectic of *theologia* which pervades
any and all church education and the special form that takes in particular matrices and modes. It must be acknowledged that the distinctive requirements of leadership education (the matrix of the present concern) do pervade and therefore unify that education.

On the other hand, because it sees theological understanding as the
subject matter and substantial unity of the course of study, this proposal departs from the clerical paradigm. Because that subject matter
is not to be *defined* by clerical education, it has its own integrity and
sets its own requirements. This also means that discrete clerical tasks
do not define ecclesial leadership. When they are permitted to do so,
education is pursued in order to learn to preach, administer, counsel,

and so forth. In the view argued here, a special facilitative carrying out of theological understanding defines ecclesial leadership, and specific responsibilities are approached through that.

4. *Theologia* in the Church and in the University

This essay culminates in a proposal to restore the *habitus* of theological understanding to the course of study which prepares the leadership of the church. As the analysis developed, it became clear that theological understanding occurs in the life of faith itself, and that leadership is only one of its modes. This simple notion has implications for educational undertakings other than simply clergy education. An early section of the essay observed serious problems attending both church and university education as a result of the loss of *theologia*. The recovery of *theologia* as a fundamental feature of Christian existence itself would issue in the reform of church and graduate as well as clergy education. These implications will be pursued in connection with three different educational enterprises: church education, undergraduate teaching of Christian studies, and graduate education.

The distinction between clergy (ordained priests, ministers) and laity is decisive in the history of the church's conception of education as a special undertaking. Worship, prayer, contemplation, confession, and hearing the Word are all for the laity. Education occurring as a special discipline and in a special institution is for the church leadership. Modern movements of "religious" and "Christian" education have changed all this. Yet a certain ambivalence about education for the laity continues to characterize the churches. Because the clerical paradigm defined theology as an undertaking of clergy education, the education left to the laity could not be "theological education." The laity must, accordingly, eat the crumbs spilling over from the hearty meal enjoyed by the clergy. The education of the laity must be conceived in some other way than a theological education and, if we do not include those traditions which still retain some version of doctrinalization through catechetics, that other way means assistance in Christian life and piety. A few decades ago and continuing in many churches, that assistance meant learning the lessons of life, piety, and morality from Scripture. In more recent, psychologically sophisticated decades it means the communication of psychic wholeness correlative to the stages of human development. The ambivalence about "Christian education" is that it is education and yet is not education. Its psychological orientation prompts it to adapt to the needs and social situation of each age group, yet there is little accumulation of knowledge or skill built into the educational program itself. This is due in part to the absence of an institution in which accumulated knowledge could occur. The Sunday morning church school and its spinoffs are clearly not such an institution.

It is also due to an absence of an educational subject matter. Even with the loss of *theologia*, clergy education continued to have a subject matter because of its retention of scholarly disciplines and its agenda of clergy education. Remnants of clergy education's subject matter make occasional appearances in adult church education, frequently to the delight of the participants, but at best this is the presence of a small educational moment dropped from a clergy course of study which itself lacks unity and coherence. Education in the truest and most serious sense of that word (*paideia*) needs to be introduced into the church. It may be surmised that as long as the church educator is conceived as a specialist in program administration and in developmental psychology, this will not occur. Further, if a Christian *paideia* is introduced into church education, it too will involve the recovery of theological understanding. The reason is simply that *theologia*, a dialectical reflection which presides over faith's self-conscious and critical responses to the world, is the heart and soul of any Christian *paideia*.

If this is the case, an educational enterprise is called for in the churches which has all three of the features ascribed to clergy education. As an education in theological understanding, it would include historical knowledge of and the ability to interpret ecclesiality, its mythos, literatures, traditions. It would also include some level of self-conscious exercise of the dialectic which comprises theological understanding. And, replacing the distinctive responsibilities and tasks which leadership requires, church education would be an education

in the mode of the believer, which means the believer's individual
and corporate praxis in the world. But to repeat an earlier point, such
a recovery of *theologia* in church education would be virtually impossible apart from a new institutionality and a new model of educational
process which permits and evokes cumulative knowledge.

As the queen of the sciences, theology's place in the university and
its validity among the sciences were once assured. This was the situation in the relatively homogeneous religious culture of the Christian
Middle Ages. The critical temper of the Enlightenment challenged
the supernatural grounds of theology as a science, and with that its
place in the university. Schleiermacher's answer to this challenge was
a defense of theology as a positive science, parallel to medicine and
law, designed to prepare a special population of cultural leaders,
namely, ministers. The price paid for this solution was the location of
theology outside the university's circle of sciences. Its validity was as
a special professional school. This historical consequence remained
relatively hidden in American higher education because most of the
original colleges and private universities were sponsored by religious
communities. Once American pluralistic culture created the secular,
private, or state university, the problem immediately surfaced. In the
religious studies movement as in the European Enlightenment, theology's legitimacy in the university and even in the study of religion
is highly suspect. The clerical paradigm and the correlation of theology
with clergy preparation only exacerbates this suspicion.

The thesis argued in this essay repudiates this correlation. It defines
theology as a *habitus* of the understanding, a dialectic of reflection
which in its ordinary setting occurs on the ground of a determinate
religious faith. This approach broadens the meaning of theology and
denies that it is clerical. We must consider, however, whether even
a higher price is paid by this solution. Does this connection of theology
with *faith* not disqualify it forever from being a valid undertaking in
higher education? Is not theology imprisoned forever in the church?
These questions sound plausible and forceful, but they suppress the
parallels between the cultural determinacy represented by theology
and faith and the cultural determinacy of most of the areas of higher
education.

Universities and their departments of religious studies do not question the validity of the study of determinate cultural traditions, including religious traditions. Jewish studies, studies of modern native American religions, and Buddhist studies all have their place. It would be arbitrary to say that Christian studies do not. But can Christian studies be studied "theologically"?

According to the approach offered here, this would mean so presenting this determinate religious faith that the student will be confronted with the critical appraisals which attend what this religion means by faith. In the author's view, this is exactly what should happen when Buddhism is taught in such a way as to do it justice. To teach Buddhism is not simply to communicate information about Buddhist history or present practices but so to stage and evoke participation in its texts and their claims that the .nsightfulness of Buddhist meditation is insightfully grasped by the student. The same holds for Romantic poetry, French existentialism, and studies in Marx and Freud. The representation of determinate historical and cultural experience, even if it is religious in character, does not disqualify a subject matter, movement, or literature from university studies. Nor is it disqualified by the potentiality of that determinacy, be it Marx, Lao-tse, or Tillich, to lay claims on the student and evoke insights. What disqualifies a subject matter is an approach to it which eschews critical method for mere authority, special pleading, or ideology. But theological understanding is stifled as much by those things as are romantic poetry and Buddhist studies.

Earlier on, the analysis argued that Christian studies occurring in colleges and universities do not escape the problem of clergy studies described in these pages. Christian studies likewise embody a remnant of the fourfold pattern and with that participate in the loss of *theologia*. These studies also need unity and coherence. They also need to dig behind merely external and phenomenal data to explore that about this particular historical faith which lays a claim on human beings. They need to do this to understand and teach that faith at all. For this reason, the recovery of *theological* understanding as a theme for teaching is crucial for the study of religion in the university.

The third educational enterprise to which the recovery of *theologia* is pertinent is the graduate education of teachers of Christian studies and clergy courses of study. When we consider the possibilities of reform, this may be the most important challenge of all. Graduate programs for Christian studies may now be the fourfold pattern's real home and its strongest institutionalization. Seminaries, church schools, and university departments of religion can all change their offerings, even the basic teaching areas (disciplines) with the welfare of their constituents in mind. But "disciplines" as sciences are the very essence of graduate programs. It is their very being. The expertise institutionalized in their divisions represents centuries of accumulated scholarship as well as decades of personally accumulated knowledge and discipline. Because they provide teacher-scholars for seminaries and universities along the lines of the traditional encyclopedia, these programs shape and maintain the way areas of teaching are conceived.

The recovery of *theologia* in theological education has implications for graduate programs in Christian studies in two ways. Both ways pertain to senses in which the graduate programs themselves need critical review. If the reform of education in church, leadership, and college education is to occur, teachers in these programs must be able to transcend their guild loyalties and specialist worlds to the type of insight and thought which serve the aims of this education. Insofar as the faculty is an instrument of reform, its members must be able to participate in the new conceptual world which reform requires. In other words, teachers in these schools must themselves be educated in the *paideia* of theological understanding.

It is just at this point that graduate schools are deficient. While the quality of scholarly accomplishment varies from school to school, there is little doubt as to the commitment of these schools to the ideals of scholarship. This commitment is acted out specifically in the linguistic and methodological world of the specialty. Graduate teachers and their students, accordingly, are not only specialists in designated literatures and areas, but their overall thinking occurs in and through the conceptual world of the specialty. The primary unit of the specialty shapes and restricts the specialists' way of thinking. Thus, thinking is dominated by literary tests, cases, ontological structures, arguments, historical details, and so forth. This primacy of unit and method in a scholar's work appears to be inevitable, even desirable, as a concomitant of serious scholarship. It becomes problematic when it cannot be transcended, when it pervades all the postures, perspectives, and thinking of the specialist.

If theological understanding is recovered in the education of clergy, the areas of pedagogy (disciplines) will be taught in such a way as to help the student draw on the contributions of specialized scholarship in that understanding. Specialist teachers must be able not only to see the rationale of the total course of study, but to teach their specialty as something which advances the whole. At present many, if not most, teachers of specialties in schools of clergy education and colleges hold not only graduate but professional (M.Div.) degrees or their equivalent. Unfortunately, the professional degree as an aggregate of independent scholarly studies does not engender theological understanding. According to the threefold scheme propounded here, the graduate and scholarly specialty should be construed as a particular matrix (graduate teacher) and mode of theological understanding. If that is the case, graduate education should go beyond the usual specialty-plus-minor to a grounding in the two major areas of education which are theological: comprehensive knowledge of ecclesiality and thematization of the dialectic of theological understanding.[6]

In the absence of a concrete proposal for a new course of study and new ways of conceiving disciplines (areas of pedagogy) and sciences (research areas), little can be said about the second way graduate education needs reformation. It should be clear, however, that if the fourfold pattern does not stand up to criticism, if theological understanding returns to the center of church and clergy education, if praxis comes to mean something much broader than clergy practice, all this has ramifications for the retention or nonretention of the traditional areas of graduate study and for the introduction of new areas. The three criteria proposed here for clergy education will surely not find implementation in an actual course of study without corresponding changes in graduate study. These criteria may call forth such areas of graduate study as interpretation and hermeneutics, theological dialectic, and situational reflection and inquiry. Graduate education in religion has already changed under the impact of the religious-studies movement. It needs now to change in relation to Christian studies and the reform of theological education.

Has this essay spoken too glibly, too easily, about the reform of theological education? So many things now converge to say it is not time for reform. It is not time because the world itself is going to pieces, waiting for the impending global holocaust. It is not time because the theological schools are so hard pressed by hard times that they cannot see past issues of existence and survival. It is not time because religion itself is such a pluralistic and eclectic stew that sufficient conditions even for a conversation about reform do not exist. Of course it is not time, because it is by definition never time for reform. Reform creates its own time and reform time is not maintenance time or even survival time.

As to world holocaust, we must assume that, short of that unspeakable event, theological schools—like churches, newspapers, scout troups, and shopping centers—will remain in business. Surely these schools will exist more responsibly under impending apocalypse if they gird up their loins, not for business as usual, but for reform. Surely a leadership which occurs through disciplined acts of theological understanding is more pertinent to the situation of global crisis than a leadership trained to refuse that discipline.

It is, therefore, time. The accumulated and unexamined presuppositions of theological education have enjoyed their dark corners long enough. They are moldy and outworn, and they have exercised hidden control too long. The institutional structures they created are too often oppressive, irrelevant, and ineffectual.

It is time then . . .

. . . to uncover and assess the deep presuppositions and dominant paradigms which determine how the unity and aims of theological education are understood;

. . . to obtain some clarity about the sense in which theological understanding (sapiential knowledge and its dialectical exercise) attends the subject matter of all education which purports to be theological;

. . . to discover how education in theological understanding can be translated into a program of studies;

. . . to sort out the ends, aims, subject matter, and unity of a course of studies designed for the leadership of the church;

. . . to explore the effects of interpreting theological education as a *paideia* of theological understanding;

. . . to discern the areas of study and teaching (disciplines) necessary to an education which is a *paideia* of theological understanding for leaders of the church.

These are not the only tasks and issues which comprise the reform of theological education. But if they are ignored, the effect can only be a trivialization of reform.

NOTES

1. In the theological encyclopedia literature this distinction was expressed in the terms *general encyclopedia* and *special encyclopedia*. It is, however, older than this literature, operative in the medieval proposals concerning the place of *theologia* in the circle of sciences. It remains operative in the present in the distinction between professional or seminary education and the college-level course of studies which that supposedly presupposes. I say "supposedly" because, while accredited seminaries do require the bachelor of arts *degree* or its equivalent for admission, they desire but do not *require* certain levels of educational competence or accomplishment as conditions of admission.

2. A fuller list of general areas of knowledge and sciences which theological understanding requires might include the following: linguistics and the nature of language; hermeneutics; sciences of human being (social, psychological, philosophical); philosophy of moral experience, language, history, world; current world situation as rooted in history; American history and culture; post-Enlightenment intellectual history (Marx, Freud, etc.); philosophy and history of world religions.

3. See the author's *Ecclesial Reflection: An Anatomy of Theological Method* (Philadelphia: Fortress Press, 1982), chap. 9, for an elaborated account of "theological portraiture," the historical description of ecclesial existence.

4. Farley, *Ecclesial Reflection*, chap. 11, contains a fuller though "ideal" account of the institutionality and activities which constitute the ecclesial community's redemptive way of persisting over time and over generations.

5. In rare instances apologetics and polemics are placed under practical theology. The only other area besides the traditional five which has occasional presence in the encyclopedia literature is missions or evangelism, thus reflecting the nineteenth-century worldwide missionary expansion of Christianity.

6. An example of a graduate education which combines comprehensive and even theological understanding with the rigor of scholarship is the ideal evi-

dently at work behind most Jewish scholarship. Rare is the Jewish scholar who is simply a narrow specialist, who lives in the specialist's world in such a way as to be unable to interpret Judaism with comprehensive historical insight and theological appraisal. In short, Jewish scholars tend to work from what we are calling theological understanding, be they specialists in Jewish Scriptures, Talmudic studies, or philosophical theology. Examples of past and present Jewish theologian-scholars come readily to mind: Abraham Heschel, Franz Rosenzweig, Jacob Neusner, Lou Silberman, Samuel Sandmel, Emil Fackenheim. The notion that specialized pursuit of scholarship would exclude the possibility of being a theological interpreter of Judaism would be utterly foreign to all of these figures.

Index

"faith development"
- a kind of semantic reductionism
- the ψ concomitants of faith w/ the
central Θ meanings of faith

- asymmetric unity
  means shaping the ψ w/i a XμΘ framework

H5 -yes - how the auxiliary science
provides the criterion for the work
and how it gets translated into (reduced
to) terms of the aux. science

PP176 & 180 - contradiction
so it is it not the <u>subj matter</u>
of all education in the ____ comm?

1. What is the theological rationale for pastoral theology?
   - i.e. its relation to Xity or Xn faith?
   - what are the criteria used

2. What is its contribution to the training of professionals?

3. What is the relationship of pastoral Θ to the other disciplines of the semin[ary]

   Θ reflection on pastoral tasks?
   Θ & Φ theory
   Θ & Φ practice
   Θ use of Φ vs. Φ of religion

   p 132 - practice or experiential knowledge was built into Θ by defi[nition]

What is it that unifies pastoral Θ as a discipline?

p 80 - 4 issues that brought about change
   1) collapse of orthodox Θ
   2) what unifies Θ - its aims, i.e. clergy ed
   3) the meaning of theology itself
   4) the place of Θ in the university

hist. crit. method
rejection of supernat'lism & authority

p 128 - external tasks abstracted/separated from its Θ rationale
p 129 - controlled by aux. sciences
   application of & satellite discipline to tasks of ministry
p 136 - liberal Θ, not KB's assumption
   144 simplistic
   - Luther, Aquinas - Calvin - didn't believe this
X phenomen.... aligned